The Chez Panisse Cookbook Library

THE CHEZ PANISSE MENU COOKBOOK

BIRTHDAY DINNER FOR LINDA · NOVEMBER 8, 1980 · FRUITS DE MER SUR LE GRIL · LES PETITES SALADES CHEZ PANISSE · CHOU ET CANARD SAUVAGE · HARICOTS VERTS ET CHANTERELLES CRESSON ET ENDIVE · COTE DE BOEUF A L'ANCHOIADE · POMMES ALLUMETTES · FROMAGE DE CHAUME ET FRUITS · MONT BLANC

THE
CHEZ PANISSE
MENU
COOKBOOK

by

Alice Waters

In Collaboration with Linda P. Guenzel
Recipes Edited by Carolyn Dille
Designed and Illustrated by David Lance Goines

RANDOM HOUSE
NEW YORK

The truth of the matter is that the restaurant and this
book exist only because our customers have constantly expanded
our horizons along with their own.

G. B.

This work was originally published in hardcover by Random House, Inc., in 1982.

Library of Congress Cataloging-in-Publication Data
Waters, Alice.
The Chez Panisse menu cookbook.
Includes index.
1. Cookery, French. 2. Chez Panisse.
I. Title.
TX719.W34 641.5944 81-40215
Paperback Edition ISBN 0-679-75818-6
Hardcover Edition ISBN 0-394-51787-3 AACR2

Manufactured in the United States of America on acid-free paper

Paperback Edition Printing
1 2 3 4 5 6 7 8 9
Hardcover Edition Printing
4 B 5 6 7 8 9

ACKNOWLEDGMENTS

This book would never have been written but for Linda Guenzel's belief in me and in Chez Panisse. She transcribed my ramblings, organized my thoughts, and overcame my doubts, all with tireless enthusiasm. I cannot thank her enough for the countless hours she has given me so generously. This book is as much hers as mine.

My sincere thanks to Carolyn Dille for extracting and codifying these recipes; to Jean-Pierre Moullé for continuing to cook dinners at the restaurant while helping me taste, evaluate, and refine the recipes; to Pat Curtan for her friendship, inspiration, and collaboration; to Fritz Streiff for his valuable finishing touches; and to David Goines for wanting to realize this cookbook design.

My gratitude to my partners, Tom Guernsey, Jerry Budrick, and pastry chef Lindsey Shere for keeping everything going at the restaurant; and to my former partner, Jeremiah Tower, my gratitude for his innovative and inspiring cooking at Chez Panisse. And I want to especially thank Gene Opton for her generosity and trust during the first precarious years of Chez Panisse.

Special thanks to Todd Koons, Steve Sullivan, Sharon Monday, Eleanor Bertino, Tom Luddy, Jean-Pierre Gorin, Nathalie Waag, Marion Cunningham, Joyce Goldstein, Barbara Carlitz, Frances Garbellano, Doris Muscatine, Victoria Wise, Craig Sutter, Greil Marcus, David Stewart, Fred Guenzel, Judy Newman, and my parents.

For their inspiration and encouragement I want to thank Gerald Asher; my friends at the Cheeseboard; Martine Labro; Kermit Lynch; Madeleine Kamman; Richard Olney; Diana Kennedy; James Beard; my friends at Tassajara, Greens, and Green Gulch; Darrell Corti; Lulu and Lucien Peyraud; Elizabeth David; Susan and Bob Lescher; Bob Finigan; Mark Miller; Dianne Johnson; M.F.K. Fisher; Judith and Evan Jones; and my editor, Jason Epstein.

INTRODUCTION

Food must be experienced, and I worry that writing about it may not make the sense I want it to! I wish I could just sit people down and give them something to eat; then I know they would understand. Since I cannot do that, I hope that an explanation of how I became involved with food and why I started Chez Panisse will allow a vicarious understanding.

I believe that many of my aesthetic principles have their roots in my early childhood. "A picky eater," my father would say, and I wouldn't eat just any old thing. I wanted green beans and rare charcoal-grilled steaks every birth-day dinner. I remember sitting out in the strawberry patch, happily devouring those fresh berries. I can still taste the applesauce made from the fruit of my apple tree, and can smell the apple blossoms. Friends of the family had a cottage up at the lake, and I was delighted by the possibilities of a seven-foot barbecue in the sand. We had clambakes, complete with roasted corn, chicken, and blueberries we had picked out on the islands. I still love corn, but that was the best. Though I never had anything unusual to eat when I was little, I was lucky to have tasted fresh fruits and vegetables from the garden.

At the age of nineteen I went eating in France—the best description of my year of study abroad. I began eating all kinds of wonderful things I'd never tasted before. It was the first time for so many foods—oysters, crayfish, mussels—and I liked *everything*. The idea of ever opening a restaurant hadn't entered my conscious mind, but I experienced a major realization: I hadn't eaten *anything,* comparatively speaking, and I wanted to taste *everything*. I began to see a pattern—a technique for looking at food, examining it, and understanding it.

In France, for the first time, I found that people would spend an hour or more deciding where to eat. My French friends would drive around on Sunday afternoon, stopping at all the restaurants in town to see who had the best of whatever was fresh and in season, and then they would agonize over the final choice, a process of selection that showed much respect for food.

A little stone house we just happened upon in Brittany was the setting for one of the most memorable meals of my life. I had eaten all over France, and it was here that I first heard usually reserved Frenchmen exclaim over the food. Elsewhere, even when I found the food to be wonderful, they would say only that it was "all right"; but after the meal in this tiny restaurant, they applauded the chef and cried, *"C'est fantastique!"* I've remembered this dinner a thousand times: the old stone house, the stairs leading up to the small dining room, which seated no more than twelve at the pink cloth-covered tables and from which one could look through the opened windows to the stream running beside the house and the garden in back. The chef, a woman, announced the menu: cured ham and melon, trout with almonds, and raspberry tart. The trout had just come from the stream and the raspberries from the garden. It was this immediacy that made those dishes so special.

I now knew that I loved to eat and that I wanted to eat certain foods of a certain quality. I bought Elizabeth David's book, *French Country Cooking,* and I cooked everything in it, from beginning to end. I admired her aesthetics of food, and wanted a restaurant that had the same feeling as the pictures on the covers of her books. It was so important that I was driven, as if I had a sense of mission. I didn't envision success. All I cared about was a place to sit down with my friends and enjoy good food while discussing the politics of the day. And I believed that in order to experience food as good as I had had in France, I had to cook and serve it myself.

The timing and the location encouraged my idealism and experimentation. This was during the late sixties, in Berkeley. We all believed in community and personal commitment and quality. Chez Panisse was born out of these ideals. Profit was always secondary.

Chez Panisse began with our doing the very best we could do with French recipes and California ingredients, and has evolved into what I like to think of as a celebration of the very finest of our regional food products. The recipes of Elizabeth David and Richard Olney provided a starting point and an inspiration to us; and we soon realized that the similarity of California's climate to that of the south of France gives us similar products that require different interpretations and executions. My one unbreakable rule has always been to use only the freshest and finest ingredients available. Our quest for the freshest and best of the region has led us to Amador County for suckling pigs and wonderful, peppery watercress; to the Napa Valley for Zinfandel made especially for the restaurant; to Gilroy for garlic; to Sonoma County for locally made goat cheeses; to the ocean daily for oysters; to the backyards of our customers where we have our own gardens; and finally, if we must, to the local produce markets for that which we cannot grow or procure ourselves. Our goal is to be totally self-sufficient so that we need not depend upon the unreliable quality and inconsistencies of the commercial food wholesalers.

My definition of fresh is that the perfect little lettuces are carefully hand-picked from the hillside garden and served within a few hours. Over the years, the notation "If Available" has frequently appeared after a particular item on our menus. This means that if the food listed is available in the best condition, we will serve it; otherwise, we will make a substitution.

When people come to the restaurant, I want to insist that they eat in a certain way, try new things, and take time with the food. Therefore, our format of serving only one five-course dinner each evening often surprises people at first, but I think the appealing aromas and the roasted flavors of food cooked over the charcoal grill, and the earthiness of those lettuces, tend to seduce the hesitant. For me food is a totally painless way of awakening people and sharpening their senses. I opened a restaurant so that everybody could come and eat; remember that the final goal is to nourish and nurture those who gather at your table. It is there, within this nurturing process, that I have found the greatest satisfaction and sense of accomplishment.

A.L.W.

CONTENTS

SEASONAL MENUS 51

MENUS FOR SPECIAL OCCASIONS

GRILLING MENUS

THE CHEZ PANISSE MENU COOKBOOK

WHAT I BELIEVE ABOUT COOKING

My approach to cooking is not radical or unconventional. It may seem so simply because we as a nation are so removed from any real involvement with the food we buy, cook, and consume. We have become alienated by the frozen and hygienically sealed foods. I want to stand in the supermarket aisles and implore the shoppers, their carts piled high with mass-produced artificiality, "Please . . . look at what you are buying!" Food should be experienced through the senses, and I am sad for those who cannot see a lovely, unblemished apple just picked from the tree as voluptuous, or a beautifully perfect pear as sensuous, or see that a brown-spotted two-foot-high lettuce, its edges curling and wilted, is ugly and offensive. It is a fundamental fact that no cook, however creative and capable, can produce a dish of a quality any higher than that of the raw ingredients.

It is unfortunate for the children who will not remember or will never know the taste of real food. They will believe that the mass-produced imitation, the phony, is the real and the genuine, and I worry that they will be deprived of so much pure pleasure. Communication around the dinner table and the sense of family which comes with it are largely missing in our society. One of my goals at Chez Panisse is to re-establish the gastronomic excitement that inspires and encourages conversation and conviviality. Depersonalized, assembly-line fast food may be "convenient" and "time-saving," but it deprives the senses and denies true nourishment.

Much of the alienation we suffer at the hands of the fast-food giants comes from the distance they create and emphasize between the food and the diners. The high plastic counters, disposable dishes, and emphasis on a minimum of contact between the foods and human hands—to ensure "cleanliness and hygiene"—also ensure distance and estrangement between the diners and those who prepare the food, to say nothing of the distance between the "cooks" and the food itself. I am reminded of a small neighborhood restaurant where I have eaten for years. It is run by an Indian man and his Mexican wife who do everything themselves: they prepare the food and serve it. The restaurant continues to support itself and thrive modestly against the prevailing winds of faster and faster food purveyors. Seated at one of their tables, I am always captivated as I watch them prepare our order in their tiny kitchen. If I should look out the window, I find my gaze captured by the scene in the doughnut shop across the street: the customers, totally isolated from one another and the food itself by the gleaming white sterility of the plastic counters, tables, and walls, are all facing in different directions. The result can be nothing but alienation from one another, as well as from the food and those who cook and serve it. It is doubly sad to me because they *could* simply have walked across the street to reap the humane benefits of this little restaurant for virtually the same price!

As I have watched the transformation of a stressed and rather uninterested diner at Chez Panisse into an involved, excited, and participatory member of his party, I have more clearly understood the necessity and importance of feedback from the kitchen to the dining room and back again. It all has to do with the opening up of the senses on the part of the diners, and I do believe that such things as flowers, food on display, lovely linens, and appealing china can greatly enhance the experience and aid in bringing about the metamorphosis of that hurried and harried diner into the relaxed patron who has submerged himself in the very pleasurable act of eating. But basically it is the genuine involvement with food that fosters this sensory receptiveness.

Flexibility is an essential component of good cooking. You should never feel locked in to a recipe or a menu unless it involves a basic principle regarding procedure or technique such as those involved in breadmaking and pastry. I don't ever want to write anything in this book that is so precise that the reader must invoke great powers of concentration on every last detail in order to ensure the success of a recipe or a dinner; ingredients are simply too variable. I want to *suggest* the expected taste; I want to *suggest* the appearance of the completed dish; I want to *suggest* the combination of ingredients; and I want to *suggest* the overall harmony and balance of the meal. Then it will be up to you to determine the correct balance and composition. Perhaps the garlic is sharp and strong and you will use it sparingly in a particular presentation, or you may find the garlic to be sweet and fresh and you will want to use twice as much!

When I mention a particular garnish, I cannot always tell you what to substitute if the suggested one is unavailable. I *can* make a definitive statement regarding my personal choice for garnishing a particular dish. In the recipe for artichoke and grapefruit salad, I have suggested garnishing the salad with chervil because I felt the need for a light, green, feathery touch of delicacy. Chervil looks right and has the requisite bit of sharpness in its distinctive flavor. At times I have substituted a small sprig of young fennel, a suitable replacement in appearance and flavor. If my recommendation is unobtainable or unreasonably expensive, your own ingenuity, resourcefulness, and personal aesthetics must come into play. When you are faced with the absence of a certain ingredient, don't panic; formulate your own acceptable or inspired replacement, always having the anticipated harmony and balance of the dish uppermost in your mind. I would like these recipes to be understood by someone who doesn't know how to cook at all. The absence of technical knowledge need not prevent a person from understanding the inspiration of rubbing the bread with garlic!

I have not attempted to oversimplify the problem of obtaining first-quality ingredients, nor have I de-emphasized the sometimes exorbitant cost demanded by those who can supply exceptional or unusual foodstuffs. In the same vein, I have not attempted to simplify the complex preparation of an apparently simple dish. Remember that the ultimate quality of a dish is determined initially by the worth of the ingredients and the time and effort expended by the cook. Certainly some dishes require a less complex presentation, but those are usually the dishes which require an additional application of diligence in the selection of the raw ingredients.

If your culinary expertise does not extend to *beurre blanc* and *demi-glace,* but you do understand and empathize with the guidelines set out here regarding freshness and excellence of ingredients, then teaching yourself to make a good *beurre blanc* would be a simple matter indeed. There are innumerable cookbooks devoted solely to the perfection of cooking techniques, but this book is not about complicated sauces. My style of cooking involves combining ingredients that harmonize because of their quality, freshness, aroma, and flavor. If you should encounter an unfamiliar technique or process in these recipes, it is the simplest thing in the world to check any of the procedurally oriented cookbooks. This is how I learned to cook!

We all cook differently. On many occasions I have tasted the same dish prepared by different cooks using the same recipe; the results were similar, but they were *not* identical! My pinch of salt may be larger than your pinch of salt; or I may prefer a slightly saltier taste, while you may, quite justifiably and correctly, fancy a more lightly salted flavor. If your ingrained philosophy tells you that an ingredient or an amount called for in a particular recipe wouldn't be right, eliminate the component or change it to one which falls into the same categories of flavor, texture, and aroma; you should alter the amount of any element you think needs change. And it is vitally important that you continually taste and retaste your ingredients, raw and cooked.

Learn to trust your own instincts. A good cook needs only to have positive feelings about food in general, and about the pleasures of eating and cooking. I have known some cooks who did not seem to discover pleasure and gratification in things culinary. At the restaurant, I look for employees who are interested in working in the kitchen for reasons above and beyond those of simply needing a job, any job. This applies equally to the home cook: a cook who dislikes food is a bad cook. Period. Even an ambivalent cook is a bad cook. Yet a person who responds to the cooking processes and the mound of fresh ingredients with a genuine glow of delight is likely to be, or become, a very good cook indeed. Technical skills can be acquired and perfected along the way, but dislike or ambivalence toward food cannot always be overcome.

In the early stages of my culinary pursuits, I cooked as I had seen cooking done in France. I copied some of the more traditional cooks, and I stayed within the bounds they had laid out so carefully because I didn't trust my own instincts yet. Having imitated their styles, I found that with time and experience, their fundamental principles had become a part of my nature and I began to understand why they had done certain things in a particular way. Then I could begin to develop a different and more personal style based on the ingredients available to me here in California.

When I cook, I usually stand at my kitchen table. I may pull a bunch of thyme from my pocket and lay it on the table; then I wander about the kitchen gathering up all the wonderfully fresh ingredients I can find. I look at each foodstuff carefully, examining it with a critical eye and concentrating in such a way that I begin to make associations. While this method may appear chaotic to others, I do think best while holding a tomato or a leg of lamb. Sometimes I wander through the garden looking for something appealing, absorbing the bouquet of the earth and the scent of the fresh herbs. Sometimes I butterfly my way through cookbooks, quickly flipping the pages and absorbing a myriad of ideas about a particular food or concept.

You can use these recipes and adapt them to your regional ingredients just as I adapt the recipes of other regions and cooks to the ingredients here in California. I enjoyed a marvelous meal at Frédy Girardet's restaurant just outside Lausanne, Switzerland; the chef had achieved a certain perfection and elegance in his use of regional foodstuffs; I admired and appreciated the meal as a work of art. Back in Berkeley I wanted to re-create a part of it. The first course was fresh foie gras—unobtainable here. So I concentrated on the technique they had used to prepare it: sautéing the goose liver, deglazing the pan with sherry vinegar, adding shallots, parsley, and walnut oil, and pouring the sauce over the liver like a vinaigrette. We prepared the dish at Chez Panisse with duck livers, which are readily available to us at an affordable cost. They do not taste the same as foie gras; but we do not pretend that they do. The dish tastes like duck livers prepared in an interesting way, and that in itself is wonderful. Careful substitutions and adaptations can considerably expand the potential applications of any recipe.

Cooking, preparing food, involves far more than just creating a meal for family or friends: it has to do with keeping yourself intact. Because most people cook and eat three meals a day, this process becomes an integral part of one's daily routine. These eating and cooking habits can either be sensually nourishing, even on an unconscious level, or they can rapidly become redundant. There is a marvelous scene in a film by Les Blank of the morning-coffee ritual of an old Southern lady. We watch her reach into her store of coffee beans for a handful, which she puts in a pan on the stove to roast. When she is satisfied with the degree and depth of roast, she shakes the fragrant beans into a hand-cranked coffee grinder and proceeds to pulverize them into a cloth napkin filter. Then she boils the water and pours it through the coffee-filled filter to produce a cup of coffee for herself—one you know must be wonderful. She sits and drinks her coffee in a totally intimate and relaxed manner, and eventually rises to wash out the napkin and hang it out to dry. This ritual is important because she is making a celebration out of the act of making coffee for herself. For others, this coffee habit can be as alienating as a Styrofoam cup of coffee from a vending machine.

So many people believe that by using a myriad of machines and equipment in their cooking, they're simplifying it and making the whole process easier. Somehow, we have been indoctrinated into believing that by making food preparation easier and less time-consuming, we're gaining valuable free time. No mention is ever made of what we lose by this whittling away at our direct contact with our food or what better thing we might do with the time thus gained. I strongly believe that much of what has gone wrong with American food has been the result of mechanization and the alienation that comes with it. The quality of the home food prepared in France has deteriorated, too. It is no longer a simple matter to find hand-kneaded and -shaped bread and homemade aïoli. The harsh sounds of the machine have replaced the rhythmic chop of the knife.

I simply don't believe that all the "gourmet" equipment and utensils are vital. To begin with, the terms "gourmet" or "gourmet cooking" have all the wrong associations for me: they somehow seem to imply that one is more interested in the gleaming copper pans and the flashy chrome and plastic of the food processors than in what one is cooking, and certainly more impressed with them than with the food itself. It is far easier to cook with good sharp knives, but you *can* cook without them. Perversely, some of the very best times to cook are those occasions when you are faced with virtually nothing in terms of equipment—you must make do, improvise, and focus primarily on the food itself. So you may gather rosemary branches from the yard and use them to skewer the meat before you put it on the charcoal grill. If you do, you will have learned something fundamental about food, unrestricted and unhampered by equipment. You need to learn to cook first, and then you will learn what equipment is genuinely important to you.

When you use a machine, you never really touch the food, a fact that deprives you of much of the sensual pleasure and sensory experience so important in developing good cooking habits. When learning to make pesto, you *need* to rub the olive oil into the pounded garlic and the basil with your pestle in hand. You *need* to be able to stick your finger into the mixture to feel the transformation of the ingredients. Otherwise the information just does not come through all your senses. The senses of smell, touch, and hearing, in addition to sight and taste, must work together to enable you to judge what is happening to the ingredients. Machines have a place, but only after you have reached a point in your cooking at which you *know* what you are sacrificing in sensory stimulation for the questionable exchange of a slight saving in time and effort.

Every time we make pesto at the restaurant, it's different. If it isn't garlic with a hotter taste or the basil with a bitterness from too much sun, it's the cook pounding it differently—or it may be that the customer who loved it last time isn't in the mood this time. Maybe every six months the waiters are in the right mood, the cooks cook it right, the customers feel like eating that particular dinner, and I feel satisfied with the results; when that happens, I know that it has been worth the effort.

COMPOSING A MENU
How to use the menus in this book

Marrying the elements of a meal correctly so as to achieve that elusive equilibrium requires an understanding of each separate course and its importance within the overall structure of the menu. To succeed, first consider what foods are at their peak that particular day. Second, consider the factors that affect the meal's reception: the guests and their gastronomic idiosyncrasies; the time of year, and the temperature; and most important, what you feel like cooking and eating yourself.

Bread
My criterion for good bread is that it be good all by itself with just the addition of some sweet butter. But wonderful homemade bread can take over a dinner so completely that by the time the entrée arrives, your guests have filled up on delicious bread! It is splendid to serve bread alone as a lunch—bread, olive oil, garlic, and a glass of wine—but I believe that one food should never be allowed to overpower a meal of which it is merely a part, however important. At the restaurant we try to use bread as an integral part of the various courses rather than serve an unlimited quantity of it on the dining-room tables. We may make little croutons to dip in the olive oil of a salad or we may serve a walnut bread with the cheese.

Hors d'Oeuvres—First Course
The first food tasted in a meal should be enticing. This course should never be heavy and filling. It could be a savory dish such as roasted red peppers and anchovies, or a goat cheese soufflé with thyme, or cold oysters and hot spicy sausages—something to get the juices flowing. Awaken and energize the palate, but don't stun it into unconsciousness.

Soup
It is very difficult to integrate a soup into a menu successfully because soups can easily assume the same role as an overwhelming quantity of bread—too much of one food at one time. I like rich, one-course dinners with soup as the main course, such as bouillabaisse with perhaps just a little *mesclun* salad before, and a bit of sherbet afterward. However, as a part of a more compli-

cated menu, the type and amount of soup become critical issues. For that reason, the soups included in this book are generally light vegetable or fish broths or purées with a minimum of cream or stock. Often the garnishes are intended to offset any richness, such as in the addition of lemon thyme in the squash soup or black pepper on a cream of leek soup.

Fish Course
Fish is wonderfully flexible; it can appear on a menu in a garlicky salt cod hors d'oeuvre, in a fish soup, or as a grilled entrée with a red wine sauce. In the menus at Chez Panisse, we often use fish instead of soup courses; for our purposes, a fish course looks lighter and less filling.

Entrée
I do not really believe in entrées in the American sense of lots of meat, potatoes, and vegetables in the center of a menu. This may be appropriate when the main dish is a suckling pig or some large bird, but I generally prefer to give a number of courses equal weight and importance. The small courses of a French service are appealing to me, and I am fascinated by the kind of menu composition found in Japanese or Chinese meals that have recurring themes, no main dish, and hot, spicy foods at the end of the meal.

I personally cannot eat massive quantities of food, so to me, heaped-up plates are truly offensive. A heavily laden plate allows one course to dominate, and the risk is that it will overwhelm the entire framework of the meal. I do like platters of food in the middle of the table, family style; a more appealing presentation can be made and those at the table can help themselves to precisely the amount they want. This encourages everyone's involvement with the food, eases serving complications in the kitchen, and evokes a communal sense about dining.

Salad
I am often asked whether to serve salads before or after the main course. This depends on the particular menu you have composed. Because I do serve a number of saladlike first courses at the restaurant, I tend to eliminate the salad after the entrée. My personal preference at this point in a meal, particularly after a very rich entrée, is for some little course that's refreshing; this serves the purpose of cleansing and piquing the palate before the cheese and the dessert.

I find that many people do not understand or appreciate two salads in one meal. I don't mind, particularly if they are considerably different in looks, texture, and taste. I like serving a salad to begin a meal, regardless of whether there is to be one after the entrée, because it is nice to have the tart pungency of a good vinaigrette to pick up your palate and awaken the senses the way the right hors d'oeuvre should. You can then proceed with the dinner and perhaps have a cheese course after the entrée, especially if you are drinking wine with the meal and don't wish to interrupt the flow of the wine with an incompatible vinegar-based dressing.

Cheese

Because cheese is one of those simple, straightforward commodities, it can be enormously appealing as a course all by itself with red wine or as the ending to a meal. When the cheese is truly at its peak, it can be a marvelous experience; but cheeses are often badly stored, or they arrive from Europe underripe and uncorrectable or overripe and ammoniated. Therefore, tasting and discrimination are essential, and so is the cultivation of your local cheese merchant.

The simple earthiness of cheese appeals to me, and its facility for making a good wine taste even better endears it to me. When I am in France I am always fascinated by the choice of cheeses, and have even had the wonderfully instructive experience of tasting a cheese in all its various stages of development and age. I like serving more than one type of cheese at a time, for the opportunity for comparison right there at the dining-room table is interesting. So is comparing and contrasting several cheeses of the same type—three or four different blue cheeses, for example.

Desserts

Where I have listed a dessert suggestion for each menu in this cookbook, I have not always included the recipe; I have often found, when testing these menus, that I did not really wish to have a dessert at the meal's end. My desire is frequently for an unexpected taste and texture—a refreshing sherbet, or a wonderfully ripe piece of fruit accompanied by some cheese, a glass of lovely Sauternes, some nuts sautéed in olive oil served hot, or a little glass of anisette.

There should be an ending to a meal, but it need not be a rich and sweet traditional dessert. When I finish a meal, I want to feel *just* satisfied, not stuffed. That stuffed feeling is anathema to me, so my inclination is for something light. At a recent meal I was treated to goat cheese and sage flowers in lieu of dessert, and was intrigued by the fact that this pairing had the very same effect a good dessert should have: it was very refreshing and seemed to aid the digestion more than a heavy dessert ever could have. Too often, dessert is a sugar fix rather than a little touch of sweetness as a change from the savory, the salty, or the piquant. This final course could also be a very dramatic change in look such as a fruit salad, not necessarily sweet, that you could conceive having had at the meal's beginning. A dish that is very hot or very cold can be highly effective: a dramatic change in temperature is quite refreshing.

Wine

Combining wine with food to achieve a perfect balance requires thought, knowledge, and experience. Occasionally a combination of food and wine will result in an almost transcendental balance, a whole greater than the sum of its parts. This is difficult to achieve because there are so many variables. You may think about a certain dish and plan on a certain wine to accompany it, but when you actually cook the dish you may find that it has taken on an entirely different character from what you expected; the wine, too, because it is a living, breathing commodity, may reveal an unexpected aspect— perhaps it is fruitier or drier than you anticipated.

When you achieve that perfect pairing, you stand in awe and never forget. A recent memory is of a St. Péray, a Côtes-du-Rhône, which, when paired with a leek and goat cheese tart, produced such a wonderful combination of flavors that it took me by surprise. On another occasion, I found that a young Château Suduiraut, accompanied by a lightly smoked salmon, made a lovely lunch. A special combination, charcoal-grilled salmon and a 1966 Château Léoville-Las-Cases, made me realize that the oily, smoky salmon needed the charming elegance of an older Bordeaux. My favorite wines are those that are never mistaken for any other. A Joseph Swan Zinfandel will always be a Joseph Swan Zinfandel, and will always jump up from the wine glass to grab my senses when I taste it. Great wines, like those from Domaine Tempier in Bandol, should have an elusive character and breed that the winemaker is able to capture in each and every vintage. I am striving to bring the same energy and dedication to my cooking.

How to Use the Menus in This Book

After most of the menus you will find recipes for all the courses; but sometimes no recipe is given. This may be because I've thought of the dish as an optional course, more an afterthought than an integral part of the meal; or it may be that the missing recipe would have been redundant or self-evident. In either case, the entry is marked with an asterisk. In the same way, the wine suggestions are usually offered as a general idea of some appropriate wines; but sometimes I've listed a wine more specifically because it's a proven success with the menu. `

The point is that if you use these menus, you, too, can be more or less specific. To execute any menu in this book will be to re-compose it; to cook any recipe will be to re-invent it. In the end, it will be your character and your taste that determine the outcome.

INSPIRATIONS
AND
ADAPTATIONS

࿐

For some years now, every Thursday I have faced the weekly dilemma of planning a different five-course meal for each evening of the following week, a chore which could rapidly have become drudgery had it not been for the creative stimulation of the wonderfully inventive cooks I have known and admired. They have influenced me with their clearly delineated likes and dislikes and their discrimination: that most desirable of qualities which combines discernment, penetration, and judgment. In helping me define my personal gastronomic aesthetics, they have supplied the motivation and encouragement that every cook needs. The result has been a personal aesthetic which is very much a patchwork—an idea borrowed from here or there, an adaptation of a particular concept, an infusion of stimulation—spurring me to create those five new menus each week. I believe this combining of styles and flavors is what has made Chez Panisse a unique establishment.

I cannot overemphasize the importance of approaching each new menu or each new dish with a fresh attitude. Never look back, burdening yourself with the memory of the dinner that didn't quite work. Nor should you endlessly repeat the comfortable dish that you have mastered: that promotes a stagnant attitude. Move away from that safe old chocolate mousse recipe to new ideas, new cookbooks, and new restaurants for inspiration, motivation, and incentive. Learn to discriminate and choose the best of everything. More than any other quality in other cooks, the one I most value is the ability to see precisely what is needed in a particular dish, dinner, or event. This discrimination and attention to detail distinguish those dedicated and perceptive cooks I most admire.

Dodin-Bouffant, the fictional *bon vivant* in Marcel Rouff's *The Passionate Epicure,* epitomizes this ability to discern and to discriminate. Everything in his life was tied in to gastronomic enjoyment. He believed that the lush greenness and scent of a freshly mowed lawn just outside the window had much to contribute to a successful dinner party, and that no more than eight guests should gather round the table, eight being the exact number needed for stimulating conversation! The paintings on the walls, the color of the wood in the dining-room furniture, and the relative comfort of the armchairs at his dining table all played a major role in cosseting his guests. The flowers had to perfume and color the room in a manner harmonious to the foods and the wines, and the temperature of the room had to be precisely 16 degrees Centigrade, summer and winter. Dodin-Bouffant believed in an overall ambience that enfolds you in its reassuring warmth.

He took great pains to achieve a harmonious effect in the pairing of a particular food and the dish it was served upon. His inspirational discourses on the subject of total eating have exhilarated and influenced me in countless ways. His premise that dining well is an art that must be preserved has made me apply his standards to many details of the restaurant and its food. A successful dinner is more than the sum of the food and the wine; it includes comfortable chairs, pleasant artwork on the walls, lovely linens, delightful dishes, a comfortable room temperature, sparkling glasses—and most of all, the receptive and participatory attitude of the guests.

Rouff's model for Dodin-Bouffant was the great French gastronome Curnonsky. The charming photographs in his cookbook *The Traditional Recipes of France* are a source of never-ending delight to me. Regional specialties are illustrated with meticulous attention to detail. Wines, silverware, dishes, linen, all harmonize with the food. The photograph of beige and brown-striped gloves laid casually on the table beside tiny striped *petits fours,* a still life of crusted old bottles of port next to a Roquefort cheese on a daintily flowered plate, a succulent goose surrounded by fresh truffles— these are the visual stimuli that inspire me.

I have a wonderful picture book called *La Belle France,* and I have spent hours examining all the details in the photographs: the old gentleman pictured in his garden as he chose a ripe peach and held it up to the camera's eye, the close-up of a strawberry patch overflowing with perfect tiny red berries, a restaurant in a garden with tables under the arbor right on the grass —images such as these have helped mold my gastronomic tastes in many ways.

While the menus that follow do not always include dishes specifically created by the cooks or writers who inspired them, they are the result of my exposure to the tastes and ideologies of these people, and in each case, their clearly defined aesthetics and their incomparable sense of food and life have inspired the menu.

For a full explanation of the use of asterisks before certain entries (meaning that recipes are not given for entries so marked), please see page 12.

Roasted Red Peppers with Anchovies
Potato and Truffle Salad
Hard-Cooked Quail Eggs
Marinated Cheese with Olives and Whole Garlic
Roast Pigeon with Purple Grapes
**Sourdough Bread with Parsley Butter*
Lindsey's Almond Tart
**Nectarines*

Picnics can be very special, indeed, if the foods are chosen carefully enough so that they last through the entire outing—or if the dishes improve with time. Then the picnickers can experience the food undistracted, discovering each dish as it is taken from the basket. So, it is important to consider every possible need when planning the picnic. Elizabeth David inspired this menu because she loves to eat out-of-doors and says she always travels with a bit of this food and that food, just in case she finds herself without access to something edible. Picnics provide diverse opportunities for experimentation with color and texture because all of the foods are laid upon the table or cloth at the same time. For example, in this menu the smooth purple skin of the grapes contrasts nicely with the crinkly brown skin of the squab, while the sleek black of the olives is a foil for the roasted skin of the bright red peppers.

SUGGESTED WINES: Red or white Provençal wine with most of the picnic, and a Muscat Beaumes-de-Venise with the dessert.

Roasted Red Peppers with Anchovies

Serves 6

3 large red bell peppers
½ cup virgin olive oil
3 whole salt-packed anchovies
6 to 8 basil leaves
Black pepper

ROAST 3 large red bell peppers directly over a medium-high gas flame on the stove top. Turn the peppers as they blacken, holding them with tongs to char the stem area. When the peppers are completely charred but still firm, about 5 to 6 minutes, remove them from the flame to a paper or plastic bag. Close the bag loosely and let the peppers steam for about 5 minutes.

Remove the peppers from the bag, cut them in half lengthwise and remove the seeds, fibers, and stems. Scrape the charred skin from the peppers with the blunt edge of a knife. Cut the peppers in 1-inch strips lengthwise, put them in a dish and cover them with ½ cup virgin olive oil.

Fillet 3 whole salt-packed anchovies and rinse them thoroughly in cold water. Add the anchovy fillets to the peppers along with 6 to 8 basil leaves. Sprinkle lightly with coarse ground black pepper and toss the basil, anchovies, and peppers to coat with oil. Arrange the dish and marinate at cool room temperature for 30 minutes to 1 hour.

Potato and Truffle Salad

Serves 6

12 red or white new potatoes, about 2 inches in diameter
1 tablespoon sea salt
3 large shallots
¼ cup white wine vinegar
Fresh black truffles
about ½ cup virgin olive oil
Black pepper

P UT 12 small red or white new potatoes in a pot and cover with water by 1 inch. Add 1 tablespoon sea salt, cover the potatoes, and bring to a boil. Reduce the heat to a strong simmer, remove the cover and cook the potatoes gently for 5 to 10 minutes. Check the potatoes frequently with a small sharp knife for doneness. When the potatoes are just done, drain them and let them cool.

While the potatoes are cooking, dice 3 large shallots and put them in a small dish. Cover them with ¼ cup white wine vinegar and sprinkle them with a little salt.

Peel the potatoes and slice them into ¼-inch rounds. Thinly slice as many fresh black truffles as you can afford and toss them gently with the potatoes. Finish the vinaigrette by adding ½ cup virgin olive oil and freshly ground black pepper to the shallots and vinegar. Adjust the vinaigrette with more olive oil, pepper, or salt if necessary. Dress the salad and cover it well so that the truffle aroma permeates the potatoes while the salad is being taken to the picnic.

Hard-Cooked Quail Eggs

Serves 6

12 to 18 quail eggs

P UT 12 to 18 quail eggs in a pot and cover with cold water by 1 inch. Bring the water to a boil. The eggs are usually done just as the water begins to bubble. Remove one egg and cut it open to test for doneness. The centers should still be soft and orange. Drain the eggs immediately and cool them under cold running water. Shell the eggs at the picnic.

Marinated Cheese with Olives and Whole Garlic

Serves 6

12- 16-ounce small goat cheeses
12 whole cloves garlic
1 pint virgin olive oil
Salt and black pepper
½ cup Niçoise olives
2 to 3 bay leaves

C HOOSE 12- to 16-ounce firm fresh goat cheeses, small enough that they can be marinated whole. Peel 12 cloves of garlic and put them in a small sauté pan. Barely cover them with virgin olive oil and sprinkle them lightly with salt and black pepper. Cook the garlic over very low heat until it is tender but still firm, about 10 minutes. Turn the garlic occasionally and do not let it color beyond a pale golden. When the garlic is tender, drain it and reserve the olive oil. Let the garlic cool to room temperature.

Put the cheese in a jar or crock just large enough to hold it. Add the garlic cloves, ½ cup Niçoise olives, and 2 to 3 bay leaves. Pour enough olive oil, including the reserved oil, over the cheese to completely cover it. Cover the container and marinate in a cool place.

To serve, spread the garlic with some cheese and some olive oil on pieces of sourdough bread.

Roast Pigeon with Purple Grapes

Serves 6

3 pigeons
Salt and pepper
4 tablespoons duck fat
Cognac
2 pounds purple grapes

REMOVE the heads and feet from 3 pigeons. Salt and pepper the pigeons. Heat 4 tablespoons duck fat over medium-high heat in a large sauté pan and brown the pigeons for about 5 minutes, turning them frequently. Flame with a little Cognac and remove from the heat.

Place the pigeons breast up on a rack in a roasting pan. Roast in a preheated 400°F. oven for 15 to 20 minutes, until the breasts are springy yet firm when pressed lightly with a finger. If the breasts are pricked, the juices will run pink. Remove the pigeons from the oven and let them cool completely to room temperature before wrapping them for the picnic. Serve the pigeons with about 2 pounds of purple grapes trimmed into clusters.

Lindsey's Almond Tart

Serves 6 to 8

1 recipe tart pastry (page 179)
1 cup blanched sliced almonds
1 cup whipping cream
¾ cup sugar
Pinch of salt
1 tablespoon Grand Marnier
1 tablespoon kirsch
2 drops almond extract

PRESS the tart pastry into a 9-inch tart form with a removable ring, reserving a small amount. Press the dough evenly over the bottom and sides about ⅛ inch thick and extend the dough ⅛ inch above the top of the ring. Prick the shell lightly, and refrigerate for at least 1 hour. The dough may be refrigerated for 8 hours, or it may be frozen.

Partially bake the tart shell in a preheated 400°F. oven for 10 minutes, until it begins to set and brown. Remove the shell to a cake rack and cool to room temperature. Patch any holes in the shell by smoothing a very small bit of reserved dough over them.

In a heavy saucepan, mix 1 cup blanched thin-sliced almonds with 1 cup whipping cream, ¾ cup sugar, a pinch of salt, 1 tablespoon each Grand Marnier and kirsch, and 2 drops almond extract. Cook the mixture over low heat until the sugar has dissolved and the texture is silky, about 10 to 15 minutes. Cool the mixture slightly and pour it into the prepared tart shell.

Line the floor of the oven with foil and preheat it to 350°F. Bake the tart on the center rack for 25 to 30 minutes. The filling will bubble up and may overflow, then it will settle and begin to caramelize. Rotate the tart frequently during the last 15 minutes of baking so the top is an even deep golden brown. Remove the tart to a cake rack and let cool to room temperature before cutting.

Whole Baked Garlic with White Cheese and Peasant Bread
Spit-Roasted Squab with Anchovy-Olive Butter
New Potatoes in Parchment
*Garden Salad
Linda's Chocolate Cups

This is a menu I cooked for James Beard when he came to the restaurant. I tried to think of a way to cook garlic he might not have tried and came up with this now infamous recipe. The chocolate cups at the end were inspired by a story he told my friend who makes chocolate: once, twenty years ago in Switzerland, when his after-dinner coffee was served, tiny molded chocolate cups filled with cream accompanied it; then the entire mold, cream and all, was dropped into the coffee, which created a divine melange of bittersweet chocolate, sweet cream, and coffee.

SUGGESTED WINES: Good California Chardonnay with the garlic, a good California Cabernet with the squab.

Whole Baked Garlic with White Cheese and Peasant Bread

Serves 6

6 whole heads of new-crop garlic (firm and unsprouting)
⅓ cup butter
⅓ cup olive oil
Salt and pepper
2 or 3 sprigs thyme
½ cup goat cheese
¼ cup heavy cream

PREHEAT the oven to 275°F. Make an incision around the head of garlic to remove the outer skin from the top half of the head, exposing the individual cloves. Arrange the heads in a baking dish that will just hold them. Dot with butter, pour the ⅓ cup olive oil over, and salt and pepper well. Put thyme sprigs in here and there. Bake, covered, for 30 minutes then take off the cover and baste every fifteen minutes. Bake an additional 1 to 1½ hours depending on the size of the heads. The garlic should be very tender and sweet.

Make a mild cream cheese to serve with the garlic. Mix ½ cup goat cheese and ¼ cup heavy cream together until it has an easily spreadable consistency.

When the garlic is done, serve the whole heads with the oil from the dish spooned over them, with peasant bread and the white cheese. Dip the bread in the oil, squeeze on the garlic, and eat warm.

Spit-Roasted Squab with Anchovy-Olive Butter

Serves 6

3 fresh squabs
2 onions
½ bunch parsley
2 cups red wine
⅓ cup brandy
3 whole salt-packed anchovies
1 cup pitted Niçoise olives
¼ pound butter
Olive oil
Salt and pepper

MARINATE 3 fresh squabs with 2 sliced onions, ½ bunch parsley, 2 cups red wine and ¼ cup brandy for several hours, turning frequently.

To make the olive-and-anchovy butter, fillet 3 salt-packed anchovies and rinse them thoroughly under cold water. Pound them in a mortar with 1 cup pitted Niçoise olives, ¼ pound butter, and the remaining brandy.

Spit the birds so that they are securely fastened on the skewer. Place the birds over a hot grill or next to a hot fire. As they turn they should be basted with the marinade. Depending on the size of the birds and the heat of the fire, they should take about 20 to 30 minutes and should have a crisp brown exterior and rare interior.

Allow the squabs to rest after cooking. Cut them in half and spread the pieces with the olive-and-anchovy butter. Serve with new potatoes in parchment.

New Potatoes in Parchment

Serves 6

1 pound new potatoes
4 tablespoons butter
2 sprigs fresh thyme
Salt

CHOOSE very fresh new potatoes. If they are very small, leave them whole; otherwise cut them into 1-inch pieces. Salt the potatoes and seal them in a double-thickness, folded parchment-paper package with 4 tablespoons butter and 2 sprigs of thyme. Bake in a preheated 425°F. oven for 25 to 30 minutes.

Linda's Chocolate Cups

About thirty cups

8 ounces Swiss bittersweet chocolate

YOU WILL NEED:

¾-inch new pastry brush
Small paper bonbon cups
Cookie sheet or muffin tin
Instant-reading thermometer

FIRST temper the chocolate by alternately heating and cooling it; this will prevent cocoa butter from rising to the surface and leaving white streaks on the finished chocolate. To do this, grate the chocolate and place it in a double boiler over hot water at 140°F. Stir frequently to ensure that it remains well-blended and that it melts more quickly. Use the thermometer to monitor the temperature of the chocolate; *never* allow it to rise over 100°F. The chocolate should be completely melted at approximately 96°F; remove the double boiler from the heat, replace the hot water with cool water, and replace the chocolate over the water.

Stirring constantly, allow the chocolate temperature to fall to 80°F. Remove the top of the double boiler, replace the cool water with warm water at between 120° and 130°F., and put the chocolate over the warm water. Stirring constantly and checking the temperature frequently, raise the temperature of the chocolate to 89°F., exactly. Remove the chocolate from over the warm water. It may be necessary during the molding of the cups to replace the chocolate over warm water to melt it slightly, but never allow it to rise over 89°F. Add hot water or replace water in the lower half of the double boiler as needed to maintain the chocolate at 86°F. to 89°F.; stir the chocolate frequently.

Take a small stack of bonbon cups and loosen the top cup. Put this cup back on the stack. Using the pastry brush, paint the inside of the top cup with the melted chocolate, keeping the coating of the chocolate as even as possible. (The paper will be removed after the chocolate cools and hardens, so the cup must be strong enough to hold its shape unaided.) Carefully remove the top cup from the stack and place it on a cookie sheet or muffin tin.

When you have used all the melted chocolate, place the cookie sheet or muffin tin in the refrigerator. It is not necessary or desirable to leave the cups in the refrigerator for a long period of time, just until the chocolate has hardened (about 10 minutes). When they are hard, remove a few cups at a time from the refrigerator.

Carefully peel away the paper cup on the outside of the chocolate.

Chocolate cups made with any dark chocolate will keep indefinitely if stored in a closed container in a cool place (but not in the refrigerator). They may then be used as needed. Eight ounces of chocolate, properly tempered, will yield approximately thirty chocolate cups, depending upon the thickness of the chocolate coating.

When you are ready to serve after-dinner espresso, place the chocolate cups on a tray and carefully fill them with heavy cream, then let each person drop a cream-filled chocolate cup into his or her coffee cup.

Pressed Caviar with Flavored Russian Vodkas
Warm Salad with Tiny Escarole and Lettuce
Coulibiac of Salmon
Mango Compote

My friend Jeremiah Tower used to tell stories about his Russian uncle when he cooked blinis and coulibiacs at Chez Panisse. To know if you had enough butter on the blini it had to be dripping off your elbows as you put it in your mouth, and he recalled his uncle washing this down with lemon-flavored Russian vodka. This menu emerged from those stories and others. I remember early coulibiacs we made together at the restaurant. We had to make ten at a time and assemble them by dinner. Needless to say, copious amounts of sweet butter and cream were used. This particular coulibiac with wild rice is a variation that provides an interesting contrast of flavor and texture to this wonderfully rich dish.

SUGGESTED WINES: After the flavored vodkas (which can be flavored with buffalo grass, lemon, peppercorns, dried wild mushrooms, fennel seed, etc.: just put the flavoring—seed, peel, herb, or whatever—into some vodka to steep for a few days or longer), serve an old bottle of Château Lafite from an odd or light vintage with the coulibiac. Serve a fine, old Sauternes at the end.

Warm Salad with Tiny Escarole and Lettuce

Serves 10

10 assorted tiny escarole and lettuce heads
2 cups pecans, in halves
4 tablespoons unsalted butter
¼ cup Balsamico vinegar
about ¾ cup virgin olive oil
1 tablespoon finely minced shallots
Salt and pepper
½ pound Smithfield ham, sliced very thin

WASH and dry 10 heads of tiny escarole and assorted garden lettuce. Sauté 2 cups of pecan halves in 4 tablespoons butter for 5 minutes and drain the pecans. Make a vinaigrette with ¼ cup Balsamico vinegar and about ¾ cup virgin olive oil. The vinegar is very flavorful, so more olive oil may be needed. Stir in 1 tablespoon minced shallots, and season the vinaigrette with salt and pepper.

Heat the vinaigrette with the pecans in a large sauté pan over medium low heat for about 1 minute. Put the lettuces and Smithfield ham in a large bowl and toss with the hot vinaigrette. Serve the salad at once.

Coulibiac of Salmon

Serves 10

4 pounds salmon
1 recipe *court-bouillon* (see page 220)
1 to 2 pounds butter
Salt, pepper, and lemon juice
1 cup wild rice
12 quail eggs
¾ pound mushrooms
3 shallots
½ cup Italian parsley leaves
6 sprigs chervil
6 sprigs tarragon
1 recipe buckwheat crêpes (see page 32)
1 recipe brioche (see page 234). Note: Prepare the dough the day before
  serving the coulibiac.
1 egg yolk
1 tablespoon whipping cream

EARLY on the serving day, poach 4 pounds of salmon in a *court-bouillon* until the salmon is *barely* cooked. Bring the *court-bouillon* to a simmer, poach the salmon about 5 minutes, remove all bones and skin, and flake it carefully into large pieces. Melt ¼ pound butter and pour it over the salmon. Season with salt, pepper, and lemon juice. Cover and refrigerate until needed.

Cook 1 cup wild rice in 3 cups of water with ½ teaspoon salt for about 45 minutes. The rice should be cooked *à point;* simmer it until it is cooked through, tender but not falling apart. Drain, cool to room temperature, and toss it with ¼ pound melted butter and salt and pepper. Set aside.

Simmer 12 quail eggs until they are *à point,* with the yolks still soft but not runny (see page 19). Peel the eggs, wrap them in a tea towel, and refrigerate.

Make a *duxelles* with ¾ pound finely chopped mushrooms and 3 minced shallots. Melt 4 tablespoons butter and slowly sauté the *duxelles* over medium heat for about 25 minutes, stirring frequently. Remove to a bowl and stir in ½ cup Italian parsley leaves which have been minced with the leaves from 6 sprigs chervil and 6 sprigs tarragon. Season with salt and pepper.

Make 6 buckwheat crêpes; the batter may be used directly from the refrigerator.

About 2 hours before serving time, assemble the coulibiac. Remove the brioche dough from the refrigerator and divide it in half. Roll about ¾ of the dough on a floured board to ¼ inch thick in a rectangle or in an oval. Place on a lightly buttered baking sheet. Arrange 3 crêpes, slightly overlapping, in a line down the center of the dough. Spread half of the wild rice on the crêpes. Remove the salmon from the refrigerator (drain it if necessary), and very carefully toss it with another ¼ pound melted butter. Place half of the salmon on top of the rice. Make a line of the eggs lengthwise down the center of the salmon and surround them with the *duxelles*. Cover with the remaining salmon, rice, and crêpes. Bring the dough on the baking sheet up around the sides of the filling, enclosing it completely. Seal well and trim any excess. Tuck in the ends of the dough neatly. Make a decorative braid by cutting three thin strips of the rolled-out dough and braiding them. Brush a little egg wash down the center seal of the coulibiac, lay the braid on top, and tuck under at the ends.

Allow the coulibiac to stand at room temperature for 30 minutes, then glaze the top and sides with 1 egg yolk lightly beaten with 1 tablespoon of whipping cream. Bake in a preheated 375°F. oven for about 45 minutes, until the brioche is a rich golden brown.

FOR THE GARNISH:

6 to 8 sprigs each of Italian parsley, tarragon, and chervil
1 to 1½ cups crème fraîche
1 to 1½ cups melted unsalted butter

ALLOW the coulibiac to rest 5 minutes before slicing, then garnish with sprigs of Italian parsley, tarragon, and chervil and accompany with crème fraîche and melted butter.

Buckwheat Crêpes

2 cups milk
½ cup butter
1 teaspoon salt
1 teaspoon sugar
¾ cup buckwheat flour
1½ cups all-purpose flour
1 tablespoon vegetable oil
4 eggs
1 cup flat beer

HEAT 1 cup of the milk, ½ cup butter, 1 teaspoon salt, and 1 teaspoon sugar in a saucepan over low heat until the butter melts. Remove from the heat and let cool to room temperature. Mix ¾ cup buckwheat flour with 1½ cups all-purpose flour in a large bowl. Make a well in the flour and put

1 tablespoon vegetable oil and 4 eggs in it. Beat thoroughly with a whisk, gradually incorporating the cooled milk mixture and 1 cup flat beer. Cover the batter and let it rest for about 2 hours in the refrigerator. Add most of the second cup of milk, stirring well, until the batter has the consistency of thick cream.

To cook the crêpes, butter an 8-inch crêpe pan very lightly and heat over medium-high heat. Pour in about 3 tablespoons of batter, enough to form a thin layer over the whole pan. Cook for 1 to 1½ minutes, until the crêpe browns nicely. (Buckwheat flour takes longer to cook than wheat flour.) Turn the crêpe over and cook for 30 to 45 seconds on the other side. Stack the crêpes. The batter will keep one to two days in the refrigerator.

Mango Compote

Serves 10

5 large ripe mangoes
about 2 teaspoons lime juice
2 cups Sauternes

PEEL the mangoes and slice them from the stones in about ⅜-inch slices. Put them in a shallow dish and sprinkle with 2 teaspoons lime juice. Pour 2 cups Sauternes over the mangoes, cover, and refrigerate for 2 to 3 hours. Remove them from the refrigerator 1 hour before serving and taste for lime juice. There should be a hint of lime flavor; add more juice if necessary.

Fresh Herring Fillets with Salt and Lemon
Salt Cod Bouillabaisse
Lamb Shank Daube
Cheeses
Marc de Provence

When I was visiting the Domaine Tempier in Bandol, in Provence, Lulu Peyraud, the proprietress, took me on one of her excursions to ferret out the freshest offerings at the harbor. We brought back some herring just out of the water which she skinned, filleted, and marinated in lemon juice with a bit of salt, and then served as an hors d'oeuvre with bread and sweet butter. The aromas of garlic, salt cod, and saffron perfumed the air as she next presented her salt cod bouillabaisse. When I came back to the restaurant I tried to re-create that dish using both salt and fresh cod because I couldn't remember exactly how she had made hers, and mine was just too salty with salt cod alone.

A little *marc* seems like the perfect conclusion to a substantial Provençal meal.

SUGGESTED WINES: Naturally, the wines of the Domaine Tempier are the perfect wines for this meal: their salmon-colored rosé with the fish, and their unforgettable red with the lamb shanks and the cheese.

Salt Cod Bouillabaisse

Serves 8 to 10

THE FISH AND THE *FUMET*:

1 pound salt cod
5 to 6 pounds whole fresh rockfish
2 medium leeks
2 onions
1 carrot
1 celery rib
3 to 4 shallots
2 medium tomatoes
4 tablespoons virgin olive oil
Bouquet garni: 6 sprigs parsley; 3 sprigs fresh thyme; 3 cloves chopped
     garlic; 1 teaspoon fennel seed; ½ teaspoon coriander seed; 10 to 12
     black peppercorns; 1 bay leaf
Pinch of saffron
Piece of orange peel
2 tablespoons Pernod

TO prepare the fish, select a piece of salt cod that is firm, white, and fresh-smelling, and soak it for 2 or 3 days, refrigerated. Change the water several times during the soaking. When it has soaked, clean it thoroughly, removing any skin, bones, and dark spots. Cut it into even, medallion-shaped pieces and set aside. Fillet the rockfish (reserve the trimmings for the *fumet*) and cut the fillets into pieces similar in thickness and size to the salt cod. Set the pieces aside.

To make the *fumet,* clean the scraps of the fish well, removing the gills and any bloody parts. Slice the leeks, onions, carrot, celery, and shallots. Dice the tomatoes. Sauté the fish frames gently in 4 tablespoons olive oil in a stock pot for 4 to 5 minutes. Add the vegetables and cook for another 5 to 10 minutes. Add the bouquet garni, a pinch of saffron, a strip of orange peel with no white pith, and 2 tablespoons Pernod. Add water to cover the fish and vegetables by a few inches. Bring the *fumet* to a boil, skim, and reduce the heat. Simmer for 30 to 45 minutes. Strain the *fumet* and reduce it slightly if a more concentrated flavor is needed.

THE VEGETABLES AND SEASONING FOR THE BROTH:

2 onions
1 clove garlic
2 medium tomatoes
1 pound white potatoes
4 tablespoons virgin olive oil
Pinch of saffron
1 bay leaf
Strip of orange peel
about 1 tablespoon Pernod
about ⅓ cup dry white wine
1 teaspoon minced fresh thyme
1 tablespoon minced parsley
about 1 tablespoon orange juice
Black pepper

BEFORE cooking the bouillabaisse, taste the salt cod for saltiness. If it is very salty, blanch the pieces in plain water for 1 or 2 minutes and drain.

Dice 2 onions and slice a clove of garlic thin. Peel, seed, and dice 2 tomatoes. Peel 1 pound of potatoes, slice them thin, and blanch them for 1 minute in plain water.

Soften the onions in 4 tablespoons olive oil. Add the garlic, a pinch of saffron, a bay leaf, the orange peel, and the salt cod pieces. Add the tomatoes and cook gently for 1 minute. Add the *fumet* (about 3 quarts), about 1 tablespoon Pernod, and about ⅓ cup white wine. Bring to a simmer, add the potatoes and minced herbs, and about 1 tablespoon orange juice. Simmer 2 or 3 minutes, then add the rockfish fillets, which have been seasoned with black pepper. When the fish is just cooked, remove it to serving bowls. Taste the broth and correct the seasoning.

GARNISHES:

18 to 24 garlic croutons (see page 95)
1 recipe aïoli (see page 219)

PREPARE the garnishes while the *fumet* is simmering. To serve the bouillabaisse, ladle the broth over the fish and garnish each serving with a little minced thyme and parsley and three or four garlic croutons. Put about 1 tablespoon of aïoli in each dish and serve the rest separately.

Lamb Shank Daube

Serves 8 to 10

3 large lamb shanks, about 6 pounds
6 to 8 cloves garlic
3 small carrots
1 large onion
3 cups red wine, preferably Bandol
1 sprig fresh thyme
1 sprig fresh marjoram
6 sprigs parsley
½ teaspoon fennel seeds
2 strips orange peel
about ½ cup virgin olive oil
about ¼ cup Cognac
3 tablespoons all-purpose flour
¼ pound salt pork
about 2 cups lamb stock (see page 199)
½ cup water
Half a pig's foot
1 ripe tomato
Salt and black pepper

To prepare the lamb shanks for the marinade, bone them and trim off excess fat and connective tissue. Cut the meat into 2-inch cubes.

Peel and chop 6 or 8 cloves garlic roughly. Peel and slice thin 3 small carrots and 1 large onion. Make the marinade of 3 cups red wine, the sliced vegetables and garlic, 1 sprig thyme, 1 sprig marjoram, 6 sprigs parsley, ½ teaspoon fennel seeds, 2 strips of orange peel with no white pith, ¼ cup of the olive oil, and 2 tablespoons of the Cognac. Put the lamb in the marinade and leave it, covered, in the refrigerator overnight, or at room temperature for 4 hours. If the lamb is marinated overnight, let it stand at room temperature for 3 or 4 hours before cooking.

To assemble the daube, remove the lamb from the marinade and pat it dry. Remove and discard the herbs, strain the marinade, and reserve the vegetables and marinade. Brown the lamb over high heat in 3 tablespoons olive oil. Pour the oil from the pan when the lamb is well-browned, and sprinkle the meat with 3 tablespoons all-purpose flour. Immediately flame the meat with 2 or 3 tablespoons Cognac and remove from the heat.

Cut ¼ pound salt pork into 1-inch cubes and blanch them in plain water for 4 or 5 minutes. Drain the pork and pat dry. Sauté the pork with the reserved vegetables in 2 tablespoons olive oil over gentle heat for 5 to 10 minutes. Add the vegetables and pork, along with the reserved marinade, to the pot with the lamb and bring to a boil over high heat. Put the hot lamb and marinade in an earthenware crock that has a lid, and add about 2 cups lamb stock and ½ cup water. Add the pig's foot and a peeled, seeded, and roughly chopped tomato. Seal the lid of the crock with a flour-and-water paste and bake in a preheated 325°F. oven for 2 to 2½ hours.

After it is done, let the crock come to room temperature, then break the seal. Remove the lid from the crock and season the sauce with salt and black pepper if necessary. The sauce should be medium thick; if it is not, ladle most of it into a saucepan and reduce it to the desired thickness.

The daube is absolutely best if it is cooked the day before serving. Cover the crock loosely and refrigerate overnight. Reheat the daube in a pot on top of the stove over medium heat. Serve with egg pasta that has been flavored with saffron.

Duck Pâté with Pistachio Nuts
Squid with Leeks and Red Wine
Rack of Lamb Roasted with Herbs and Served with White Purée
*Garden Lettuces with Hyssop and Rocket Flowers
Olive Oil and Sauternes Cake

This menu is a combination of dishes from a menu Richard Olney proposed for a Chambertin-Clos de Bèze tasting at the restaurant some years ago and from a lunch he prepared for me at his home in Provence. The salad was actually served as a first course with green beans just picked from his garden, nasturtiums, and hyssop and rocket flowers, all tossed with olive oil and his homemade vinegar. The lamb was grilled in his stone fireplace. I couldn't resist adding this olive oil and Sauternes cake, which could easily accompany a lovely old Sauternes at the end of this dinner. The amazing part is that the cake neither tastes of olive oil nor Sauternes, but is a moist and rich marriage of the two.

SUGGESTED WINES: Begin with a white Burgundy, and drink a succession of Chambertins, from young to old, with the squid and the lamb. And of course, an old Sauternes with dessert.

Duck Pâté with Pistachio Nuts

Serves 10 to 12

1 fresh 5-pound duck
⅓ cup Cognac
1 large shallot
Optional: 1 tablespoon minced black truffle
Salt and pepper
½ pound salt pork, rind removed
¾ pound lean pork
2 eggs
1 clove minced garlic
¼ teaspoon powdered ginger
¼ teaspoon freshly grated nutmeg
about ½ teaspoon dried thyme
about ½ teaspoon rubbed sage
about ½ teaspoon freshly ground black pepper
1 small carrot
½ cup shelled unsalted green pistachio nuts
3 bay leaves

TO fill a 1½ quart terrine, bone a 5-pound duck. Peel off the skin in as large pieces as possible and reserve. Cut the breast meat crosswise into ¼-inch strips and marinate for 4 hours in ⅓ cup Cognac with 1 large minced shallot and about 1 tablespoon minced black truffle. Season the marinade with salt and pepper.

To make the forcemeat, remove the sinews from the leg meat and grind it with ½ pound salt pork and ¾ pound lean pork through the fine blade of the meat grinder. The texture should be fine but not mashed or puréed. To the ground meat add 2 beaten eggs, 1 minced clove garlic, ¼ teaspoon ginger, ¼ teaspoon nutmeg, ½ teaspoon dried thyme, ½ teaspoon rubbed sage, and ½ teaspoon ground black pepper. Peel 1 small carrot and cut it into ¼-inch dice. Add the diced carrot and ½ cup shelled pistachio nuts to the forcemeat and mix well. Check the seasoning by frying a small bit of the forcemeat. More herbs and spices may be needed.

Line the terrine with the reserved duck skin. Make a layer of half of the forcemeat on the bottom and place the marinated strips of duck breast down the center. Cover with the remaining forcemeat, pat the mixture down, and put 3 bay leaves on top. Cover the top of the terrine tightly with foil and put it in a roasting pan. Add hot water to the roasting pan to a level 1 inch below the top of the terrine. Bake in a preheated 325°F. oven for about 1½ hours. The pâté is done when the internal temperature is 150°F. Remove the pâté from the bain-marie and let stand at room temperature for about 4 hours. Weight the terrine and refrigerate for at least 6 hours.

Squid with Leeks and Red Wine

Serves 6

16 squid, about 6 inches long
about 4 tablespoons virgin olive oil
Salt and pepper
1 tablespoon Cognac
about 1¼ cups light-bodied, fruity red wine
1 ripe medium tomato
2 medium leeks
1 large minced shallot
1 minced clove garlic
2 teaspoons all-purpose flour
Bouquet garni: 2 sprigs fresh thyme; 4 to 5 sprigs parsley; 1 bay leaf; a
    strip of orange peel
about 2 tablespoons minced parsley
12 garlic croutons (see page 95)

CLEAN the squid and cut the bodies into 1-inch rings. Leave the tentacles whole. Pat the squid very dry between paper towels. Sauté the squid in 2 tablespoons olive oil over medium-high heat for 1 to 2 minutes. Season the squid with salt and pepper, and flame the pan with 1 tablespoon Cognac. Deglaze with ½ cup of the red wine and remove from the heat.

Peel, seed, and dice the tomato, and clean and roughly chop the white parts of 2 leeks. Soften the tomato and leeks, 1 minced shallot, 1 minced clove garlic, and a little salt and pepper in 2 tablespoons of olive oil over medium-low heat. After about 10 minutes, add the squid and its pan juices, 2 teaspoons all-purpose flour, about ¾ cup red wine and enough water (about ¼ cup) to barely cover the squid and vegetables. Add a bouquet of 2 sprigs fresh thyme, 4 to 5 sprigs parsley, 1 bay leaf, and a strip of orange peel to the pan. Cover and simmer for about 1 hour, until the squid is tender. Correct the seasoning, adding more olive oil if needed for sweetness. Garnish with minced parsley and garlic croutons.

Rack of Lamb Roasted with Herbs

Serves 6

2 racks of lamb (6 chops to each rack)

FOR THE MARINADE:

½ bottle dry white wine
½ cup virgin olive oil
1 medium yellow onion
½ teaspoon fresh, minced thyme
½ teaspoon fresh, minced marjoram
10 to 12 cracked black peppercorns
1 crumbled bay leaf

TRIM the racks thoroughly and marinate them for several hours in ½ bottle white wine, ½ cup olive oil, 1 sliced onion, ½ teaspoon each of thyme and marjoram, 10 to 12 cracked black peppercorns, and 1 crumbled bay leaf.

Remove the lamb from the refrigerator 3 to 4 hours before roasting it. Put the meat on a rack in a shallow roasting pan and season it lightly with salt and pepper. Roast it in a preheated 450°F. oven for 20 to 25 minutes. The internal temperature of the meat should be 130°F. Let the racks rest for 10 minutes at room temperature and prepare the sauce.

FOR THE SAUCE:

The reserved pan juices from the lamb
½ cup lamb *demi-glace* (see p. 199)
¼ cup Burgundy
4 tablespoons unsalted butter

TO make the sauce, skim the fat from the roasting pan and add the juices to a saucepan with ½ cup lamb *demi-glace* and ¼ cup Burgundy, and heat until briskly boiling. Whisk in 4 tablespoons butter at room temperature.

Carve the racks and spoon a little sauce on warm serving plates. Put two chops on top of the sauce on each plate and serve with a white (vegetable) purée (see page 205).

Olive Oil and Sauternes Cake

Serves 6

5 eggs plus 2 egg whites
¾ cup sugar
1 tablespoon mixed grated orange and lemon peel
1 cup sifted flour
½ teaspoon salt
½ cup good quality Sauternes
½ cup plus 2 tablespoons extra virgin olive oil

PREHEAT the oven to 375°F. Separate the 5 eggs and beat the egg yolks with ¾ cup sugar in a bowl with a whisk for 3 to 5 minutes until light-colored and well-beaten. Add the orange and lemon peel and set aside.

Combine 1 cup sifted flour and ½ teaspoon salt, and then add bit by bit to the sugar-and-egg mixture, beating continually until it is incorporated. Add the Sauternes and the olive oil in the same fashion.

Beat the 5 egg whites and 2 additional egg whites until they stand in stiff peaks, and then fold them into the mixture thoroughly.

Pour this batter into an 8-inch spring-form pan whose bottom has been lined with parchment and whose entire interior has been well buttered. Bake for 20 minutes, rotating the cake if necessary to ensure even cooking. After 20 minutes, lower the oven temperature to 325°F. and bake for another 20 minutes. Then turn off the oven, cover the cake with a round of buttered parchment, and leave the cake in the closed oven for 10 minutes more while the cake deflates like a fallen soufflé.

Remove the cake from the oven, invert it onto a flat surface, remove the spring-form pan, and allow it to cool completely.

This cake can be stored, well sealed, in the refrigerator. Serve with fresh peaches and a glass of Sauternes.

Deep-Fried Squash Blossoms
Corn Soup with Roasted Poblano Chiles
Charcoal-Grilled Rockfish with Onion and Tomato Relish
*Papayas with Fresh Lime

Whenever I think of corn and peppers I am immediately drawn to Diana Kennedy's cookbooks on regional Mexican cuisine for inspiration. The corn soup in this menu is actually a variation on one from her book. I found that if the corn is sweet and wonderful, there is only need for a little pure water and some roasted peppers to add roasted flavors. I think that the repetition of certain tastes within a menu—corn in the hors d'oeuvres and corn in the soup, and the grilled flavor of the peppers recalled by the grilled fish—can be surprisingly effective and unifying as a recurring theme. The repeated yellow of the courses only intensifies the sunny summer feeling of this menu.

SUGGESTED WINES: This menu would be well served by a white California Zinfandel.

Deep-Fried Squash Blossoms

Serves 6

¼ cup Italian parsley leaves and 12 sprigs Italian parsley
4 to 5 cloves garlic
12 fresh open squash blossoms
½ pound tasty Italian Fontina cheese
2 eggs
¼ cup milk
1 cup fine cornmeal
about ½ cup black olives

MINCE ¼ cup Italian parsley together with 4 to 5 cloves garlic. Open up the individual blossoms wide enough to insert a piece of cheese about ½ inch thick and 1½ inches long. Add a pinch of the garlic-and-parsley mixture and twist the ends of the blossoms together gently.

Beat 2 eggs together with ¼ cup milk. Dip each blossom into the mixture and then roll quickly and evenly in the cornmeal. Refrigerate for a few minutes.

Deep-fry the blossoms at 350° to 400° F. for about 3 minutes, or until they begin to brown and the cheese is melted. Drain on paper towels and serve immediately, garnished with lots of Italian parsley sprigs and black olives.

Corn Soup with Roasted Poblano Chiles

Serves 6

6 ears of sweet corn (the fresher the better)
4 tablespoons sweet butter
Salt and pepper to taste
3 cups spring water
½ cup cream
2 roasted poblano chiles

WITH a sharp knife, remove all the corn kernels from the cobs. Melt 4 tablespoons butter in a heavy-bottomed pot and add the corn, salt, and finely ground pepper. Toss the corn in the butter over medium heat. After a few minutes, add the spring water and cook over low heat, stirring occasionally so that the corn does not stick to the bottom. After 15 minutes, remove from the heat and cool slightly; pour in a blender and blend until smooth. Press through a medium-fine sieve to smooth the coarse texture. Add the cream, correct the seasoning, heat until just hot, and garnish with minced poblano chiles that have been roasted and peeled.

Charcoal-Grilled Rockfish with Onion and Tomato Relish

Serves 6

2 large cloves garlic
3 to 4 sprigs fresh lemon thyme
Salt and pepper
1½ cups olive oil
1 whole very fresh rockfish, about 2½ pounds, cleaned and scaled
1 red onion
1 large ripe tomato
Vinegar

POUND together 2 garlic cloves, 3 to 4 sprigs fresh lemon thyme, salt and pepper. When you have made a paste, incorporate 1 cup of the olive oil. Rub this mixture inside and outside the fish. Allow the fish to marinate while the fire is being prepared.

For the garnish, dice fine 1 red onion and 1 large tomato. Mix them together and season with ½ cup olive oil, vinegar, salt and pepper.

To cook the fish, make sure the fire is hot but not flaming. Remove the fish from the marinade and place it on the grill. Allow it to cook for about 5 to 8 minutes on each side. Baste frequently.

SEASONAL MENUS

&

Keep it seasonal. There is nothing simpler or more economical than buying what is in season—if you *know* what is in season. Unfortunately, going to the supermarket, which tries to supply all of the produce all of the time, and looking at all the waxed and treated fruit will not give you the answer; learning comes from critically tasting and evaluating the produce on a month-to-month basis. If you could embark upon a long-term program of buying a tomato in the supermarket every month, you would eventually find that in one particular month the tomato would taste like a tomato; the remainder of the time it would bear an unfortunate resemblance to watery mush.

If you feed your appetite with second-best foodstuffs for most of the year, you will miss the joyous experience of savoring the tomato during its peak season. You have really missed a great deal: delayed gratification, anticipation, and the big extra thrill of waiting to eat it *only* when it is good. Not only is this pleasurable to the senses, but it allows you to give proper consideration and attention to the other produce *only* when it is good. In addition, once you have tasted the delights of a truly peak-time tomato, you will willingly abandon the second-best at other times of the year, for eating tomatoes or corn *must* be seasonal. The season for both corn and tomatoes is so short that when you are able to acquire some of either that is really wonderful, you can't stop eating it. Fresh corn on the cob at its absolute peak, roasted over the charcoals and then drowned in sweet butter, with a little salt and pepper, can be a great pleasure—especially if you have not dulled your palate with a monthly procession of mediocre or inferior corn.

The seasonal concept is also the point at which to begin, for it tells you that you shouldn't even be looking for corn in December. By the same token, it gives you plenty of advance warning and time for anticipation, so that by June your mouth will be watering for the corn to come in late July. For me, the seasons are the starting points: I just pick and choose foods for a menu, guided by the stimuli of perfectly ripe tomatoes, succulent spring lamb, a new garlic harvest, or fragrant fresh basil.

By paying attention to these seasonal considerations, you will be able to create a menu mood that is appropriate to the weather and satisfies your own desires as well. If it is boiling hot and you're trying to cool off, you'd never give goose fat and cabbage a second thought. Even though cabbage, goose fat, and beans, too, are available all year long, you will wait until the fall to cook the cassoulet. Instead you will think light, fresh, and cool, so the mint and melons in the garden will become the designing influence for that late-summer menu.

I cannot stress another point strongly enough: the importance of developing an approach to marketing for food that will heighten your discrimination and, I hope, result in an increased demand for higher-quality foodstuffs from the supermarket. If the American public continues to purchase bruised, over-sized lettuces from the produce sections of supermarkets across the country, management will have no incentive whatsoever to increase and intensify its efforts to offer higher-quality produce.

Naturally, maintaining your own garden, be it ever so small, can considerably ease the difficulty you face in finding absolutely fresh ingredients in excellent condition. At the restaurant, growing these foods ourselves has been the only way in which we could obtain sufficient quantities of particular ingredients of the type, variety, and quality which we desired. It may well be the answer for you, too, if you want to benefit fully from the cyclical changes of the seasons.

This seasonal calendar gives you an idea of the ingredients that have been available at Chez Panisse over the past ten years. Some of them are commercially available and others come from our gardens. We are fortunate to be in California, where we have a long growing season and easy access to major food markets. However, I'm convinced that with persistence it is possible to find unusual and interesting ingredients anywhere in the country.

MARCH: Asparagus . . . red Mexican garlic . . . Belgian endive . . . spring lamb . . . vine cuttings for grilling . . . herring and herring roe . . . tiny bay scallops . . . mint, chervil, thyme, sorrel . . . mandarin oranges . . . Japanese eggplants . . . young beets . . . first strawberries . . . artichoke hearts . . . triple-crème cheeses

APRIL: Violets . . . field-grown rhubarb . . . dandelion greens . . . snow peas . . . new potatoes . . . rocket . . . salmon . . . Gulf Coast red snapper . . . Hawaiian shrimps . . . Oregon morels . . . quail eggs

MAY: Nasturtiums . . . sugarsnap peas . . . baby leeks . . . sweet basil . . . blood oranges . . . red onions . . . local squid . . . borage flowers . . . *haricots verts* . . . mangoes . . . Louisiana crayfish . . . goat cheeses

JUNE: Sonoma red onions . . . peaches . . . cantaloupe and French melons . . . *haricots verts* . . . basil . . . golden zucchini . . . baby halibut

. . . Oregon salmon . . . Crenshaw melon . . . Queen Anne cherries . . . Bing cherries . . . olallieberries . . . boysenberries . . . thyme, sage, and rocket flowers . . . nectarines . . . soft-shell crabs

JULY: Herbs in bloom . . . sweet red onions . . . garlic harvest . . . Silver Queen corn . . . squash and squash blossoms . . . Jerusalem artichokes . . . green peppers . . . Better Boy and Early Girl garden tomatoes . . . dill and tarragon . . . grape leaves . . . blackberries . . . ripe avocados . . . Oregon peas . . . Oregon blueberries . . . lavender . . . rockfish . . . goat cheese . . . sunrise papaya

AUGUST: Fresh tuna . . . new potatoes . . . red cherry tomatoes and yellow tomatoes . . . Walla Walla onions . . . lemon cucumbers . . . Silver Queen and Illini Chief corn . . . Santa Rosa plums . . . cheeses from Normandy like Pont L'Evêque . . . Bordeaux wines arrive . . . figs . . . white Babcock peaches

SEPTEMBER: Chardonnay harvest . . . purple grapes . . . fresh squid . . . Sacramento Delta crayfish . . . eggplants . . . yellow, green, and red peppers . . . oysters . . . Mission and Calmyrna figs . . . walnut-oil production . . . Boursault, Camembert, Fontina cheeses

OCTOBER: Zinfandel grapes . . . muscat grapes . . . white truffles . . . savoy cabbage . . . spinach . . . wild mushrooms (chanterelles) . . . Albacore tuna . . . Eastern shellfish . . . end of garden tomatoes . . . Comice pears . . . Bluelake green beans . . . artichokes . . . nasturtium flowers . . . Reblochon, Gruyère, Époisses cheeses . . . Dungeness crab season opens

NOVEMBER: White truffles . . . goose . . . turnips and turnip greens . . . black radishes . . . red peppers . . . pumpkins . . . butternut squash . . . chestnuts . . . fennel . . . Belgian endive . . . horseradish . . . raspberries . . . sorrel . . . winter melons . . . Vacherin and Montrachet cheeses

DECEMBER: Black truffles . . . fennel . . . red and white cabbage . . . snow peas . . . persimmons . . . limestone lettuce . . . lamb's-lettuce . . . tangerines . . . pearl onions . . . pears . . . celery root . . . oysters . . . spiny lobster . . . steelhead salmon . . . Zinfandel Nouveau . . . Stilton and Roquefort cheeses

JANUARY: Shellfish: Maine lobster, spiny lobster, crab, oysters, clams . . . wild mushrooms . . . winter lettuces: romaine, watercress, lamb's-lettuce . . . quince . . . artichokes . . . red cabbage . . . pink grapefruit . . .

Explorateur and Pont L'Evêque cheeses . . . smoked trout . . . herring . . . red apples . . . tangerines . . . leeks . . . turnips and turnip greens

FEBRUARY: Meyer lemons . . . oranges . . . beginning asparagus . . . artichokes . . . East Coast scallops . . . local Monterey prawns . . . early spring lamb . . . cardoons . . . pineapple . . . celery root . . . sorrel . . . rocket . . . Camembert, Saint-Marcellin, Beaufort and blue cheeses . . . last of the black truffles

SPRING

Wild Mushrooms on Croutons
Thin Pasta with Spring Vegetables
Charcoal-Grilled Salmon with Grilled Red Onions
Buckwheat Crêpes with Tangerines, Glacéed Fruit Butter, and Eau-de-Vie

When I think of spring, I immediately think of salmon—those first young delicate-fleshed fish that seduce everyone in the dining room. This menu is meant to directly complement the salmon: little croutons with the last of the fresh morels; the first peas and asparagus with very delicate thin pasta; and buckwheat crêpes that are interesting in flavor but not overwhelmingly rich.

SUGGESTED WINES: This menu calls for new, young wines—perhaps a fresh Bourgogne Aligoté and a Beaujolais with the grilled salmon.

Wild Mushrooms on Croutons

Serves 6

about ⅓ pound fresh wild mushrooms (boletus, chanterelles, or morels;
    do not substitute dried mushrooms)
9 thin slices *pain de mie* (see page 233), crusts removed
½ cup melted butter
2 tablespoons light olive oil
2 tablespoons unsalted butter
½ teaspoon minced garlic
4 to 5 sprigs Italian parsley

P REHEAT the oven to 350°F. Carefully clean and trim ⅓ pound fresh
wild mushrooms. Cut them into ¼-inch slices and set aside. Cut 9 thin
slices *pain de mie* in half diagonally and brush both sides lightly with the
melted butter. Bake the bread slices for 10 minutes, until the croutons are
golden brown.

While the croutons are baking, sauté the mushrooms over medium-low
heat in 2 tablespoons oil and 2 tablespoons butter with ½ teaspoon garlic for
5 to 7 minutes, until they are tender but not limp.

Arrange the mushrooms on the croutons and garnish with 4 or 5 sprigs
Italian parsley leaves. Put three croutons on each of six warm plates and serve.

Thin Pasta with Spring Vegetables

Serves 6

1½ pounds fresh unshelled fava beans
12 ounces tender unshelled peas
½ pound asparagus
8 tablespoons unsalted butter, at room temperature
12 to 15 chervil sprigs or 8 to 10 basil leaves
6 to 8 sprigs Italian parsley
Salt and pepper
1 to 2 cloves garlic
3 tablespoons virgin olive oil
1¼ pounds fresh pasta cut very fine or spaghettini

S HELL 1½ pounds fava beans and remove the outer skin from each bean. Shell 12 ounces peas and mix with the fava beans. Snap the tough ends from ½ pound asparagus, peel just to the tips, and julienne. Blanch the vegetables together in an abundant amount of boiling salted water for 10 seconds.

Make an herb butter with 8 tablespoons softened butter, 12 to 15 minced chervil sprigs or 8 to 10 minced basil leaves, and 6 to 8 minced sprigs of Italian parsley. Season.

Bring plenty of salted water to boil for the pasta. Mince 1 to 2 cloves of garlic, and heat with the blanched vegetables in 3 tablespoons virgin olive oil over low heat.

Cook the pasta *al dente,* about 40 seconds. Drain, and toss off the heat with the vegetables and the herb butter. Serve on warm plates.

Charcoal-Grilled Salmon with Grilled Red Onions

Serves 6

2 pounds salmon fillets
2 medium red onions
about ¼ cup light olive oil
2 tablespoons virgin olive oil
Salt and pepper

P REPARE a medium-hot wood charcoal fire. Cut 2 pounds salmon fillets into 6 pieces of equal thickness. Slice 2 red onions about ⅜-inch thick crosswise. Mix ¼ cup light olive oil with 2 tablespoons virgin olive oil.

Salt and pepper the onion slices, brush with the oil mixture, and put on the grill in a place where the heat is low. Grill the onions for 5 minutes, turn, and grill for 5 minutes.

Salt and pepper the salmon fillets and brush them with the oil mixture. Put them on the grill over medium-hot fire and grill for 3 minutes, turn, and grill for 3 more minutes, until they are firm and springy when pressed with a finger. Serve the salmon and onions on warm plates.

Buckwheat Crêpes with Tangerines, Glacéed Fruit Butter, and Eau-de-vie

Serves 6

12 buckwheat crêpes (see page 32)
6 tablespoons minced glacéed citrus fruit preserved in eau-de-vie
9 tablespoons unsalted butter, at room temperature
3 to 4 tablespoons eau-de-vie
6 to 8 tangerines or blood oranges, sectioned from membrane and seeded
  (there should be 6 to 8 sections for each crêpe)

MAKE the crêpes and allow them to cool. Mix 6 tablespoons glacéed citrus fruit with 8 tablespoons of the softened butter and 2 tablespoons eau-de-vie. Section 6 to 8 tangerines or blood oranges, or enough for 6 to 8 sections per crêpe. Marinate the tangerine sections in the remaining eau-de-vie.

Just before serving the crêpes, spread each one with about a tablespoon of the butter and fruit mixture. Roll the crêpes and put them side by side in a lightly buttered shallow baking dish. Strew the tangerine sections over the crêpes and dot with the remaining butter. Bake in a preheated 375°F. oven for 5 to 7 minutes, until the crêpes are hot through. Serve two crêpes and several tangerine sections per person.

SUMMER

Tomato and Rocket Salad
Yellow Squash and Blossom Soup
Grilled Whole Filet of Beef with Deep-Fried Onion Rings
Honey Ice Cream with Lavender

Tomatoes, corn, and honey are summer for me. I like to eat outside and cook everything there, or have it ready to bring to a table outdoors. Ideally, I would like to eat deep-fried onion rings with this menu; but practically, I would probably grill them instead so that there would be effortless service from the grill to the table.

SUGGESTED WINES: This meal could begin with a young, straightforward Chardonnay such as a Macon Blanc. With the grilled beef, drink a big, generous Zinfandel.

Tomato and Rocket Salad

Serves 8

10 ripe tomatoes
2 big handfuls very young rocket leaves
½ cup or more virgin olive oil
Salt and pepper to taste

CHOOSE 10 very ripe and red, but firm, tomatoes. Cut them crosswise into 4 thick slices each. Arrange the tomatoes slightly overlapping on a serving platter, and salt and pepper them lightly. Strew the rocket leaves over the tomatoes and drizzle ½ cup of olive oil over the salad. There should be a liberal amount of olive oil; use more if necessary. Salt and pepper the salad lightly and serve.

Yellow Squash and Blossom Soup

Serves 8

4 shallots
4 tablespoons unsalted butter
4 pounds yellow squash (4- to 5-inch crookneck or yellow zucchini)
2 to 3 quarts light chicken stock
Salt and pepper to taste
8 to 12 squash blossoms

MINCE 4 shallots and sweat them in 4 tablespoons butter in a large covered pot for 10 minutes. Roughly chop 4 pounds young firm yellow squash. Toss the squash with the shallots and sweat it covered over low heat for 5 minutes. Add enough light chicken stock to barely cover the squash and cook, uncovered, over medium-low heat until the squash is just tender, 10 to 15 minutes.

Remove the pan from heat and cool for 5 minutes. Purée the soup in a blender and season with salt and pepper. Add more hot chicken stock if the soup is too thick.

Cut the petals of 8 to 12 squash blossoms into fine strips. Serve the soup in warm soup plates and garnish with the squash blossoms.

Grilled Whole Filet of Beef

Serves 8

1 6- to 8-pound filet of beef
2 medium yellow onions
2 bay leaves
10 to 12 black peppercorns
1 bottle red wine (Beaujolais or Chianti)
½ cup virgin olive oil
10 to 12 sprigs Italian parsley
Salt and pepper

COMPLETELY trim a 6- to 8-pound filet of beef of its fat and connective tissue. Place the meat in a large, wide dish. Slice 2 medium onions and lightly crush 2 bay leaves and 10 to 12 black peppercorns. Put them around the filet, then add the 1 bottle of red wine, ½ cup virgin olive oil, and 10 to 12 sprigs Italian parsley. Marinate the filet at cool room temperature for several hours or overnight, turning it several times.

Prepare a medium-hot wood charcoal fire. Remove the filet from the marinade and rub it with a little olive oil and salt and pepper. Fold the thin tail of the filet toward the center and tie it securely to form a roll of even thickness.

Put the filet over the hot coals when the flames have just subsided. Cook the filet for about 25 minutes, turning it 5 or 6 times for even cooking. The filet is done when its internal temperature is 130°F. or when the meat is firm yet springy when pressed lightly with a finger. Remove the filet from the fire and cut off the strings. Let the meat rest on a platter for 5 minutes, then carve it into ⅜-inch slices on a slight diagonal. Nap the meat with its juices, and serve with deep-fried onion rings.

Deep-Fried Onion Rings

Serves 8

4 medium red onions
about 2 cups milk
1 to 2 quarts peanut oil
about 2 cups flour
Salt

PEEL and trim 4 medium red onions and slice them ¼-inch thick. Soak the onions in 2 cups milk, or enough to barely cover, for 1 hour. Drain the onions and separate them into rings.

Heat 1 to 2 quarts peanut oil in a wok over medium-high heat. (Using more oil allows more onion rings to be fried at a time.) Attach a deep-fry thermometer to the side of the wok and heat the oil to between 385° and 390°F.

While the oil is heating, spread 2 cups of flour on a large platter, and flour ¼ to ⅓ of the onion rings on both sides. (The number of onion rings to flour at a time depends on the quantity of oil.) Shake the onions free of excess flour and drop them in the hot oil. Turn them when they are medium golden brown and fry them until golden brown on the other side. Remove the onion rings to paper towels, and allow the oil to reach 385° to 390°F. again. Finish flouring, frying, and draining the onion rings in batches. Salt them and serve.

Honey Ice Cream with Lavender

Serves 8

4 cups whipping cream
½ cup strong-flavored honey (thyme, heather, and tupelo are good)
5 egg yolks
Optional: a few lavender blossoms

MIX together 3 cups of the cream, ½ cup honey, and 5 egg yolks, and cook in a double boiler over very hot water. Stir constantly with a wooden spoon until the mixture thickens to the consistency of a crème anglaise, about 10 minutes. Add the lavender blossoms about the last minute or two of the cooking time. Strain the mixture and stir in 1 cup cream. Cover the cream and chill completely, then freeze in an ice cream freezer.

FALL

Smoked Trout Mousse with Chervil Butter
Warm Salad of Curly Endive and Artichoke Hearts
Champagne Sauerkraut
Pear Tarte Tatin

People must have unpleasant associations with sauerkraut; at the restaurant we have always had to entice our customers with champagne by describing this dish as "an Alsatian specialty with sausages and champagne." Think of it here in small portions among other regional and seasonal dishes given equal importance in this menu.

SUGGESTED WINES: Drink a succession of Alsatian white wines with this meal.

Smoked Trout Mousse with Chervil Butter

Serves 6

FOR THE MOUSSE:

10 ounces sole, halibut, or sea bass
6 ounces scallops
1 egg
1 egg white
2 tablespoons unsalted softened butter
½ to ¾ cup whipping cream
Salt and pepper to taste
2 ounces flaked smoked trout

REMOVE all bones and bits of skin from 10 ounces of sole, halibut, or sea bass, and dice the fish into ½-inch cubes. Trim 6 ounces of scallops and dice into ½-inch cubes as well. Grind the fish and scallops through the finest screen of a meat grinder, or chop with an off-and-on motion in a food processor with a steel blade. Put the fish mixture through the grinder a second time, or scrape the sides of the processor bowl and keep chopping until the fish is almost a purée. Force the fish through a very fine sieve.

Put the fish in a large bowl over ice. Work in 1 egg and 1 egg white for 5 to 10 minutes with a wooden spoon. Add 2 tablespoons butter, ½ cup heavy cream, and salt and pepper to taste. Continue to work the mixture for 5 to 10 minutes, adding more cream if necessary. The longer the mixture is worked, the lighter the mousse will be. When the mixture is light, stir in 2 ounces of flaked smoked trout. Cover the mixture and chill thoroughly.

To check for seasoning and cooking time, fill a chilled, buttered ½-cup ovenproof mold with mousse, and bake in a preheated 375°F. oven for 15 minutes, partly immersed in a barely simmering bain-marie. Check for doneness with a toothpick inserted in the center of the mousse. The mousse should be set but not completely dry. Taste a little of the cooked mousse and correct the seasoning in the rest of the mousse if necessary. Butter and fill six more ½-cup molds. Put them in the bain-marie and bake until done. Remove them from the water when they are done and set aside.

FOR THE CHERVIL BUTTER:

2 shallots
1 cup Alsatian white wine
6 to 8 chervil stems
½ pound unsalted butter
Salt and pepper to taste

GARNISH:

12 chervil sprigs
1 ounce fresh black caviar

MAKE the chervil butter while the mousse is cooking. Fine chop 2 shallots and put them in a saucepan with 1 cup Alsatian white wine. Reduce over high heat until about 1 tablespoon of liquid remains. Add 6 to 8 chervil stems halfway through the reduction. Cut ½ pound butter into bits. Whisk the butter (which should be about 60°F.) bit by bit into the wine-shallot mixture over low heat. Remove from the heat, season with salt and pepper, and strain the mixture through a fine sieve. Keep warm in a bain-marie.

To serve the mousse, run a knife around the edges of the molds and invert each one onto a warm plate. Spoon a tablespoon or so of chervil butter over each mousse and garnish with chervil sprigs and a teaspoon of fresh black caviar.

Warm Salad of Curly Endive and Artichoke Hearts

Serves 6

6 medium-large artichokes
2 to 3 tablespoons lemon juice or tarragon vinegar
1 pound curly endive (chicory)
¼ pound prosciutto
2 shallots
¼ cup sherry vinegar
1 tablespoon Dijon mustard
½ cup virgin olive oil
Salt and pepper to taste
about ¼ cup duck fat

TRIM the leaves completely from 6 artichokes, so that only the hearts remain. Remove the chokes, cut off the stems, and pare the outside of the hearts to remove any green. Slice the hearts into ¼-inch pieces and put them in a bowl with cold water and 2 or 3 tablespoons lemon juice or vinegar.

Trim and wash about 1 pound of curly endive, using just the center leaves if the head is large. Dry the endive and break it into small pieces. Thin-slice ¼ pound of prosciutto.

Make the vinaigrette by fine-dicing the shallots and mixing them with ¼ cup sherry vinegar and 1 tablespoon Dijon mustard. Whisk in ½ cup virgin olive oil and season with more mustard if necessary, and salt and pepper.

To assemble the salad, cook the artichokes in boiling water with a little salt and lemon juice added. They should be cooked *al dente,* about 1½ to 2 minutes. Drain the artichokes and toss them, still hot, into some of the vinaigrette. Toss the endive with some vinaigrette in a large salad bowl. Heat about ¼ cup duck fat over low heat until it is very warm. Add the artichoke slices to the endive and drizzle the duck fat over the salad. Toss and season with salt and pepper. Garnish with the prosciutto.

Champagne Sauerkraut

Serves 6 to 8

FOR THE SAUERKRAUT:

4 pounds sauerkraut, packed in brine
Salt and pepper
about ¼ cup duck fat
¼ pound ham rind or bacon rind
1 medium carrot
2 small onions
1 whole clove
2 cloves garlic
1 bay leaf
6 juniper berries
6 ounces bacon in one piece
2 suckling-pig's feet
a small piece of prosciutto bone about 3 inches long
½ bottle champagne
about 1½ quarts chicken stock

TO prepare the sauerkraut for baking, soak 4 pounds of sauerkraut in about 2 quarts of water for 1 to 3 hours, depending on its saltiness. Drain the sauerkraut and squeeze it dry in fistfuls about the size of tennis balls. Break the balls apart and dry the sauerkraut completely on towels. Season with salt and pepper.

Cover the bottom of a 6- to 8-quart oven casserole with about 3 table-spoons of duck fat. Cut the ham rind or bacon rind into strips about ¼ inch thick and 1 inch wide and put them on top of the duck fat. Divide the sauerkraut into two batches and layer one batch over the ham rind. On top of the sauerkraut, arrange 1 whole peeled carrot, 2 small whole peeled onions stuck with 1 whole clove, 2 whole peeled cloves of garlic, 1 bay leaf, and 6 juniper berries. Put 6 ounces bacon in one piece, 2 suckling-pig's feet, and the small piece of prosciutto bone on top of the vegetables and sauerkraut. Cover with the rest of the sauerkraut and pour over ½ bottle of champagne. Add about 1 quart of chicken stock, enough so that the sauerkraut is thoroughly wet but not floating or soupy. Dot the top with the remaining duck fat. Cut a piece of bakers' parchment to fit inside the casserole and put it on top, then cover with a lid. Bring the mixture to a boil on top of the stove over medium-high heat, then bake in a preheated 375°F. oven for 3 to 4 hours. Check the liquid from time to time. The sauerkraut should not dry out on top. Add more chicken stock if necessary.

MEAT-AND-POTATO GARNISH:

1 to 2 pounds new potatoes, about 2 inches in diameter
1 pound suckling-pig loin chops, about ¾ inch thick
1 pound Virginia ham, cut into ½-inch slices
½ pound garlic sausage in one piece
¼ pound champagne sausages (see page 75)

TO cook the meats and potatoes, remove the casserole about 40 minutes before serving. Scrub the potatoes and bury them in the sauerkraut. Arrange 1 pound suckling-pig chops, 1 pound Virginia ham slices, and a ½-pound garlic sausage on top of the sauerkraut. Bake for 15 minutes, uncovered, basting the meat 2 or 3 times. Turn the meat and baste, and then bake for about 15 minutes longer. Ten minutes before serving, add ¼ pound champagne sausages to the casserole and turn them after 5 minutes. Serve some meat, potatoes, and sauerkraut to each person.

Pear Tarte Tatin

Serves 10 to 12

FOR THE CRUST:

1 cup all-purpose flour
1 tablespoon sugar
⅛ teaspoon salt
5½ tablespoons unsalted butter
3 to 5 tablespoons ice water

MIX 1 tablespoon sugar and ⅛ teaspoon salt into 1 cup of flour. Cut 5½ tablespoons butter into small pieces and cut them into the flour until the pieces of dough are the size of small peas. Add 3 tablespoons of ice water and gather up the dough. If it does not hold together, sprinkle with a tablespoon or two of ice water. When the dough just holds together, flatten it into a round about 5 inches in diameter, and cover with plastic wrap. Refrigerate for at least 30 minutes.

FOR THE FILLING:

5 to 6 pounds Comice or Bosc pears, a little underripe (there should be
    14 cups of pear slices)
½ cup sugar
½ cup melted butter
1 to 2 tablespoons half-and-half

PEEL and core 5 to 6 pounds Comice or Bosc pears and cut each pear into twelfths. Measure 14 cups sliced pears into a large bowl and toss them with ¼ cup sugar.

Pour ¼ cup melted butter into a 12-inch cast-iron skillet or tarte tatin pan and sprinkle with ¼ cup sugar. Place the pear slices in concentric circles, a layer at a time. Pour ¼ cup butter over the pears.

Roll out the crust to about a 13½-inch-diameter circle. Trim the uneven edges to leave about an inch of overhang around the pears. Turn the extra dough under and cut several slits or small holes in the crust so the steam can escape. Bake the tarte in a preheated 450°F. oven for 10 minutes. Brush the crust with about 1 tablespoon of half-and-half. Bake another 15 to 20 minutes, until the crust is deep golden brown.

Remove the tarte from the oven and remove excess juice with a bulb baster. There should be about ½ inch of juice left in the bottom of the pan. Put the pan on top of the stove over the highest heat. Cook the tarte, revolving it frequently, until the bottom caramelizes, about 10 to 15 minutes.

The edge of the tarte will caramelize before the bottom does, so the tarte will smell almost burned. Keep loosening the sides of the tarte with a spatula while it is caramelizing so that they do not stick.

Cool the tarte for 15 minutes before unmolding. After the tarte has cooled, loosen it again with a spatula. Invert a large flat serving plate over the tarte pan, set the plate on a table, and lift the pan off the tarte.

WINTER

Oysters on the Half Shell with Victoria's Champagne Sausages and
Mignonette Sauce
Roast Duck Stuffed with Corn Bread and Wild Mushrooms
Red Onion Tarts
Garden Lettuce Salad with Roquefort Vinaigrette
Lemon Clove Cookies

I can't think of winter without thinking of oysters and wild mushrooms, both very fine in Northern California this time of year. And a winter menu should be warming and aromatic—here I smell the sausages sautéing and the corn bread baking and the irresistible aroma of the *mirepoix*—the carrots, onions, and celery with bay leaves and thyme—gently cooking for the stuffing.

SUGGESTED WINES: Begin with champagne, and drink an older Cabernet or Zinfandel with the duck.

Oysters on the Half Shell with Victoria's Champagne Sausages and Mignonette Sauce

Serves 2

12 to 16 very fresh oysters
6 to 8 champagne sausages (see recipe below)

SHUCK 12 to 16 oysters and put them on ice. Grill or sauté 6 to 8 champagne sausages over medium heat, turning frequently, for 10 minutes, or until they are crisp on the outside and juicy inside.

FOR THE SAUCE:

½ cup champagne vinegar
½ cup dry white wine
1 tablespoon minced shallots
Cracked black pepper to taste

TO make the mignonette sauce, mix ½ cup champagne vinegar with ½ cup dry white wine, 1 tablespoon minced shallots, and the cracked black pepper.

Serve the oysters on ice, the sausages on a warm serving plate, and the mignonette sauce on the side for dipping.

Victoria's Champagne Sausages

(Victoria Wise was the first chef at Chez Panisse. She left to start a charcuterie across the street called Pig-by-the-Tail.)

Makes 14 to 16 sausages

1½ pounds pork butt, well-marbled
1 egg
½ teaspoon minced garlic
½ teaspoon salt
¼ teaspoon ground black pepper
½ teaspoon pâté spice made from 2 ounces white pepper, 2 ounces black
 pepper, 1 ounce coriander seed, 1 ounce ginger, ½ ounce cloves, and
 ¼ ounce ground nutmeg, ground together
½ ounce black truffle, roughly chopped
½ cup demi-sec champagne
12 feet sheep casing
Butter for sautéing

TRIM most of the outside fat from a pork butt, then grind once, using the finest plate of the meat grinder. Add the rest of the ingredients and mix thoroughly. Taste for seasoning by frying a small bit.

Fill sheep casing and tie off the ends. Twist at 4-inch intervals, or coil. (Slice after cooking.) Or shape into small patties.

To cook, melt butter and sauté on moderately low heat for about 10 to 15 minutes.

Roast Duck Stuffed with Corn Bread and Wild Mushrooms

Serves 2

1 4- to 5-pound duck

FOR THE MARINADE:

1 onion
2 carrots
1 celery rib
10 to 12 sprigs parsley
3 to 4 sprigs thyme
2 cloves garlic
3 cups rich red wine (Burgundy or Cabernet Sauvignon)

REMOVE the head, neck, and feet from the duck, and be sure to leave enough neck skin to cover a little stuffing. Reserve the head, neck, and feet for stock. Peel and roughly chop 1 onion, 2 carrots, and 1 celery rib. Put them in a dish large enough to hold the duck, and add 10 to 12 sprigs parsley, 3 to 4 sprigs thyme, and 2 cloves lightly crushed garlic. Put the duck in the dish and add about 3 cups rich red wine. There should be enough to come halfway up the duck. Marinate in a cool place overnight up to 24 hours and turn the duck six to eight times. Then strain the marinade, reserving the vegetables for the stock and the wine for the sauce.

FOR THE STOCK:

Head, neck, and feet of duck, and leftover duck pieces or 2 chicken
  backs and 1 neck
The reserved vegetables from the marinade

PUT the duck's head, neck, and feet, along with leftover duck pieces or 2 chicken backs and 1 neck into a stock pot. Add the vegetables and herbs from the marinade. Barely cover with water and bring to a boil. Reduce heat immediately to a simmer and skim the stock. Cook for about 1 hour, skimming as necessary. Strain the stock and reserve.

FOR THE STUFFING:

½ pound fresh chanterelles or boletus mushrooms
7 tablespoons unsalted butter
2 cloves garlic
2 cups crumbled corn bread
½ medium red onion
1 celery rib
1 teaspoon fresh minced thyme
2 tablespoons fresh minced Italian parsley
Salt and pepper
about 2 tablespoons heavy cream

CLEAN the wild mushrooms and slice them crosswise about ¼ inch thick. Cook them over low heat in 4 tablespoons melted butter with 1 clove minced garlic for 5 to 7 minutes, until they are just done. Coarsely crumble enough corn bread to measure 2 cups.

Dice ½ red onion and 1 celery rib very fine and cook them gently with 1 clove minced garlic in 3 tablespoons melted butter until they just soften, about 3 minutes. Drain the mushrooms in a fine sieve and reserve the juice, discarding any sandy residue. Mix the mushrooms and juice, sautéed vegetables, and corn bread in a bowl. Add 1 teaspoon fresh minced thyme and 2 tablespoons fresh minced Italian parsley, and season with salt and pepper. Stir in 2 tablespoons heavy cream, or enough to just bind the stuffing.

To prepare the duck for roasting, preheat the oven to 475°F. and bring the strained stock to a simmer. There should be enough stock to just cover the duck; add water if necessary. Prick all the fatty deposits of the duck and poach it in the stock for 10 minutes, turning it three or four times. Drain the duck (reserving the stock) and pat it dry. Salt and pepper inside and out. Fill the duck cavity and the neck loosely with stuffing and sew the flaps closed.

Put the duck on a rack in a shallow baking dish, breast up. Bake for 20 minutes and turn, draining fat if necessary. Brown the back for 15 to 20 minutes and turn again. Cook the duck for another 10 to 15 minutes, for a total of 50 to 60 minutes. Prepare the sauce while the duck is roasting.

FOR THE SAUCE:

Duck stock
1 ounce dried wild mushrooms
⅔ cup hot water
½ red onion
½ carrot
½ celery rib
2 tablespoons duck fat
1 cup reserved marinade
Salt and pepper

REMOVE all fat from the duck stock and reduce to 3 cups. Soak 1 ounce dried wild mushrooms in ⅔ cup hot water for 10 minutes. Pick over the mushrooms carefully for grit, strain their liquor through triple, rinsed cheesecloth, and mince the mushrooms. Fine-dice ½ red onion, ½ carrot, and ½ celery rib. Sauté the vegetables over medium heat in 2 tablespoons duck fat for 3 to 4 minutes. Add the mushrooms and their liquor, the vegetables, and 1 cup of the reserved marinade to the 3 cups of duck stock, and cook over medium heat for 15 minutes. Strain the sauce and reduce to 1½ cups. Season with salt and pepper.

To serve the duck, let it stand for 10 minutes out of the oven before carving. Remove the thighs and legs at the thigh joint and slice the meat from them so that some skin remains with each slice of meat. Slice the meat from the breast on the diagonal. Arrange the slices on warm plates and nap with some of the sauce. Serve the stuffing beside the duck with a red onion tart on each plate.

Red Onion Tarts

Serves 2

⅛ of puff pastry recipe (page 147)
2 medium red onions
3 tablespoons unsalted butter
½ cup Zinfandel
¼ cup sherry vinegar
1 to 2 tablespoons cassis
Pinch of sugar
Salt and pepper to taste

DIVIDE in half the ⅛ piece of puff pastry recipe. (Reserve the rest of the puff paste for another use.) Roll the pieces into 2 rough oval shapes large enough to fit into 4-inch-long oval-shaped forms. Press the puff paste gently into the forms and trim it, leaving ⅛ inch above the rims. Prick the dough well, and bake on a baking sheet in a preheated 400°F. oven for 10 minutes. Reduce the heat to 350°F. and prick the dough again if necessary. Bake for another 5 to 10 minutes, until the shells are completely done. Leave the shells in the forms on a cake rack until they are completely cool. Remove the shells from the forms and set aside.

To make the red onion mixture, thin-slice 2 medium red onions. Sweat them in 3 tablespoons unsalted butter over medium heat for 10 minutes. Add ½ cup Zinfandel and ¼ cup sherry vinegar, cover, and cook for about 30 minutes over low heat. Add 1 to 2 tablespoons cassis for color, a pinch of sugar, and salt and pepper to taste, and cook, uncovered, for 5 minutes over medium heat. The onions should have just a tablespoon or so of liquid. Divide the onion mixture between the tart shells and serve with the duck and stuffing.

Garden Lettuce Salad with Roquefort Vinaigrette

Serves 2

about 2 big handfuls mixed garden lettuces (romaine, chicory, dandelion
    greens, red-leaf, oak-leaf lettuces, etc.)
¼ cup virgin olive oil
2 tablespoons heavy cream
about 2 teaspoons lemon juice
about 1 tablespoon crumbled Roquefort cheese
Black pepper

CAREFULLY wash and dry the garden lettuces. Put them in a bowl, cover with a tea towel, and crisp in the refrigerator.

Mix ¼ cup virgin olive oil with 2 tablespoons cream, 2 teaspoons lemon juice, and 1 tablespoon crumbled Roquefort cheese. Season with coarsely ground black pepper. Adjust the vinaigrette with more lemon juice, Roquefort, or cream, as necessary.

Just before serving, toss the vinaigrette with the lettuces and arrange on salad plates.

Lemon Clove Cookies

Makes about 3 dozen cookies

½ pound unsalted butter
¾ cup sugar
1 teaspoon vanilla
1 egg
1 tablespoon lemon zest
Pinch of salt
2⅓ cups all-purpose flour
¼ teaspoon ground cloves, or to taste

CREAM ½ pound softened butter and ¾ cup sugar with an electric mixer at medium speed. Beat in 1 teaspoon vanilla, 1 egg, and 1 tablespoon lemon zest at medium speed. Changing to low speed, gradually work in a pinch of salt, 2⅓ cups flour and ¼ teaspoon ground cloves. The dough will be rather soft.

Divide the dough in half and roll each part into a cylinder about 2 inches in diameter. Wrap the cylinders with plastic wrap, then with foil, and chill from 2 to 12 hours.

Preheat the oven to 350°F. Remove the wrap and slice the dough ¼ inch thick. Place the cookies on baking sheets with about ½-inch space between them and bake for 8 to 10 minutes, until they are light golden brown on the bottom and pale golden brown on top.

MENUS FOR
SPECIAL OCCASIONS

Any special treat—fresh tomatoes or suckling pig—whose arrival you welcome can be cause for a special meal or a celebration of the season, any season. Opening a wonderful old bottle of wine is a very special occasion indeed. Anything that tantalizes you into commemorating that particular occasion with a noteworthy effort is reason enough.

Chez Panisse's "garlic gala" owes its genesis to a longtime customer who has written a garlic cookbook. His timely suggestion that we initiate a celebration dedicated to garlic came as I was working on the menu for Bastille Day, July 14. This annual festivity was launched when it suddenly occurred to me that since the garlic crop is harvested shortly before July 14 and comes in right around that time, why not combine the two events?

Like bread, garlic is fundamental in its nature. It is associated, in my mind, with many of the dishes I love: a big plate of fresh pasta, tossed with olive oil and lots of the new-crop garlic, or charcoal-grilled croutons rubbed with garlic and splendidly fruity olive oil. Many of our customers have succumbed to garlic's heady charms, and I have delighted in watching the transformation of those who were horrified at the prospect of dealing with an entire baked head of garlic on the plate in front of them, but who loved it when they discovered the toasty sweetness of its baked flavor.

Each year our friends at the Joseph Phelps Winery in Napa Valley make a Zinfandel Nouveau for us, and we design a menu to complement the wine that is dispensed from barrels in the restaurant's dining room. The yearly arrival of the newly made wine always heralds a uniquely regional and seasonal experience which our customers have come to anticipate with enthusiasm.

The pungency that permeates the kitchen whenever fresh truffles arrive at the restaurant is incentive enough to build an entire meal around those delectable fungi. I will always remember a very special dinner in Milan which began with white truffles with just melted Parmesan cheese; the meal continued with pasta with grated white truffles followed by risotto with white truffles; ultimately, we had white truffles with melted cheese again! The earthy aromas and flavors of those incredibly fresh white truffles were imparted to every dish with a slightly different effect. I also recall with pleasure and delight the evening's meal at which six of us consumed the entire 1980 crop of the Texas truffles offered to the restaurant by our most loyal patrons.

Aside from wine and food celebrations, we have planned menus around such unlikely events as the 100th birthday of Alice B. Toklas. All of the recipes were adapted from *The Alice B. Toklas Cookbook:* guests ate Madame Loubet's Asparagus Tips, Bass for Picasso, Braised Pigeons on Croutons, "Vent Vert" Salad, Scheherezade's Melon, and Alice's Cookies. And on the seventieth birthday of M.F.K. Fisher, we assembled a group of restaurant diners who had a meal composed around the titles of her books: the first course, *Consider the Oyster,* inspired a selection of four varieties of oysters on the half shell; *A Considerable Town* featured California snails with Pernod, tomatoes and garlic, followed by whole Pacific rockfish charcoal-grilled with wild herbs and anchovies, young spit-roasted pheasant with new potatoes, a bitter lettuce salad with goat cheese croutons, and three plum sherbets with orange rind boats; *A Cordiall Water* suggested the last course, a Muscat de Beaumes-de-Venise, coffee and candies.

Music is often a feature of the special events held on the Chez Panisse Birthday, August 28. Last year we held a day-long food extravaganza during which guests ranged upstairs and down, through the kitchen and outside in the yard, exchanging tickets purchased at the door for sushi, bowls of chile with buttered tortillas, fresh oysters on the half shell, white and green pasta with green beans, and corn on the cob. Guests perched on tables in the kitchen or on the stairs as they devoured homemade ice cream and fruit tarts. Kebabs of fish, marinated in red chile, were grilled over the charcoal, and we spit-roasted chickens. A Cajun band played Cajun music upstairs, while downstairs other friends played traditional folk music on mandolins.

A special occasion is any occasion you wish to be special. It's as simple as that.

CHAMPAGNE DINNER

Oysters on the Half Shell with Mignonette Sauce
Blinis à la Russe
Sautéed Duck Livers with Celery Root
*Red Leaf and Radicchio Salad
Fresh Pineapple Sherbet with Champagne Sabayon and Candied Rose Petals
Escoffier

This was one of the most successfully balanced menus we ever served at Chez Panisse. All the courses seemed to be equally important. It was a dinner designed to launch Billecart Salmon Champagne in Northern California, so every course was meant to complement fine champagne.

SUGGESTED WINES: Serve a succession of champagnes.

Oysters on the Half Shell with Mignonette Sauce

Serves 6

5 to 6 dozen very fresh tiny oysters
¾ cup champagne vinegar
¾ cup dry white wine
2 shallots, finely minced
½ teaspoon cracked black pepper, or to taste

WITH an oyster knife, shuck the oysters curved side down to save their juices. Loosen the oysters from their muscles with the knife. Mix the champagne vinegar with the white wine, the minced shallots, and the cracked black pepper. Serve the sauce in three or four small bowls so that people may dip their oysters in the sauce if they like.

Blinis à la Russe

Serves 6

½ tablespoon dry yeast
3 cups milk
1 cup buckwheat flour
1 cup all-purpose flour
2 teaspoons sugar
½ teaspoon salt
3 egg yolks
3 egg whites
2 tablespoons butter
1 cup clarified butter
about ⅔ cup crème fraîche
3 to 4 ounces yellow whitefish caviar

TO make the blinis, dissolve ½ tablespoon dry yeast in 1½ cups luke-warm milk. Mix together ½ cup buckwheat flour, ½ cup all-purpose flour, 2 teaspoons sugar, and ½ teaspoon salt in a large bowl. Make a well in the center of the flour mixture and add 3 slightly beaten egg yolks and the milk-and-yeast mixture. Stirring in one direction, slowly incorporate the wet and dry ingredients to form the sponge. Cover the sponge and let it rise in a warm place until double in bulk, about 1 hour.

Mix the remaining ½ cup of buckwheat flour with the remaining ½ cup of all-purpose flour. When the sponge has doubled in bulk, add the flours alternately with 1½ cups of room-temperature milk to form a smooth batter. Strain the batter through a medium-fine sieve or chinois and let it double in bulk. This will take about 1 hour at warm room temperature, but the batter can sit for 4 or 5 hours at cool room temperature.

Just before making the blinis, beat the 3 egg whites to soft peaks. Fold the beaten whites into the batter. Using about ⅓ cup of the batter at a time, cook the blinis on a very hot griddle or in a crêpe pan very lightly coated with butter. Cook the blinis for about 40 seconds on the first side and about 30 seconds on the second side. Stack the blinis and keep them warm.

For each serving, stack three or four blinis, drizzling each one generously with clarified butter. Top each serving with about 1½ tablespoons of crème fraîche and garnish with about 1½ teaspoons of yellow caviar.

Sautéed Duck Livers with Celery Root
(From a Troisgros recipe)

Serves 6

12 very fresh duck livers
Salt and pepper
1½ pounds celery root (celeriac)
2 tablespoons duck or goose fat (or 2 tablespoons clarified butter)
3 tablespoons port
½ cup duck *demi-glace* or 1 cup duck stock (see page 76)
1 teaspoon minced black truffle
2 tablespoons unsalted butter
6 slices foie gras (if available)

TO prepare the duck livers, trim the fat from them, separate the two lobes, and cut off all attaching veins. Season the livers with salt and pepper.

To prepare the celery root, peel and trim it carefully and cut it into garlic-clove shapes. Steam the celery root over boiling salted water for 2 to 3 minutes, until it is tender but firm. Remove the celery root from the steaming pan and keep warm.

Sauté the prepared livers in 2 tablespoons of fat over medium-high heat until they are browned and just cooked, about 2 to 3 minutes. Remove the livers and keep them warm. Flame the pan with 3 tablespoons port, then add ½ cup duck *demi-glace* and 1 teaspoon minced truffle to the pan and reduce the sauce slightly. Whisk 2 tablespoons butter into the sauce and add the livers and celery root to the pan. Place the slices of foie gras on warm plates and serve the livers, celery root, and sauce over the foie gras.

Fresh Pineapple Sherbet with Champagne Sabayon and Candied Rose Petals Escoffier

Serves 6 to 8

FOR THE CANDIED ROSE PETALS:

about 3 dozen unsprayed large fragrant rose petals
1 egg white
about 1 cup superfine sugar

CHOOSE the rose petals for color and beauty and make sure they are completely dry. Beat the egg white very lightly. Brush each petal with egg white on both sides and dip it lightly in the sugar. Put the petals on cake racks and dry them in a cool dry place for 2 to 3 hours or overnight.

FOR THE SHERBET:

1 large, very ripe pineapple
⅔ cup sugar
½ teaspoon kirsch

PEEL and remove the eyes from the pineapple. Cut it into quarters lengthwise and core. Purée the pineapple in the food processor or blender and measure the purée. There should be at least a quart for ⅔ cup sugar. If there is more, add sugar to taste. Over low heat, dissolve the sugar with just enough purée to keep it liquid. When the sugar has dissolved, remove it from the heat and stir in the rest of the purée and ½ teaspoon kirsch, or to taste. Blend well and freeze in a 2-quart ice cream freezer.

FOR THE CHAMPAGNE SABAYON:

4 tablespoons sugar
4 egg yolks
¼ cup champagne

COMBINE the 4 tablespoons sugar, the 4 egg yolks, and the ¼ cup champagne in a copper bowl. Put the bowl in a pan with hot water so that the bowl does not touch the water and put the pan over medium heat. Whisk the mixture continuously until it is light and foamy and triple in volume, about 5 minutes.

   To serve the dessert, arrange the candied rose petals on serving dishes, put one or two scoops of sherbet in the center of the petals, and pour the sabayon over the sherbet.

A MENU FOR THE ZINFANDEL FESTIVAL

Ragoût of Wild Mushrooms with Veal Stock and Red Wine
Confit of Duck
*Escarole Salad
Poached Pears and Figs in Zinfandel with Cassis Cream

Ideally, this menu calls for fresh wild mushrooms. We are sometimes able to get chanterelles, bluets, lepiota and boletus mushrooms, morels, and oyster mushrooms fresh from the Berkeley hills, from Mendocino, or from around San Jose. To walk around in the woods in search of wild mushrooms is one of the most satisfying endeavors that a gastronome can undertake, but it takes an expert mycologist to appraise the varieties in one's basket. Every year more varieties of wild mushrooms appear, fresh and dried, in specialty markets; these will give the non-initiate access to tastes beyond that of the watery mushroom of commerce.

SUGGESTED WINES: This menu is designed to celebrate the arrival of the new Zinfandel just a few months after the harvest. For almost ten years Walter Schug, the winemaker at the Joseph Phelps Vineyards, has been making new Zinfandel for us by the traditional carbonic maceration method. Like Beaujolais Nouveau, the wine is fruity, fresh, light, and alcoholic. Now a variety of "nouveau"-style wines are becoming available that would complement this meal.

Ragoût of Wild Mushrooms with Veal Stock and Red Wine

Serves 4

¼ cup dried wild mushrooms (boletus or *truffes des pauvres*)
1 cup veal stock
4 to 5 large fresh chanterelles
6 to 8 medium cultivated mushrooms
4 to 5 tablespoons unsalted butter
1 shallot
½ clove garlic
Salt and pepper
1 to 2 tablespoons Zinfandel, or rich red wine
1 to 2 tablespoons whipping cream
Black pepper
1 to 2 tablespoons roughly minced parsley

SOAK ¼ cup dried wild mushrooms in 1 cup hot veal stock for 20 to 30 minutes. Pick over the soaked mushrooms, rinsing them if necessary, and slice them into ⅜-inch slices if they are large. Strain the veal stock through a fine strainer covered with doubled cheesecloth and set aside. Slice 4 to 5 chanterelles, enough to equal about 3 cups, and 6 to 8 cultivated mushrooms, enough to equal about 1 cup.

To cook the ragoût, melt 2 tablespoons of the butter in a sauté pan over medium heat. Sauté the dried soaked mushrooms for about a minute, then add the chanterelles and cultivated mushrooms. Stir together for a minute, then add 1 shallot and ½ clove garlic, both finely minced, and salt and pepper to taste. Add 1 or 2 tablespoons Zinfandel and the strained veal stock, and bring the ragoût to a boil.

Finish the ragoût with the remaining 2 to 3 tablespoons butter and 1 to 2 tablespoons whipping cream and remove from the heat. Taste for salt and add an ample amount freshly ground black pepper. Serve in a warmed bowl with 1 to 2 tablespoons roughly minced parsley sprinkled over.

Confit of Duck

Serves 4

1 fresh duck, 4½ to 5 pounds
1 cup rock salt
3 bay leaves, crushed
2 teaspoons dried thyme, lightly crushed
about 6 cups duck or goose fat
Parsley stems
10 to 12 black peppercorns
1 head of garlic

PRESERVE the duck in salt and herbs first. Remove the backbone from a 4½- to 5-pound duck and quarter the duck. Blend together 1 cup rock salt, 3 crushed bay leaves, and 2 teaspoons lightly crushed dried thyme. Rub the duck with the salt-and-herb mixture and put it in a crock with the remaining salt on top. Cover the duck and weight it, and leave it in a cool place for 1 to 2 days.

To finish the confit, remove the duck from the cure and clean each piece well. Melt about 6 cups duck or goose fat in a pan that will hold the duck pieces close together in one layer. The fat should cover the duck. When the fat is hot, add the duck pieces and a bouquet garni of some parsley stems, 10 to 12 black peppercorns, and a head of garlic cut in half crosswise. Simmer gently for about 1½ hours. Test for doneness by inserting a bamboo skewer through the thickest part of the leg; it should pass through with no resistance.

Remove the duck from the fat and let it cool. Carefully pour the fat through a fine strainer, taking care to stop before getting to the juices and debris which have settled to the bottom. Clarify the fat by boiling to remove any liquids, skimming frequently. Watch carefully that it does not brown. When it is clean, strain it again and let it cool to room temperature. When the duck is cooled, partially bone the breasts and pack the pieces in an earthenware crock. Pour the cooled fat over the duck and refrigerate for at least a week.

The confit can be kept, refrigerated, for up to six months. It is usable at any time, but the flavor improves if it is aged for a few months. If it is to be kept for some time, it is very important that the fat be well clarified and that the duck be well packed in the crock, completely covered with fat.

To cook the preserved duck, remove the pieces from the fat and put them on a rack in a roasting pan. Bake the duck in a preheated 350°F. oven for about 15 to 20 minutes. Heat a cast-iron skillet with no fat over medium heat and cook the duck pieces on the skin side for about 5 minutes, until they are well browned. Serve with a flageolet gratin: cook some flageolet beans with onion, carrot, thyme, and bay leaf; combine with some chopped garlic and a peeled, seeded, and chopped tomato; and gratiné under a layer of bread crumbs dotted with butter until golden brown.

Poached Pears and Figs in Zinfandel with Cassis Cream

Serves 4 to 6

FOR THE PEARS:

6 firm pears (Bosc or Comice are best)
1 bottle Zinfandel
1 cup sugar
1½ cups water
1 vanilla bean

PEEL the pears and leave the stems on. To poach them, bring a bottle of Zinfandel, 1 cup sugar, 1½ cups water, and 1 vanilla bean, split, to a boil. Stir to dissolve the sugar in the poaching liquid, add the pears, and reduce the heat. Poach the pears at a simmer until their outer coating is slightly translucent and they are a little soft but still firm. Remove the pears from the heat and let them cool in the poaching liquor for about 20 minutes. They should be soft to the core but not mushy, and should retain their shape.

FOR THE FIGS:

2 cups Zinfandel
3 tablespoons honey
1 pound dried black Mission figs

TO poach the figs, bring 2 cups Zinfandel with 3 tablespoons honey to a slow boil. Add 1 pound black Mission figs and reduce the heat to a simmer. Let the figs simmer until they are plump and soft, about 1 hour. Cool the figs in the poaching liquor. Remove them and reduce the liquid until it is slightly thickened.

FOR THE CASSIS CREAM:

1 cup whipping cream
1 or 2 tablespoons cassis

BEAT the 1 cup of whipping cream until it barely forms soft peaks. Flavor with 1 to 2 tablespoons of cassis.
    To serve the dessert, place each pear on a dessert plate with two or three figs, pour some of the reduced poaching liquid over them, and spoon some cassis cream on top.

JEAN-PIERRE'S BIRTHDAY

Mussels Baked with Cream and Pineau de Charentes
Fish Ragoût with Garlic Croutons
Roast Squab with Sauternes Sauce
*Curly Endive Salad
Apple and Apple Cider Sherbet

Jean-Pierre Moullé is the chef at the restaurant and this is a menu of specialties of his native Charentes that he proposed for his birthday. There is a wonderful sequence of flavors in this menu, but it is complicated to cook without assistance in the kitchen.

SUGGESTED WINES: A white Graves to begin, and "Y" (Yquem's drier wine) with the squab.

Mussels Baked with Cream and Pineau de Charentes

Serves 6

6 to 8 dozen mussels
2 yellow onions
2 cloves garlic
Bouquet garni: 4 or 5 sprigs parsley; 1 bay leaf; 1 teaspoon fennel seed;
    10 to 12 black peppercorns; a pinch of dry tarragon
2 cups dry white wine
3 large egg yolks
1 cup whipping cream
½ cup Pineau de Charentes (fortified white wine from Charentes)
Pinch each saffron and cayenne
Lemon juice to taste
2 or 3 tablespoons minced parsley

CLEAN 6 to 8 dozen mussels. Chop 2 onions and 2 cloves of garlic roughly and put them in a shallow pan with the bouquet garni and 2 cups dry white wine. Bring the mixture to a boil and add enough mussels to cover the pan in one layer. Cover the pan and steam the mussels open. Remove them to a baking tray as they open and keep it in a warm place. Finish steaming all the mussels open, then remove the top shell of each mussel and debeard if necessary. Strain the cooking juices and reduce them to 1 cup over high heat.

Beat 3 large egg yolks lightly and beat in a little of the mussel juice; set aside. Add 1 cup whipping cream to the pan with the reduced juices and cook over low heat. Stir in ½ cup Pineau de Charentes and season the sauce with a pinch each of saffron and cayenne. Stir in the beaten egg yolks and cook over low heat, stirring constantly, until the sauce thickens. Adjust the seasoning and add lemon juice to taste. Transfer the sauce to a bain-marie or a double boiler and keep it warm.

Put the mussels on a baking sheet in a preheated 350°F. oven and heat them through, about 5 minutes. When the mussels are hot, arrange them on warm plates, pour a little sauce over each one, and sprinkle with parsley.

Fish Ragoût with Garlic Croutons

Serves 6

6 pounds fresh whole fish (three or four varieties deepen the ragoût's
 flavor: rock cod, halibut, red snapper, or sea bass)
2 medium onions
3 or 4 shallots
3 cloves garlic
6 tablespoons unsalted butter
4 tablespoons virgin olive oil
6 2-inch sprigs fresh thyme
½ cup dry white wine
2 cups fish *fumet* (see page 124)
Salt, pepper, and lemon juice to taste
1 tablespoon minced parsley

FILLET the fish and cut the fillets into equal pieces. Reserve the bones
for the *fumet*. Dice 2 onions, 3 or 4 shallots, and 3 cloves garlic and soften
them over low heat in 2 tablespoons of the unsalted butter and 4 tablespoons
virgin olive oil with 1 sprig of thyme. When the vegetables are soft, add the
fish, seasoned with salt and pepper, blend well and sauté gently for 1 minute.
Turn up the heat and add the white wine. Let it reduce a little, then add the
hot *fumet* and 1 more sprig of thyme. Bring the ragoût to a very gentle
simmer, cover, and cook until the fish is just tender, about 3 or 4 minutes.
Remove the fish and vegetables to a warm serving bowl.

Finish the broth over a high flame by whisking in the remaining 4
tablespoons softened butter. Season to taste with salt, pepper, and lemon juice.
Spoon the broth over the fish and garnish with the remaining thyme sprigs,
1 tablespoon of minced parsley, and garlic croutons.

Garlic Croutons

24 slices day-old baguette, ¼ inch thick
about ½ cup melted butter
2 or 3 cloves garlic

TO prepare the croutons, brush each slice of baguette with melted butter
and bake in a preheated 350°F. oven for 5 to 7 minutes, until the
croutons are light golden brown. Rub each crouton with a cut clove of garlic
while they are still warm.

Roast Squab with Sauternes Sauce

Serves 6

3 1½-pound squabs, necks and legs cut off and reserved

FOR THE MARINADE:

1 medium onion
1 medium carrot
1 medium celery rib
Bouquet garni: 8 to 10 sprigs parsley; 2 bay leaves; 4 sprigs fresh thyme
    or 2 teaspoons dried thyme; 15 to 20 cracked black peppercorns
1 bottle Sauternes

MARINATE the squabs, including the necks and legs, for 24 hours. Make the marinade of 1 onion, 1 carrot, and 1 celery rib finely diced. Add the bouquet garni, 1 bottle of Sauternes and the squabs and marinate, covered, in the refrigerator.

FOR THE STOCK:

1 medium onion
1 medium carrot
1 medium celery rib
2 tablespoons butter
2 quarts water

MAKE a stock before roasting the squabs. Finely dice 1 onion, 1 carrot, and 1 celery rib and soften the vegetables in 2 tablespoons butter. Add the bouquet garni from the marinade, the squabs' necks and legs, and 2 quarts water. Bring the stock to a boil, reduce the heat and skim the stock. Simmer for 45 minutes, then strain the stock and reduce it by half.

TO ROAST:

4 to 5 tablespoons unsalted butter
2 tablespoons light olive oil
Salt and pepper to taste
Optional: 1 tablespoon truffle juice

TO roast the squab breasts, pat them dry, and brown them in 2 tablespoons butter and 2 tablespoons light olive oil over medium-high heat.

Salt and pepper the breasts and roast them in a preheated 450°F. oven for 12 to 15 minutes.

Meanwhile, deglaze the browning pan with ½ cup Sauternes from the marinade and 1 tablespoon truffle juice if available. Bring the mixture to a boil and add about 1½ cups reduced squab stock. Reduce the sauce by half, and finish it by whisking in 2 or 3 tablespoons softened butter.

Slice the breasts into ⅜-inch diagonal slices and arrange on a serving platter and pour the sauce over the meat. Serve with red cabbage which has been blanched briefly and braised with a little duck fat and duck stock and a few garlic cloves for 1½ to 2 hours over low heat.

Apple and Apple Cider Sherbet

(An adaptation of a Linda Guenzel recipe)

Serves 6

12 to 15 apples (pippins or Granny Smiths)
2 bottles sparkling apple cider
¼ teaspoon ground cinnamon or 3 cinnamon sticks
3 vanilla beans (cut and scraped)
¼ to ½ cup lemon juice
Zest of 1 to 2 lemons
¾ cup sugar per quart of apple purée
Pinch of salt
Optional: A touch of clove or nutmeg for a musty, autumnal flavor

CORE the apples and cut them into twelfths into a bowl of acidulated water (about 3 tablespoons lemon juice per cup of water); do not peel. Drain them and stew them in a large saucepan with 2 cups of the sparkling cider, the cinnamon, and the vanilla beans. Bring to a boil and cook for approximately 10 minutes, or until the apples are quite soft. Purée the apples in a very fine sieve, using a wooden pestle to force the mixture through the holes. Discard the peels.

Combine the apple purée, the rest of the apple cider, the lemon juice and the zest, the sugar, and the salt. The purée should still be hot so that the sugar will dissolve. The amounts of lemon and cider will vary depending on the tartness of the apples.

Let the mixture cool well and adjust for flavor before freezing. Freeze according to the directions for your ice cream freezer.

After freezing, store the sherbet in a covered container. This sherbet is best served the same day it is made; ice crystals begin to form after one day.

TRUFFLES

Eggs Cooked with Truffles
Crayfish Salad
Filet of Beef Lucien Tendret
Pommes Anna
*Raw Milk Camembert

When I think of truffles I think of very classic *haute cuisine;* and by experimentation over the years, we've learned that their flavor is most pronounced with eggs, pasta, and potatoes. This menu begins with classic truffled scrambled eggs, followed by the classically prepared crayfish salad and an extravagant whole truffled filet of beef adapted from Lucien Tendret's nineteenth-century recipe. The cheese at the end of the meal allows the truffle flavors to linger. Along with the raw-milk cheese smelling of white truffles, maybe a few pears could complete the dinner.

SUGGESTED WINES: This is a dinner for great old wines—the rarest old Meursaults, the finest old Bordeaux.

Eggs Cooked with Truffles

Serves 8

12 large eggs (preferably organic and as fresh as possible)
1 small black truffle
¼ pound unsalted butter
about ¼ cup heavy cream
Salt and pepper to taste

"TRUFFLE" 12 very fresh large eggs by putting them in a bowl with 1 small black truffle. Cover the eggs tightly and refrigerate overnight.

To cook the eggs, crack them into a bowl and beat well with a fork. Melt 2 tablespoons of the butter in a double boiler over hot water and pour in the eggs. Stir continually for about 20 minutes. The eggs should become a creamy mass with no curds. The water must stay hot but not boil. If the eggs begin to form curds, add a little cream to reduce the heat. While the eggs are still creamy, stir in the thinly sliced truffle and the rest of the butter bit by bit. Season very lightly with salt and pepper and serve with rye-bread croutons.

Crayfish Salad

Serves 8

THE CRAYFISH AND THE BOUILLON:

about 48 very lively crayfish, 6 to 8 per person
2½ quarts water
2 lemons
about 1 tablespoon coarse sea salt
1 teaspoon red pepper flakes

TO cook the crayfish, make a strong *court-bouillon* by adding 2 lemons thinly sliced, about 1 tablespoon coarse sea salt, and 1 teaspoon red pepper flakes to 2½ quarts water. The bouillon should be very salty and boiling rapidly. Rinse about 48 crayfish in cold water and put them in the bouillon. Boil them for 1 minute and remove them with a strainer. Let the crayfish cool, remove the shells from the tails and set aside. Reserve the heads, claws, and shells for the sauce. Strain the *court-bouillon* and reserve for the sauce.

THE CRAYFISH SAUCE:

1 small carrot
1 small onion
1 small celery rib
2 shallots
3 tablespoons virgin olive oil
Reserved crayfish shells, claws, and heads
1½ tablespoons Armagnac or Cognac
about ⅓ cup dry white wine
Pepper and cayenne to taste
Optional: 1 small tomato, peeled, seeded, and diced
Salt
Reserved *court-bouillon*

TO prepare the sauce, finely dice 1 small carrot, 1 small onion, 1 small celery rib, and 2 shallots. Heat 3 tablespoons olive oil over medium-high heat and sauté the shells and heads of the crayfish for 4 to 5 minutes. Turn the heat to high and flame the pan with 1½ tablespoons Armagnac or Cognac for 1 minute. Reduce the heat to medium and add the diced vegetables. Sauté for 4 or 5 minutes, then add ⅓ cup white wine and season with pepper and cayenne. (Add 1 tomato, peeled, seeded, and diced, if available.)

Barely cover the crayfish and vegetables with some strained *court-bouillon* and taste for salt. Simmer the *fumet* for 10 to 15 minutes. Put the shells, claws, and heads in a blender with a little broth and break up the crayfish. Pound the shells in a mortar and force the paste through a very fine sieve. Strain the *fumet,* add the paste, and reduce the sauce by half. Remove the sauce to a bowl and let cool.

THE VINAIGRETTE AND THE SALAD:

Reduced crayfish sauce
3 to 4 tablespoons tarragon vinegar
½ cup virgin olive oil
Lemon juice to taste
Optional: 3 to 4 tablespoons heavy cream
8 handfuls garden lettuces and curly endive (chicory)

MIX about 1 cup of the reduced crayfish sauce with 3 tablespoons tarragon vinegar. Stir in ½ cup virgin olive oil and lemon juice to taste. The vinaigrette may need adjusting with more vinegar, more crayfish sauce, or if it is very salty, 3 to 4 tablespoons heavy cream. Marinate the crayfish tails in the vinaigrette for at least 30 minutes, then remove and set aside.

Trim, wash, and dry 8 handfuls garden lettuces and curly endive. Toss the greens with some of the vinaigrette and arrange them on salad plates. Garnish the lettuces with the crayfish tails and drizzle a little vinaigrette over them.

Filet of Beef Lucien Tendret

Serves 8

8-pound filet of beef, untrimmed (5½ to 6 pounds trimmed)
½ cup olive oil
2 cups dry white wine
a few sprigs of parsley and thyme
½ cup pistachio nuts, roasted and salted, shelled and skinned
½ cup pitted Niçoise olives
2 or 3 large chanterelles, about 1½ cups sliced or 2 ounces dried morels
    or boletus mushrooms
3 tablespoons unsalted butter
½ teaspoon minced garlic
Optional: 1 or 2 small black truffles
about ¾ pound pork fatback, cut into sheets ⅛-inch thick

TO prepare the meat, have the butcher trim the fat completely from an 8-pound filet of beef. The filet should stand a few hours at room temperature in a marinade of about ½ cup olive oil, 2 cups dry white wine, a few sprigs of parsley, and a few sprigs of thyme. Butterfly the meat lengthwise, cutting just to the center, and spread it flat with the cut part facing up. With the tip of a paring knife, make small incisions and stud the meat liberally with ½ cup pistachios and ½ cup pitted Niçoise olives.

Slice 2 or 3 chanterelles about ⅛ inch thick and sauté them gently for 2 or 3 minutes in 3 tablespoons butter with ½ teaspoon minced garlic. If dried mushrooms are used, soak 2 ounces morels or boletus mushrooms in 1 cup very warm water for about 30 minutes. Strain the liquor through cheesecloth in a fine sieve and discard any tough or sandy parts of the mushrooms. Rinse the mushrooms lightly and pat dry, slice them, and sauté gently in 3 tablespoons butter with ½ teaspoon garlic for 3 to 4 minutes. Add about ¼ cup mushroom liquor to the mushrooms. (Add 1 or 2 thinly sliced black truffles if available.)

Spread the mixture over the filet and close the meat together. Fold the thin tail of the filet toward the center of the meat to ensure even cooking, and cover completely with thin sheets of pork fatback. Tie the meat securely.

To cook the meat, prepare a hot mesquite charcoal fire. Spit the meat and roast it in front of or over the fire with a pan to collect the juices. Baste frequently with the juices. It will take about 25 minutes to cook, or until the internal temperature is about 128° F. When the filet is done, remove it from the spit and let stand for 10 minutes. Skim all the fat but 1 tablespoon from the basting juices. Mix the basting juices with the juices which have collected around the filet. Slice the meat in ½-inch pieces and spoon a little juice over the slices.

Pommes Anna

Serves 8

2 pounds white potatoes (Castle Rock or russet are best)
about 1 cup clarified butter
Salt and pepper

PEEL the potatoes and cut them evenly about ¹/₁₆ inch thick. Rinse the slices in cold water and pat them dry. Spread 1 to 2 tablespoons clarified butter in each of two 8-inch cast-iron skillets. Arrange some potato slices in an overlapping spiral design on the bottom of each pan. Season the potatoes with salt and pepper and dribble 1 tablespoon clarified butter over them. Repeat the layering for a total of three layers.

Bake the potatoes in a preheated 425° F. oven for approximately 40 to 45 minutes. Press the potatoes flat six or seven times during the baking to make an even "cake." Remove the potatoes from the oven when the undersides are a deep golden brown, gently loosen them from the pans, and reverse onto two warm serving dishes.

CASSOULET

Vegetable Hors d'Oeuvres
Chez Panisse Cassoulet
*A Glass of Young Sauternes

It isn't easy to make room for anything else on the same menu as a cassoulet. I immediately choose a vinaigrette salad before or after, and possibly a simple fresh fruit sherbet for dessert. Here, however, I thought a glass of young Sauternes might serve as a digestive after the rich and complex cassoulet.

Every time we have made this dish it has been different, to the delight of our cassoulet customers who come and compare every cassoulet we cook. There are partisans of the unclassic flageolet bean, which remains more firm, and those who insist on white beans that absorb more of the juices. We have used both Great Northern white beans and Italian white cannelini beans. What is most important is that the ingredients be properly cooked and seasoned before they're put together, and that the earthenware container be wide enough to allow enough of a crust to form.

SUGGESTED WINES: Serve a light red wine, a Beaujolais or a Cahors.

Vegetable Hors d'Oeuvres

Serves 12 to 15

Celery Root with Mustard Mayonnaise

1½ pounds celery root (celeriac)
1½ cups homemade mayonnaise
Pepper
Lemon juice
2 to 3 tablespoons Dijon mustard

PEEL and trim a 1½ pound celery root. Quarter it crosswise and slice each quarter into ¼-inch slices. Cut the slices into 1-inch squares and discard any uneven pieces. Blanch the celery root in plenty of boiling salted water for 2 to 3 minutes. Drain the celery root, refresh it under cold water, and pat dry.

To make the mayonnaise, follow the recipe for aïoli (see page 219), but omit the garlic. Season the mayonnaise lightly with pepper and lemon juice. When the mayonnaise has emulsified, stir in 2 to 3 tablespoons Dijon mustard, or to taste.

Toss the celery root with ½ cup mayonnaise and mound it on a serving platter. Serve the rest of the mayonnaise on the side.

Red Onion and Cucumber Vinaigrette

3 medium red onions
1 cucumber (preferably Japanese, 6 to 7 inches long)
about ½ cup rice wine vinegar

PEEL and thinly slice 3 medium red onions and 1 cucumber. Toss the vegetables with ½ cup rice wine vinegar and arrange on a serving platter.

Beets in Orange Vinaigrette

2½ pounds small beets with tops
½ cup light olive oil
¼ cup virgin olive oil
¼ cup sherry vinegar
Zest of 1 medium orange
2 to 3 tablespoons orange juice
Salt and pepper

CUT the tops from 2½ pounds small beets, leaving about 1½ inches on the beets. Boil the beets in an abundant amount of slightly salted water until they are tender, about 20 minutes.

Make the vinaigrette by mixing together ½ cup light olive oil, ¼ cup virgin olive oil, ¼ cup sherry vinegar, the zest of 1 orange, 2 to 3 tablespoons orange juice, and salt and pepper to taste.

Drain the beets, cool them under cold water, and peel them. Slice them into ⅛-inch rounds and toss them gently with the vinaigrette. Arrange the beets on a serving platter.

Cauliflower with Anchovy Mayonnaise

1½ pounds cauliflower (2 small heads are best)
1½ cups homemade mayonnaise
Pepper
Lemon juice
3 to 4 salt-packed anchovy fillets

TRIM 1½ pounds cauliflower and break it into flowerets. Blanch the cauliflower in lots of boiling salted water for 3 to 4 minutes. Drain, then refresh the cauliflower under cold running water and pat it dry.

Use the aïoli recipe (page 219), omitting the garlic, to make the mayonnaise. Season the mayonnaise with pepper and lemon juice. Rinse 3 to 4 salt-packed anchovy fillets very well and pat them dry. Pound them in a mortar to a smooth paste. Blend most of the anchovy paste into the mayonnaise and correct the seasoning with more lemon juice or anchovy paste.

Toss the cauliflower with ½ cup of the mayonnaise and arrange it on a serving platter. Serve the rest of the mayonnaise separately.

Garden Salad

4 large handfuls mixed garden lettuce (equal amounts of red-leaf and
  oak-leaf lettuce, rocket, and chervil make the best mixture)
2 to 3 tablespoons red wine vinegar
½ cup virgin olive oil
Salt and pepper

WASH and dry the lettuce and salad herbs. Make the vinaigrette by mixing 2 to 3 tablespoons red wine vinegar with ½ cup virgin olive oil. Season the vinaigrette with salt and pepper. Toss the salad with enough vinaigrette to lightly coat it and serve it in a salad bowl.

Chez Panisse Cassoulet

Cassoulet is best if made in large amounts; this recipe will serve 15 people. It is quite wonderful if reheated a day or two after it is made.

TO COOK THE BEANS:

3 pounds cannellini or Great Northern beans
2 carrots
1 large onion
1 stalk celery
2 heads garlic
Bouquet garni: 2 bay leaves; 1½ teaspoons dried thyme or 6 to 8 sprigs
    fresh thyme; 10 to 12 sprigs parsley; 15 black peppercorns
6 quarts duck stock, made from duck bones, heads, and feet left over
    from the confit (see below)
½ cup goose or duck fat
Salt and pepper

SOAK 3 pounds cannellini or Great Northern beans overnight in plenty of cold water. Drain and rinse the beans, and pick them over for odd beans and stones. Chop 2 carrots, 1 onion, and 1 stalk celery into large pieces. Peel the cloves of 1 head of garlic. Make a strong bouquet garni with 2 bay leaves, 1½ teaspoons dried thyme or 6 to 8 sprigs fresh thyme, 10 to 12 sprigs parsley, and 15 black peppercorns. The flavor of the beans depends on the strength of the duck stock and the herbs, so the stock should be well made and the herbs should be abundant.

Put the beans in a large pot with the vegetables and bouquet garni and cover by 1 inch with duck stock. Bring to a slow boil and reduce the heat. Simmer the beans, covered, for 1½ to 2½ hours, adding duck stock as necessary. The beans should be cooked *à point,* not mushy, but completely done, as they do not become more done in the final cooking. Drain the beans when they are done and reserve the liquid. Remove the vegetables and the bouquet garni. While the beans are still warm, stir in ½ cup goose or duck fat, 1 head of garlic, peeled and finely chopped, and season well with salt and pepper to taste.

THE MEATS FOR THE CASSOULET:

5 pounds lamb neck and shoulder meat with bones
2 large onions
3 tomatoes, peeled and seeded
6 tablespoons duck fat
3 sprigs thyme
6 to 8 cloves garlic
about 3 cups dry white wine
about 3 cups water
Salt and pepper
1½ pounds sausages (fresh garlic or Toulouse)
Confit of 2 ducks (see page 91)
Optional: Leftover roast suckling pig, fat piece, or foot

MAKE the lamb stew while the beans are cooking. Cut the meat into pieces about 2½ by 2½ inches. Roughly chop 2 large onions and 3 tomatoes. Heat 6 tablespoons of duck fat in a large stock pot over medium heat. Sauté the lamb and the onions in the fat over medium heat for 10 minutes or until the lamb is well browned. Add the tomatoes, 3 sprigs thyme, and 6 to 8 peeled garlic cloves.

Cover the lamb by 1 inch with a mixture of half white wine and half water, about 3 cups of white wine and 3 cups of water. Season with salt and pepper, bring to a boil, reduce to a simmer, and skim the froth and fat. Simmer until the lamb is tender but not falling from the bone, about 1 hour. Drain the lamb and reserve the stock, reducing if necessary to concentrate the flavor. Discard the vegetables and herbs. Keep the lamb moist with a little stock.

Blanch the 1½ pounds of sausages in plain boiling water for 5 minutes. Drain and cut into 1-inch pieces when the sausages are cool enough to handle. Remove the pieces of duck from the confit of 2 ducks and reserve all duck fat.

TO ASSEMBLE THE CASSOULET:

The beans
The meats
6 to 8 sprigs thyme
about 2 cups reduced lamb stock
about 4 cups duck stock
8 cups fresh bread crumbs
2 cups duck or goose fat

MAKE the cassoulet in 2 earthenware casseroles, each 4 to 6 quarts and about 4 to 5 inches deep. Layer about one sixth of the beans in each pot and put 1 sprig thyme on the beans. Arrange one fourth of the duck confit pieces on top of each layer of beans. Arrange one fourth of the lamb and sausages on top of the confit and put 1 sprig thyme on top. Cover the meats with one sixth of the beans in each casserole. Layer again with duck confit, lamb, sausages, and thyme, and cover with the remaining beans.

Taste a mixture of duck and lamb stock with the proportions of twice as much duck stock as lamb stock. The mixture should be tart and flavorful and not too salty (it will reduce and concentrate in the final cooking); adjust as necessary. Pour enough stock in each casserole to come about ½ inch below the top layer of beans. Cover each casserole with 4 cups fresh bread crumbs and drizzle with 1 cup melted duck or goose fat.

Bake the cassoulet in a preheated 250°F. oven for 4 to 5 hours, turning the casseroles in the oven so that the crumbs brown evenly. The crust should be a deep rich golden brown. Add stock on the sides of the casseroles as necessary to keep the level of liquid ½ inch below the crumbs.

Let the cassoulet stand for about 10 minutes out of the oven, then serve some crust, beans, and variety of meats to each person.

GARLIC DINNER

Garlic Soufflé
Baked Fish with Garlic Confit
Roast Squab with Garlic-and-Liver Sauce
*Fettuccine with Fresh Chestnuts
*Romaine and Rocket Salad with Garlic
*Two Wine Fruit Sherbets

This menu emerged from one of our last Garlic Festival dinners, when the public had demanded more and more garlic. We even infused two fruit sherbets with garlic to satisfy the frenzy. As a menu, this dinner was amusing, but the individual dishes are inviting, complex in flavor, and definitely aromatic.

SUGGESTED WINES: Not a menu for great wines, but any of your lesser favorites will taste even better with this meal: the garlic enhances the wine.

Garlic Soufflé

Serves 6

6 tablespoons unsalted butter
5 tablespoons all-purpose flour
1½ cups half and half cream
1 cup whipping cream
Salt
Bouquet garni: 1 small onion, peeled and quartered; 2 to 3 cloves
    unpeeled garlic; ½ teaspoon dried thyme; 1 bay leaf; 4 sprigs
    parsley; 10 black peppercorns
2 large heads garlic
about ½ cup light olive oil
about ½ cup water
2 to 2½ teaspoons dried thyme
2 bay leaves
5 egg yolks
3 ounces freshly grated Gruyère
5 ounces freshly grated Parmesan
1 heaping tablespoon of the garlic purée
Salt, cayenne, and black pepper to taste
1 cup unbeaten egg whites

MAKE a roux of the butter and flour and cook it gently for 5 to 8 minutes. Mix the creams and scald them. Remove the roux from the heat and cool slightly before whisking in the scalded creams. Transfer the resulting béchamel to a double boiler and salt it lightly. Tie the onion, 2 to 3 cloves garlic, ½ teaspoon dried thyme, 1 bay leaf, 4 sprigs parsley, and 10 black peppercorns in cheesecloth. Add the bouquet garni to the béchamel, cover, and cook slowly for about 1 hour, stirring occasionally. Cool the béchamel slightly and remove the bouquet garni before adding the rest of the soufflé ingredients.

For the garlic purée, break up 2 heads of garlic. Put the garlic in a shallow baking dish and barely cover with the olive oil and water. Stir in ½ teaspoon dried thyme and 2 bay leaves and season with salt and pepper. Cover the dish and bake at 250° F. for about 1½ hours, or until the garlic is completely tender. Baste the garlic often while it is baking. When the garlic is done, strain it from any remaining liquid and purée it through a food mill, or push it through a medium-fine sieve with a pestle.

Stir the 5 egg yolks into the béchamel. Mix in 3 ounces Gruyère, 2 ounces of the Parmesan, and a generous tablespoon of the garlic purée. Season the mixture with salt, cayenne, and black pepper, and blend well. Butter some gratin dishes well (either one 12-inch oval platter with a slight lip or six 6-inch low gratin dishes) and coat them lightly with a little Parmesan cheese. Beat the egg whites very stiff and fold three quarters of them into the cheese-garlic mixture. The mixture should be fairly loose, but not runny. (If it is runny, add more egg white.) Pour the soufflé gently into the prepared platter or individual gratin dishes. Sprinkle with the remaining Parmesan cheese, and then with the rest of the dried thyme over the Parmesan. Bake on the top shelf of a preheated 450° F. oven for approximately 10 minutes. The platter allows the soufflé to cook more quickly than in a regular soufflé dish and provides more browned crust. The soufflé in the small gratin dishes will cook in about the same amount of time. The top and sides of the soufflé should be well-browned, and the inside warm and creamy.

Baked Fish with Garlic Confit

Serves 6

FOR THE GARLIC CONFIT:

4 large heads garlic
3 sprigs fresh thyme or 1 teaspoon dried thyme
2 sprigs fresh marjoram or 1 teaspoon dried marjoram
2 bay leaves
about 2 cups rendered duck or goose fat (light olive oil or clarified
    butter may be substituted for the fat)
2 bay leaves

BREAK the 4 heads of garlic into cloves and leave them unpeeled. Put the cloves into a heavy-bottomed pan in one layer, add 3 sprigs thyme, 2 sprigs marjoram (or 1 teaspoon dried thyme and ¾ teaspoon dried marjoram), and 2 bay leaves. Cover the garlic with the fat or oil. Cook very slowly for about 30 minutes, until the garlic is completely tender. Remove the cloves from the fat and let cool; then peel and slice them about ⅛ inch thick.

FOR THE FISH:

2 pounds fish fillets (rockfish, sea bass, halibut, or salmon would work
    well in this recipe)
Zest from 1 lemon and 1 lime
3 medium-sized ripe tomatoes
8 sprigs fresh parsley
1 sprig marjoram
6 pieces baking parchment, each about 9 by 12 inches
Reserved fat from the confit
Salt
6 tablespoons unsalted butter

CUT the 2 pounds of fish fillets into six even portions, about 1 inch thick. Thinner pieces of fish should be sandwiched to keep the same thickness. Blanch the zest of the lemon and the lime for 10 seconds and drain. Peel and seed the tomatoes, and dice them finely. Stem 8 parsley sprigs and 1 sprig marjoram and mince finely.

Arrange the parchment so the fish will be placed on the center of one half of the shorter side. Brush this center of each piece of parchment with a little reserved fat. Place 3 pieces of garlic confit in the center of the fat on each piece of parchment. Put the fish fillets on the garlic. Sprinkle the fish with salt, then put 3 more slices of garlic confit on each piece of fish. Divide the diced tomatoes evenly among the fish, spreading them over each fillet. Sprinkle the fillets with the minced herbs, and strew about 1 teaspoon of the combined zests on each fillet. Put 1 tablespoon of butter on each piece of fish and fold the parchment loosely over the top; roll and crimp the edges of the parchment well. Place the packets on a large baking sheet and bake in a preheated 450° F. oven for 5 to 8 minutes, or until the parchment just begins to puff and turn brown.

Roast Squab with Garlic-and-Liver Sauce

(Adaptation from a Troisgros recipe)

Serves 6

3 1- to 1¼-pound whole squab
3 heads garlic
4 to 6 sprigs fresh thyme or 2 to 3 teaspoons dried thyme
2 bay leaves
6 sprigs parsley
about 2 cups virgin olive oil
about 2 cups dry white wine
1 onion
1 leek
1 carrot
1 celery rib
5 to 6 tablespoons Cognac or Armagnac
about 1 quart chicken stock
6 tablespoons unsalted butter

TO marinate the squab, cut off the heads and feet and reserve the livers. Break up 1 head of garlic, peel the cloves and reserve 3 of them. Make a marinade with the peeled garlic, 2 or 3 sprigs of fresh thyme or 1½ teaspoons dried, 2 bay leaves, 6 sprigs parsley, ½ cup olive oil, and 1½ cups white wine. Marinate the squab for 2 to 4 hours or overnight.

To make the squab stock, peel and trim the onion, the leek, the carrot, and the celery, and chop them roughly. Brown the squab heads and feet in 3 tablespoons olive oil over moderate heat and add the vegetables and the reserved peeled garlic cloves. Cook over medium-low heat until the vegetables are soft and golden brown. Add 2 tablespoons of Cognac or Armagnac and 2 tablespoons of white wine and flame the pan. Add enough of the chicken stock to just cover and bring to a boil. Reduce heat immediately, skim, and simmer for about half an hour. Strain the stock and reduce it by half.

To make the garlic-and-liver purée for the sauce, break up 2 heads of garlic. Put the garlic in one layer in a small roasting dish and cover with a mixture of about ¾ cup each olive oil and water. Add 2 or 3 sprigs fresh thyme or 1½ teaspoons dried thyme, cover the dish and roast at 300° F. for about 1½ hours, or until the garlic is completely tender. Remove the cooked garlic from its cooking liquid and purée through a very fine sieve with a pestle. Sauté the reserved squab livers in 2 tablespoons of butter over medium heat for 2 to 3 minutes until they are just done. Flame the pan with 1 tablespoon Cognac or Armagnac and set aside to cool slightly. Purée the livers with their pan juices and 2 tablespoons softened butter through a fine sieve, and add the garlic purée to taste. Begin with 1 teaspoon of the purée and keep in mind that the purée will be thinned with stock to make the sauce.

To cook the squab, remove them from the marinade, pat dry, and season with salt and pepper. Heat 3 tablespoons olive oil and 2 tablespoons butter in a heavy sauté pan over moderate heat. Brown the squab, turning frequently for even browning, for 5 to 8 minutes. Pour the fat from the pan and flame with 2 tablespoons Cognac or Armagnac. Put the birds in a roasting pan and roast in a preheated 475° F. oven for 12 to 15 minutes, until the breasts are just cooked and still quite pink.

Meanwhile, finish the sauce by deglazing the sauté pan with 1 cup reduced squab stock for about 3 minutes. Cool slightly and whisk in the liver-garlic purée to a medium consistency. Do not allow the sauce to boil. Rest the squab for 5 minutes when they come out of the oven. Collect any juices and add them to the liver-garlic sauce. Slice the breast meat from the bone and put the slices on warm plates along with a leg and thigh joint for each serving. Surround each portion with some sauce. Serve the squab with fresh fettuccine with fresh chestnuts, the noodles cooked *al dente* and tossed in cream, with the chestnuts—roasted, peeled, and chopped—added at the last minute to just heat through.

GRILLING MENUS

એ

The appeal of a charcoal grill is a mysterious combination of its warmth, the sight of the fire, the aromas, and the smoky taste of the foods cooked over it. The primeval appeal of cooking over an open fire first made itself known to me when I watched my father barbecue steaks; I was entranced.

For many, cooking over charcoal is a summer event, but it is not only that—it can and should be undertaken at any time during the year that the inclination strikes. At the restaurant we have a large grill, which is 4 feet by 2 feet wide, with a firebox that can be raised or lowered beneath the stationary grill. A vertical firebox is set at right angles to this grill, and has a spit in front of it. However, it is not necessary to have a complicated built-in arrangement. Grilling or cooking over an open fire is the oldest way of cooking, and as such it has, over many years, been done in the simplest, most straightforward manner or in the most complicated and involved. I prefer the simpler form.

You can improvise a grill over just about any fire: the one in your living-room fireplace, a campside fire, or the one in the portable barbecue grill and hibachi out on the back porch. There are also small battery-operated camping spits available. You simply thread your food onto the spit, set it on the small holder, put the drippings pan underneath, and place the entire assembly immediately adjacent to your fireplace. Its slowly turning spit would be ideal for little birds or meat, or even a few fresh peppers.

I have grilled under just about every circumstance imaginable, including a fancy country inn where there was no kitchen, only a fireplace in the room. I went down to the local grocery, bought all the foods I could find that could be cooked on a grill-type arrangement, hurried back to my room to put papers down in front of the fireplace, and cooked right there. It was wonderful to have something delicious to eat when the dining accommodations could not provide it: grilled tortillas; tomatoes, sliced and grilled; red peppers, red onions, and chicken pieces, all cooked over the aromatic open fire.

At Chez Panisse, we primarily use mesquite charcoal, although any kind of natural hardwood charcoal works well, as long as the fuel you use has no chemicals of any kind on it. Avoid the use of briquette-type charcoal, as it is chemically treated and produces little heat. Mesquite charcoal is made in a time-consuming manner by the Yaqui Indians in north central Mexico; the trees, dense hardwood trees, thirty to forty feet high and nearly four feet in diameter, are hand-felled. The mesquite logs are then stacked into a 20-by-20-foot pyramid, two air shafts are created for ventilation, and the entire construction is sealed within adobe clay. The stack is then lit and allowed to burn and cure for two to three weeks. This one stack of mesquite logs will produce five to eight tons of mesquite charcoal, which burns very hot to sear quickly and seal in the natural juices and flavors of the food cooked over it.

Learning the techniques of charcoal-grilling requires nothing more complicated than practice and the experience that comes with it. You need to become accustomed to whatever fuel you are planning on burning. There are so many fuel options open to you: you can burn oak until it makes coals; you can gather all the little twigs from around your apartment building and use them to make a small fire; or you can use vine cuttings, which are wonderful because they burn very hot, like mesquite, and as the flames subside, the smoke permeates the meat in the same way that hickory wood does when used for cooking.

Rigging a spit is much a matter of trial and error, depending on the size of the spit and on the food you're cooking. Over the years at the restaurant, we have spitted everything from whole wild boars to baby pheasants. We have discovered that the larger the animal, the more difficulty there is in properly affixing it to the long metal spike. Because the equipment is not commercially available, we have had it made especially for each size of beast, though this will not be a factor for you if you are spitting smaller items. Electric rotisseries are available, which do provide a good method of cooking, even though they will not, of course, impart that wonderfully smoky quality you get when cooking over a charcoal fire.

In all spit-roasting it is important to keep the spitted foods as evenly spaced and balanced on the spit as possible, and to use foods as uniform in size and shape as you can find. If the diameter of the birds, for example, varies greatly, you will have wings sticking out and getting burned as they pass the fire, or you may well find that the unbalanced weight will interfere with the mechanism. As with grilling, the perfection of these techniques comes only with experience and practice. Once you understand and appreciate the value of continual self-basting, which moistens and flavors the food while it cooks, the desire to perfect a million techniques will overcome that initial frustration.

Grilling can be a participatory form of cooking and eating that allows a deeper understanding of the transformation of raw ingredients into the finished dish. Obviously, it is more convenient and practical if your grill is fairly close to your stove, and if your stove is reasonably near where you're serving the meal. A kitchen design in which the fire, the grill, the stove, and the table are all contained in one wonderfully warm and appealing room is ideal. The importance of communication between the kitchen and the dining room cannot be overstated—be it in the restaurant or the home. I feel this so very strongly: I *must* know the response of those in the dining room from firsthand observation. This sort of direct feedback is imperative to every good cook I know. It is the allure of the open fire that will encourage the contact between the cooks and the diners.

The traditions of grilling go back to the very beginnings of cooking, and they hold an appeal that is so basic and fundamental that they continue to survive. The nearly hypnotic quality of the flames, the warmth, and the smoky aromas and tastes meet and mingle to create an unconscious desire to eat. Who could resist the enticing aromas of garlic baking in the coals or the rosemary and bay marinade dripping from the lamb into the fire?

Charcoal-Grilled Oysters with Chervil Butter
and Yellow Caviar
Squab Salad with Garden Lettuces
Loin of Lamb Sautéed in Walnut Oil
*Tangerine Sherbet in Tangerine Shells

In California we were used to very large oysters that were difficult to eat on the half shell, but easily and wonderfully grilled. The chervil butter and yellow caviar are refinements, but the oysters can also be done very simply with melted butter and pepper. This menu incorporates a recurrent theme of the restaurant: oysters, lamb, and garden lettuces.

SUGGESTED WINES: A crisp young Chablis with the oysters, and a Bordeaux or Burgundy with the lamb.

Charcoal-Grilled Oysters

Serves 8

5 dozen oysters

FOR THE *FUMET:*

1 carrot
1 small leek
1 small celery rib
½ medium onion
5 medium shallots
1 cup dry white wine
Bouquet garni: 3 4-inch sprigs fresh fennel tops or 1 teaspoon fennel
    seeds; 6 to 8 sprigs parsley; 2 3-inch sprigs fresh thyme or 1
    teaspoon dried thyme; 1 bay leaf; 10 to 12 black peppercorns
6 to 8 chervil stems

TO make the *fumet,* shuck 2 dozen of the oysters and save their liquor. Clean and peel the vegetables. Cut the carrot, leek, celery and onion into quarters lengthwise. Roughly dice the 5 shallots. Tie the fennel, parsley, thyme, bay leaf, and peppercorns in cheesecloth to make the bouquet garni. Put the 2 dozen shucked oysters and their liquor, the cup of wine, the prepared vegetables, and the bouquet garni in a stainless or enameled pot and barely cover with cold water. Bring the *fumet* to a boil, reduce heat immediately, skim the *fumet,* and simmer it for ½ hour. Strain the *fumet,* add the 6 to 8 chervil stems, and reduce by one-third.

FOR THE SAUCE:

½ pound unsalted butter
¾ cup reduced *fumet*
2 tablespoons heavy cream
Lemon juice and white pepper to taste

FOR the sauce, the ½ pound butter should be a little cooler than room temperature. Cut the butter into tablespoon-sized bits. Remove the chervil stems from the reduced *fumet* and measure ¾ cup of it into a small heavy saucepan. Bring the *fumet* to a boil, reduce the heat, and whisk the butter in bit by bit as you would for a *beurre blanc.* Add the 2 tablespoons cream, and lemon juice and pepper to taste. The sauce should have a light syrupy texture.

GARNISH:

36 chervil sprigs
3 to 4 ounces yellow whitefish caviar

HEAT the grill with mesquite wood charcoal so that the flame is licking about an inch over the grill. Meanwhile, heat two or three large platters or shallow casseroles spread with ½ inch of rock salt in a very hot oven for 15 minutes. When the fire is ready, put 3 dozen oysters, curved side down, directly on the grill. When the shells just open slightly or begin seeping or bubbling (2 to 4 minutes), remove the oysters from the fire. Finish opening them with an oyster knife, and discard the flat top shell. Arrange the oysters on the hot rock salt and put a teaspoon or so of sauce over each oyster. Garnish each oyster with a sprig of chervil and half a teaspoon or so of caviar.

Squab Salad with Garden Lettuces

Serves 8

3 squab, about 1 pound each, livers reserved
¾ cup virgin olive oil
2 tablespoons unsalted butter
4 tablespoons Armagnac
½ cup squab stock
1 tablespoon port
7 medium shallots
2 tablespoons to ½ cup sherry vinegar
Salt and pepper
Reserved pan juices from the squab
8 handfuls of 2- to 3-inch lettuces and salad herbs (rocket, garden cress,
   watercress, chicory, dandelion greens, red leaf or oak leaf lettuces)
Optional: Minced black truffle
                1 to 2 tablespoons walnut oil

TO cook the squab, heat 4 tablespoons of the olive oil over medium-high heat and brown them turning frequently. Add the 2 tablespoons butter halfway through the browning. When the squab are browned (about 7 minutes), flame the pan with 3 tablespoons of Armagnac. When the flame dies, move the squab, breast up, to a roasting pan. Pour off the oil from the sauté pan and deglaze with ½ cup squab stock and 1 tablespoon port. Roast the squab in a preheated 475° F. oven, basting them three or four times with the deglazing juices, for 12 to 15 minutes. The squab are done when the breast meat is still quite pink. Cool the squab at room temperature and reserve all juices.

Heat 2 tablespoons of the olive oil over medium-high heat and sauté the 3 reserved livers with 5 diced shallots. Turn the livers once or twice and sauté for 1 to 2 minutes only. Flame the pan with 1 tablespoon Armagnac and add the reserved juices from the roasted squab. Remove the livers to cool at room temperature and strain the pan juices.

For the vinaigrette, fine-dice the remaining 2 shallots, and combine them with the remaining olive oil, the reserved pan juices, and vinegar and salt and pepper to taste. The amount of vinegar used will depend on the strength of the juices from the squab. Let the vinaigrette stand for 15 to 20 minutes, then strain. Add the truffles and walnut oil if desired and correct the seasoning.

To assemble the salad, wash and dry the lettuces and herbs carefully. Remove the breasts from the squab and slice each breast on a diagonal into ⅜-inch slices. Slice the livers into ⅜-inch slices. Reserve the juices from slicing and stir them into the vinaigrette. Toss the lettuce leaves with enough vinaigrette to coat lightly, and put them on salad plates. Arrange the breasts on the lettuce and garnish the salad with the livers.

Loin of Lamb Sautéed in Walnut Oil

Serves 8

6-pound saddle of lamb
Salt and pepper to taste
½ cup walnut oil
1 cup dry white wine
1 bay leaf
2 3-inch sprigs fresh thyme
2 medium shallots
4 tablespoons virgin olive oil
½ cup lamb stock

SEPARATE the loins and tenderloins from the saddle, and trim them completely. Season lightly with salt and pepper and marinate them in 2 tablespoons of the walnut oil, the cup of wine, the bay leaf, the thyme, and 2 sliced shallots, for 2 to 3 hours or overnight in a cool place; do not refrigerate.

Remove the meat from the marinade and pat dry. Heat 4 tablespoons of olive oil with 2 tablespoons of walnut oil in a heavy sauté pan over high heat. Sear the loins first and then the tenderloins. The meat must be seared very quickly, about 5 minutes in all. The tenderloins take about half as long to cook as the loins. Transfer the meat to a preheated 450° F. oven and roast for 6 to 10 minutes; add the tenderloins after 3 minutes. The meat should be rare; after 5 minutes, test it by feeling it, or with an instant-reading thermometer (internal temperature should be 128° F.).

Transfer the lamb to a platter and remove the oil from the sauté pan. Add the juices from the roasting pan to the sauté pan and deglaze with ½ cup of lamb stock. Reduce to thicken slightly, strain, then whisk in remaining walnut oil to taste. After the lamb has rested for about 5 minutes, slice the meat and pour the sauce over it. Serve with a vegetable, such as fresh chanterelles or Belgian endive, sautéed quickly in butter.

Goat Cheese Soufflé
Bourride
Charcoal-Grilled Loin of Pork with Grilled Leeks and Red Peppers
*Two Plum Sherbets

With its Bourride and grilled peppers, this menu seems very Provençal in feeling. It's a suitable menu for the late summer, when all the ingredients are available. It is also a very fragrant dinner with the smells of garlic, fresh fish, and burning charcoal in the air.

SUGGESTED WINES: A succession of Rhône or Provençal wines: white with the soufflé, a rosé with the Bourride, and a red with the pork and grilled vegetables.

Goat Cheese Soufflé

Serves 6

6 tablespoons unsalted butter
5 tablespoons all-purpose flour
1½ cups half-and-half
1 cup whipping cream
Salt, nutmeg, cayenne, and black pepper to taste
5 egg yolks
6 ounces strong-flavored goat cheese (Bûcheron, Montrachet, Lezay, etc.)
1 cup egg whites
light sprinkle dried thyme

MAKE a roux of the butter and flour and cook it gently for 5 to 8 minutes. Mix the creams and scald them. Remove the roux from the heat and cool slightly before whisking in the scalded creams. Transfer the resulting béchamel to a double boiler and season it lightly with salt, nutmeg, and black pepper. Cover and cook slowly for about 1 hour, stirring occasionally. Allow to cool slightly before adding the rest of the soufflé ingredients.

Stir the 5 egg yolks into the béchamel, then add 4 ounces of crumbled goat cheese; season with salt, nutmeg, cayenne, and black pepper and mix together well. Put the remaining 2 ounces of crumbled cheese on top of the mixture and sprinkle with black pepper. Beat the cup of egg whites very stiff and fold three quarters of them into the cheese mixture. The mixture should be fairly loose, but not runny. (If it is runny, add more beaten egg white.) Pour the soufflé gently onto a well-buttered 12-inch oval platter or into six buttered 6-inch shallow gratin dishes. Sprinkle the dried thyme over the soufflé and bake on the top shelf of a preheated 450° F. oven for 10 to 12 minutes. The top and sides should be well-browned, and the inside warm and creamy.

Bourride

Serves 6

6 pounds assorted rockfish (three or four different kinds deepen
    the flavor)
1 onion
1 carrot
1 leek
1 celery rib
3 to 4 large fresh mushrooms
2 cloves garlic
3 tablespoons light olive oil
Bouquet garni: 10 to 12 parsley sprigs; 1 bay leaf; ½ teaspoon fennel
    seeds; ½ teaspoon dried tarragon; 10 to 12 black peppercorns; 6 to 8
    coriander seeds
½ cup dry white wine
1½ quarts water
Salt and pepper
1 recipe aïoli (see page 219)
18 garlic croutons (see page 95)

To make the *fumet* for the Bourride, fillet 6 pounds of rockfish or other
inexpensive local, very fresh fish. Skin the fillets and cut them into
pieces of even thickness, about 2½ inches wide; reserve the trimmings for
the *fumet*. Cover the pieces and refrigerate. Remove the gills from the fish,
rinse them well, and snap their backbones in half.

Peel 1 onion and 1 carrot, and wash and trim 1 leek and 1 celery rib. Brush
3 to 4 large mushrooms. Chop the vegetables roughly, along with 2 cloves
of peeled garlic. Put 3 tablespoons light olive oil in a nonaluminum stock
pot and add the vegetables. Cover and cook over low heat for 15 to 20
minutes.

Make a bouquet garni of 10 to 12 parsley sprigs, 1 bay leaf, ½ teaspoon
fennel seeds, ½ teaspoon dried tarragon, 10 to 12 black peppercorns, and 6
to 8 coriander seeds. Add the bouquet garni, the fish frames (include heads
and tails), ½ cup dry white wine, and 1½ quarts water. Bring the *fumet* to
a boil, then reduce the heat immediately to a simmer. Skim the *fumet* and
let it simmer for 30 minutes. Meanwhile, prepare the aïoli and croutons.

Strain the *fumet* through a fine sieve into another pot and season with salt
and pepper. Bring the *fumet* to a bare simmer and add the pieces of fillet.
Poach for 3 to 4 minutes, until the fish is firm yet springy when pressed with
a finger.

Remove the poached fish to warm serving bowls and ladle the broth over
it. Float about ¼ cup aïoli per serving in the center of each bowl and serve
the garlic croutons on the side.

Charcoal-Grilled Loin of Pork

Serves 6

½ cup sugar
¼ cup salt
about 2 gallons warm water
5 coriander seeds
10 to 12 black peppercorns
5 juniper berries
6 to 8 bay leaves
2 to 3 sprigs fresh thyme
2 to 3 sprigs fresh marjoram
6-pound boned loin of pork
¼ to ⅓ cup virgin olive oil
½ cup beef or pork stock

MAKE a brine by dissolving ½ cup sugar and ¼ cup salt in 2 gallons warm water. Slightly crush 5 coriander seeds, 10 to 12 black peppercorns, 5 juniper berries, 6 to 8 bay leaves, and 2 to 3 sprigs each fresh thyme and marjoram in a mortar. Stir the herbs into the brine. When the brine is cool, put the loin into it. The meat must be completely submerged; put weights on top of a plate if necessary. Refrigerate the loin for 2 days.

About 4 hours before cooking the loin, remove it from the brine and trim the fat. Rub the loin with the olive oil and let it come to room temperature.

Prepare a medium-low charcoal fire so that the loin will cook without flaming. Put the loin on the grill and cook for about 30 minutes, turning frequently. The loin is done when the internal temperature is 137°F. The meat will be pinkish because the brine affects its color, but it is done and safe to eat at this temperature. Remove the loin to a platter and let it rest for 5 minutes or so.

To make the sauce, collect the juices from the platter and add them to the ½ cup of beef or pork stock in a small pan and reduce the sauce slightly. Slice the loin and spoon a little sauce on each serving. Serve with grilled leeks and red peppers (see pages 210 and 172–73).

Charcoal-Grilled Shellfish with Red Wine Butter Sauce
Risotto with White Truffle and Pork Kidneys
Roast Suckling Pig with Garden Lettuce Salad
*Frozen Anise Soufflé

This is a complicated but very successful dinner. Fortunately, the pig can be cooked and allowed to sit for some time before the skin loses its crispness. This will give the cook the time to attend to the quickly grilled fish and the risotto. This is definitely a fall menu when the shellfish are good and the white truffles are fresh.

SUGGESTED WINES: Drink a light cool Italian red with the shellfish, a Barbaresco with the risotto, and an old Barolo with the pig.

Charcoal-Grilled Shellfish with Red Wine Butter Sauce

The shellfish should be very fresh. The amounts given are approximate and may vary according to availability and taste. This recipe serves 12. Rock and Jonah crabs (Maine) would grill up fine; so would Florida stone crabs, Alaska king crabs, Alaska tanner or "snow crabs," and the Atlantic blue crab, Callinectes sapidus Rathbun.

THE SHELLFISH:

1 live lobster, about 1½ pounds
1 large live Dungeness crab, about 2 pounds
2 dozen oysters
2 dozen mussels
½ to ¾ pounds scallops

BRING a large pot of salted water to a boil and cook the lobster and crab in it for about 2 minutes. Remove them from the pot, cool enough to handle, clean them and disjoint them with a sharp knife. Leave the shells on and cut the lobster tail into about 1-inch rounds; leave the crab legs as they are and divide the body into four to six pieces, depending on the size of the crab. Reserve the tomalley and coral for another use. Scrub the oysters and mussels and debeard the mussels.

THE RED WINE BUTTER SAUCE:

6 medium shallots
1 small onion
1 pound and 3 tablespoons unsalted butter
½ bottle light red wine (Chianti or Beaujolais)
about 1 tablespoon red wine vinegar
Salt and black pepper to taste

FINE-DICE the 6 shallots and the small onion. Cook them in 3 tablespoons butter over low heat for about 10 minutes, until they are translucent. Cut 1 pound butter into tablespoon-sized bits and soften slightly. Add ½ bottle of red wine and about a tablespoon of red wine vinegar to the pan. Reduce over medium-low heat until the liquid is syrupy and about ¾ cup remains. Taste for acidity and add a little more red wine vinegar if necessary. Increase the heat to medium-high and whisk in half of the softened butter bit by bit. When the butter has been incorporated, lower the heat, and add the rest of the butter in four or five additions, whisking constantly. Season the sauce with salt and lots of freshly ground black pepper. Keep the sauce warm in a double boiler.

Prepare a charcoal fire that is very hot in one area, flames just licking above the grill, and medium hot in another area. Put the oysters and mussels over the hot fire and cook for about 5 minutes, until they are about half open. Remove them from the fire and finish opening them with an oyster knife if necessary. Put them on warmed platters or plates and spoon a little red wine butter over each. Cook the crab and lobster pieces and the scallops over the medium fire for 3 to 5 minutes, turning frequently. The cooking time will vary, the lobster and scallops taking less time, the crab legs more. Arrange the lobster, crab, and scallops on warm platters, and brush them lightly with a little red wine butter. Serve the rest of the sauce in small bowls.

Risotto with White Truffle and Pork Kidneys

Serves 12

1 or more white truffles
3 cups Italian Arborio rice
2 medium onions
1 sprig fresh thyme
1 bay leaf
2 cloves garlic
½ pound unsalted butter
Salt and pepper
1½ to 2 quarts chicken stock
3 or 4 dried boletus mushrooms
about ½ cup light olive oil
2 small pork kidneys
2 tablespoons minced parsley

BURY the truffle(s) in 3 cups Arborio rice and cover tightly a day before making the risotto.

Begin the risotto by dicing 2 onions very finely and cooking gently with 1 sprig fresh minced thyme, 1 bay leaf, and 1 whole garlic clove in 3 tablespoons butter for about 10 minutes. Season with salt and pepper and set aside.

Heat 2 quarts chicken stock with 3 or 4 dried boletus mushrooms to a bare simmer. Keep the chicken stock simmering and near the risotto pan.

To cook the risotto, heat ⅓ cup olive oil and ¼ cup butter in a heavy-bottomed pan and stir in the truffle-perfumed rice. Reserve the truffle(s). Cook the rice, stirring constantly, for about 5 minutes, until it begins to become translucent. Add the onions and enough boiling chicken stock to just cover the rice. Reduce the heat to a simmer and cook until the liquid is nearly absorbed. Add more hot broth, enough to just cover the rice each time, until the broth is absorbed and the rice is done. This will take from 18 to 25 minutes. The rice is cooked *al dente* when the density of the risotto is loose but not soupy. Turn off the heat and correct the seasoning. Add a good lump of sweet butter, cover, and let it rest for 5 minutes.

While the risotto is resting, sauté the pork kidneys in 2 tablespoons olive oil and 2 tablespoons butter over medium heat. Season with salt and pepper and cook for about 5 minutes, turning frequently. Add 1 minced garlic clove and 2 tablespoons minced parsley during the last minute of cooking. The kidneys are done when their texture has firmed and they are still pink in the center.

Remove the kidneys from the pan and slice them thinly. Toss them into the risotto with their pan juices and add a little butter to taste. Serve on heated plates and shave the white truffle(s) over the risotto at the table.

Roast Suckling Pig with Garden Lettuce Salad

Serves 12

1 10- to 15-pound dressed suckling pig, at room temperature
3 to 4 cloves garlic
4 to 5 sprigs fresh thyme or 2 teaspoons dried
4 to 5 sprigs fresh rosemary or 2 teaspoons dried
about ½ cup virgin olive oil for rubbing the pig
1 cup virgin olive oil for the vinaigrette
4 large minced shallots
¼ to ⅓ cup red wine vinegar
8 handfuls garden lettuces (all rocket is especially good for this salad; or
   a mixture of rocket, lamb's lettuce, 2- to 3-inch romaine, oak leaf or
   red leaf lettuces, dandelion greens, watercress, or ground cress)
Salt and pepper to taste

RUB the pig inside and out with the 3 to 4 cloves garlic and the thyme and rosemary. Put the remaining garlic and herbs inside the pig, season it with salt and pepper, and rub it with about ½ cup olive oil. Wrap the ears and tail with foil and roast the pig on a flat tray in a preheated 450°F. oven for about 50 minutes. Rotate the pig three or four times so that it browns evenly. The meat should not be overdone; the haunch when tested with a finger should spring back, or a meat thermometer should read 137°F. when inserted into the haunch. Allow the pig to rest for 10 to 15 minutes out of the oven before collecting the juices for the vinaigrette.

To make the vinaigrette, skim the fat from the pig's juices and stir them into 1 cup virgin olive oil. Add the 4 minced shallots and ¼ to ⅓ cup red wine vinegar (or more if the vinaigrette calls for more acidity). Season the vinaigrette with salt and pepper to taste.

To assemble the salad, carefully wash and dry the lettuces. Slice the meat from the roasted pig shoulders and haunches. Toss the lettuces with enough vinaigrette to lightly coat them. Put the lettuce leaves on salad plates and arrange the meat in the center of the plates. Drizzle some vinaigrette over the meat and serve the salad.

Fall Vegetable Ragoût
Salt Cod Ravioli in a Fish Consommé
Charcoal-Grilled Duck Marinated in Red Wine
*Lime Soufflé

This menu includes what we've found to be one of the most flavorful ways to cook a duck—especially the commercially available kind. I see this menu served on big platters and in big tureens, because it all happens at the last minute, after a good deal of advance preparation. This menu also includes one of the very few original dishes we have cooked: salt cod ravioli that bring together the rather simple elements of pasta, salt cod, and broth, and elevate them into a sophisticated preparation; the whole seems better than the sum of its parts.

SUGGESTED WINES: Serve a white Hermitage with the salt cod ravioli, and a red Hermitage with the duck.

Fall Vegetable Ragoût

Serves 4

1 large, very ripe tomato
1 red onion
6 to 8 mushrooms
1 small zucchini
¼ pound green beans
1 medium sweet red pepper
12 to 14 fresh basil leaves
2 to 3 sprigs parsley
2 sprigs fresh thyme
1 clove garlic
¼ cup virgin olive oil
about ½ cup chicken stock
Salt and pepper to taste
Unsalted butter to taste
Lemon juice

PEEL, seed, and dice 1 very ripe tomato. Thin-slice 1 red onion, and quarter 6 to 8 mushrooms. Slice 1 small zucchini into ¼-inch rounds. Top and tail ¼ pound green beans and French-cut them. Stem and seed 1 red pepper and cut it into thin slices. Stem 6 or 7 basil leaves, 2 to 3 sprigs parsley, and 2 sprigs thyme, and mince them finely with 1 clove of garlic.

Blanch the green beans for 1 minute, refresh, drain, and set aside. Heat ¼ cup olive oil over medium heat in a heavy-bottomed sauté pan and add the sliced mushrooms, the onion, the red pepper, and a little salt and pepper. Cover and cook for about 5 minutes over medium-low heat. When the vegetables have softened slightly, add the tomato, the minced herbs, the zucchini, and a little chicken broth for moisture. (At this point, only about ¼ cup of the broth will be needed.) Season again lightly with salt and pepper. Light seasoning should follow each addition, as it helps the vegetable flavors come together.

Lower the heat, cover and cook for 3 to 4 minutes, until the vegetables are just crisp and tender. Add the blanched green beans, and season with salt, pepper, and lemon juice. Add 6 to 7 whole basil leaves and more olive oil and unsalted butter to taste, and stir the ragoût over high heat for ½ minute. The vegetables' flavors should marry in a rich spicy sauce, but the vegetables should remain crisp.

Salt Cod Ravioli in a Fish Consommé

Serves 4

FOR THE FILLING:

½ pound boneless fillet of salt cod, uniform in color and firm in texture
1 head garlic
⅓ cup whipping cream
1 cup virgin olive oil
Black pepper
Lemon juice
Optional: 1 medium potato, boiled and riced

THE cod must be soaked for 2 days in cold water in the refrigerator. Change the water two or three times. After the cod is desalted, rinse it and poach it in barely simmering water for about 8 minutes, until the fish is tender but not overcooked. Lift it out of the poaching water and flake it while it is still warm. Remove all bones and dark spots from the cod.

Peel the cloves of 1 head of garlic and crush 3 cloves slightly. Heat the crushed cloves over low heat with ⅓ cup cream. Pound the rest of the cloves to a purée in a mortar. Warm 1 cup olive oil over very low heat. Put about ⅓ cup of the oil, all of the flaked cod, and about 2 teaspoons of the garlic purée in a pan over very low heat, and work the mixture to a rough paste with a pestle or wooden spoon. Put the pan over simmering water in a double boiler and finish the purée by alternately adding the warm cream and olive oil to make a rich, homogeneous paste. Depending on the texture of the purée, it may or may not require all the cream and oil; it should not be too wet. Season the mixture with more garlic if necessary, and add black pepper and lemon juice to taste. If the purée is too salty, add enough of a boiled and riced potato to balance the flavor. Let the filling cool to room temperature (cover and refrigerate for a short time if necessary). The filling must be dry and firm for the ravioli.

FOR THE PASTA:

3 cups all-purpose flour
3 large eggs
½ teaspoon salt
1 to 2 tablespoons water

MAKE a well in a mound of 3 cups of flour. Beat 3 eggs lightly with ½ teaspoon salt and add them to the well. Incorporate as much flour as possible into the center of the well with a large fork. Knead the dough very well by hand to form a stiff dough, sprinkling in a little water as necessary. At the beginning of the kneading, the dough will seem dry and crumbly. It will become smooth by the end of the process. Be careful to add only enough water to make a workable but very firm dough. Work it thoroughly for a good 20 minutes on the table. Cover the dough and let it rest at room temperature for 1 hour.

To form the ravioli, divide the dough in half and roll one part through to the thinnest setting of a pasta machine. Avoid flouring the pasta during the rolling unless absolutely necessary. Cut the strip of pasta into 2-foot sections. Working on a lightly floured table, take one section at a time and fold it in half lengthwise. Unfold it and use the center crease as guideline to add the cod purée. Put 1 teaspoon of it every 2 inches just under the center line of one half of the strip of pasta. Spray the pasta with a fine mist of water or use a pastry brush to lightly moisten the dough between and below the filling. Fold the top half of the dough over the paste and bottom half of dough and press firmly between the dots of filling, taking care to avoid air pockets. Lightly flour the strip of ravioli, and using a cutter-crimper, cut off the uneven bottom end along the strip and then cut in between each dot of filling to form the individual ravioli. Repeat the process until all of the pasta and filling are used. Set the finished ravioli on a lightly floured baking sheet so that they do not touch each other and refrigerate until they are ready to be cooked.

TO COOK AND SERVE:

1½ quarts clarified fish *fumet* (see page 124)
The ravioli
8 sprigs chervil

HEAT the *fumet* over low heat and keep it warm. Cook the ravioli in 8 to 10 quarts lightly boiling water, preferably in a 12-inch-diameter pot, for about 2 minutes, until they are tender. Remove the ravioli carefully with a slotted spoon to four warm soup plates, and ladle some fish consommé over each serving. Garnish each serving with 2 sprigs of chervil.

Charcoal-Grilled Duck Marinated in Red Wine

Serves 4

1 fresh duck, about 5 pounds
3 carrots
3 onions
15 to 20 black peppercorns
Several sprigs fresh thyme, marjoram, and parsley
2 bay leaves
1 teaspoon sea salt
1 bottle rich red wine
Salt and pepper

To marinate the duck, first cut out the backbone so the duck can be spread flat. Lean on the duck heavily to crack the breast and rib bones. Be careful not to break through the breast meat and skin.

Roughly chop 3 carrots and 3 onions and spread half of them in a dish large enough to hold the flattened duck. Put the duck on top of the vegetables, and spread the rest over the duck. Lightly crush the black peppercorns and scatter them with the thyme, marjoram, and parsley over and around the duck. Add the 2 bay leaves and sprinkle with 1 teaspoon sea salt. Pour 1 bottle of red wine over the duck and marinate for 12 to 24 hours, turning once.

To cook the duck, preheat the oven to 500°F. Remove the duck from the marinade, dry it, and prick it thoroughly in the fat deposits around the wings and legs. Place it on a rack in a roasting pan, season with salt and pepper, and roast it for about 20 to 25 minutes. Meanwhile, prepare a medium-low charcoal fire, which should be hot enough to spit at the duck as the fat drips, but not hot enough to flame up.

Season the duck again lightly when it comes from the oven and put it skin side down on the grill. Ninety percent of the cooking should be done with the skin toward the fire so that the skin will be crisp and the flesh will remain juicy, rare, and tender. Turn the duck once and cook for 3 to 4 minutes with the split side down.

When the duck is done, after about 20 to 25 minutes, remove it to a platter and let it rest in a warm place for 5 minutes. Quarter the duck, then bone and slice the breast. Serve with an onion-shallot confit and roasted chestnuts.

FOR THE CONFIT AND CHESTNUTS:

3 onions
4 shallots
6 tablespoons unsalted butter
Salt and pepper
Pinch of sugar
¼ cup red wine
¼ cup red wine vinegar
1 to 2 tablespoons cassis or brandy
2 dozen chestnuts

Slice 3 onions, mince 4 shallots, and sauté them gently together in 6 tablespoons unsalted butter which has been allowed to brown for about 15 minutes. Season with salt, pepper, and sugar and allow the vegetables to caramelize over medium-low heat. Add ¼ cup red wine and ¼ cup red wine vinegar and 1 to 2 tablespoons cassis or brandy to flavor, reduce the heat, and simmer for about 1 hour, until the liquid is almost completely reduced and absorbed. Split 2 dozen chestnuts and roast them on the grill beside the duck.

Artichoke and Grapefruit Salad
Leek and Goat Cheese Tart
Charcoal-Grilled Lobster
*Poached Figs and Coffee Ice Cream

Charcoal-grilling a lobster brings a smoky aroma and flavor to the meat that makes it seem less rich and filling.

SUGGESTED WINES: A St. Péray Blanc with the tart is a wonderful combination; and the lobster will be best with a rich, full-bodied white wine.

Artichoke and Grapefruit Salad

Serves 6

6 extra large artichokes
1 lemon
4 handfuls red-leaf lettuce hearts
3 ripe pink grapefruit
about 1 teaspoon salt
1 cup virgin olive oil
¼ cup raspberry vinegar
Salt and pepper to taste
about ½ cup chervil sprigs

TRIM the leaves completely from 6 very large artichokes so that only the hearts remain. Remove the chokes, cut off the stems, and pare the outside of the hearts to remove any green. Squeeze the juice of 1 lemon into a bowl and add the artichoke hearts, the lemon rinds, and cold water to cover.

Wash and dry the red-leaf lettuce hearts. Section 3 ripe pink grapefruit and remove all membranes and seeds.

Slice the artichoke hearts into ¼-inch slices and cook them in boiling salted water with a little lemon juice for 1½ to 2 minutes, until they are *al dente*. Drain them and refresh with cold water. Marinate the hearts in ½ cup olive oil.

Make a vinaigrette with ½ cup of olive oil, ¼ cup of raspberry vinegar, or to taste, and salt and pepper to taste.

Toss the lettuce with some of the vinaigrette and arrange it on salad plates. Alternate grapefruit sections with artichoke slices on top of the lettuce. Drizzle the salads with more vinaigrette and a little of the olive oil from marinating the artichoke hearts. Garnish with chervil sprigs.

Leek and Goat Cheese Tart

For this tart, only ¼ of the puff pastry recipe is required. It is, however, very difficult to make good pastry in quantities smaller than 1 pound of flour and 1 pound of butter. Puff pastry freezes very successfully. It should be wrapped very well, and defrosted slowly in the refrigerator for 24 hours. If not to be frozen, it should be used within a day or two at the most.

Serves 6

FOR THE PUFF PASTRY:

1 pound all-purpose flour
1½ teaspoons salt
1 cup plus 2 tablespoons ice water
1¼ pounds unsalted butter

MIX 1 pound flour with 1½ teaspoons salt and make a mound of it on a work surface. Make a well in the mound and add 1 cup plus 2 tablespoons ice water to the well. Incorporate the flour into the water from the center of the well. When the dough forms a soft mass, add ¼ pound soft butter and knead once to form a soft dough. Cover, refrigerate, and let rest for 1 hour.

On a floured table, spread the dough into a symmetrical cross shape, keeping the center part thicker than the four flaps. Put 1 pound cool but soft unsalted butter in the center and fold the flaps over the butter, like a package, to completely encase it. Flour lightly and roll the dough into a rectangle approximately 18 by 9 inches. Brush the flour off the dough. Fold it in three equal parts, one over the other like a letter. Turn the dough 90 degrees, roll out again to a rectangle and fold in three. Cover and refrigerate for 1 hour. Repeat the process of rolling and folding twice more. Cover, refrigerate, and let rest another hour. Give the dough a final two turns, making a total of six turns. Let it rest for another hour in the refrigerator, before you start the final assembly.

FOR THE FILLING:

3 to 4 pounds leeks (about 12 to 14 small leeks)
8 tablespoons sweet butter
Salt and pepper
¼ pound pancetta
1 egg
¾ cup crème fraîche or ½ cup heavy cream
2 teaspoons Dijon mustard
Pinch of curry powder
¼ pound goat cheese
⅓ cup fresh bread crumbs

TRIM the green stems and the roots from the leeks. Julienne the leeks, rinse them well in cold water, drain them, and cook them in 6 tablespoons butter over gentle heat for 20 to 30 minutes. Season with salt and pepper, then cover the pan after 10 minutes and let the leeks sweat. Thin-slice ¼ pound pancetta, unroll the slices, and cut them into ½-inch pieces. Render the pancetta over low heat for 10 to 15 minutes and drain off the fat and water.

To make the custard, beat the egg lightly in a large bowl and stir in ¾ cup crème fraîche or ½ cup heavy cream, 2 teaspoons Dijon mustard, and a pinch of curry powder. Crumble half of the trimmed cheese into the custard. When the leeks and pancetta are cool, stir them into the custard.

To assemble the tart, roll out one quarter of the dough to an 11½-inch-diameter circle about ⅛ inch thick. Prick the dough and transfer it to a baking sheet lightly moistened with water. Roll up the circumference of the dough to form a free-standing tart shell with sides 1½ inches high. Refrigerate the shell for 15 to 30 minutes. The tart shell may be covered and refrigerated overnight if desired.

To bake the tart, fill the shell with the cool leek-custard mixture. Crumble the remaining goat cheese over the filling. Sprinkle the tart with ⅓ cup fresh bread crumbs and 2 tablespoons melted butter. Remove the bottom from a 10-inch tart or flan ring and place the ring upside down over the tart to help it keep its shape in the oven. Bake in a preheated 400°F. oven for 10 to 15 minutes. When the sides have puffed and set, remove the ring, reduce the temperature to 350°F., leaving the oven door ajar for a few minutes to ensure the rapid temperature change, and bake for another 30 to 40 minutes until the pastry is a beautiful golden brown. Serve the tart immediately.

Charcoal-Grilled Lobster

Serves 6

6 1- to 1½-pound lobsters
¾ cup coarse sea salt
½ pound unsalted butter
Reserved coral (if any) from the lobsters
Salt and pepper to taste
Optional: Lemon juice to taste
                3 to 4 tablespoons heavy cream

TO prepare the lobsters for the grill, bring 10 to 12 quarts of water with ¾ cup coarse sea salt to a rapid boil. The water should be very salty. One by one, plunge the lobsters into the boiling water for 1 minute.

Prepare a low wood charcoal fire and put the lobsters on it. Cook them for 10 to 12 minutes, turning frequently. To serve the lobsters, cut them in half lengthwise through the center of the head and tail and remove the gravelly stomach sac and the coral. Reserve the coral for the sauce, and remove the lobster to a warm serving platter.

Gently melt ½ pound butter and whisk the reserved coral into it. Season the sauce with salt and pepper. Add lemon juice to taste and 3 or 4 tablespoons heavy cream to the sauce if desired. Serve the sauce in small dishes.

Salade Niçoise
Mexican Garlic Soup
Charcoal-Grilled Veal with Mustard Herb Butter
Straw Potato Pancakes
*Black Currant Ice Cream

This is a very informal menu meant to be served when the tomatoes, garlic, and green beans are at their best. It is also easy to serve because everything can be prepared in advance—everything except the veal, and the potato pancakes, which take only a few careful minutes at the end. This is a fresh, light, aromatic menu, and predictable if the ingredients are impeccably chosen.

SUGGESTED WINES: This meal would go well with a simple red wine served chilled throughout.

Salade Niçoise

Serves 6

1½-pound fresh tuna steak
1 carrot
1 onion
1 celery rib
4 cloves garlic
2 to 3 sprigs thyme
about ½ cup virgin olive oil
Salt and pepper

COOK the tuna before preparing the vinaigrette and vegetables. Preheat the oven to 350°F. Roughly chop 1 carrot, 1 onion, 1 celery rib, and 4 cloves of garlic. Sweat the vegetables with 2 or 3 sprigs of thyme in 4 tablespoons virgin olive oil over low heat for about 10 minutes. Put the vegetables in a small baking dish. Rub a 1½-pound tuna steak well with olive oil, and salt and pepper lightly. It is important that the tuna be of even thickness. Put the tuna on the vegetables and bake, for a piece about 1½ inches thick, about 15 to 20 minutes, turning once. The tuna should be barely warm inside. Remove the tuna to a plate when it is done and let cool to room temperature. Remove the skin and any bones, and barely flake the tuna. Drizzle lightly with olive oil.

THE GARLIC VINAIGRETTE:

2 to 3 cloves very fresh garlic
1 cup virgin olive oil
¼ to ⅓ cup flavorful red wine vinegar
2 tablespoons capers, rinsed and drained
Salt and pepper

USING a mortar and pestle, crush 2 to 3 cloves peeled garlic with 1 teaspoon of olive oil. Mix the garlic paste with ¼ cup red wine vinegar, and whisk in the rest of the olive oil. Add 2 tablespoons capers, and season the vinaigrette with salt and pepper and more vinegar if necessary.

THE VEGETABLES AND ACCOMPANIMENTS (CHOOSE ONLY THE BEST OF THE FOL-
LOWING VEGETABLES):

¼ pound *haricots verts*
½ pound tiny new potatoes
¼ pound shelled fava beans
3 to 4 artichokes and 1 lemon
1 red pepper
6 to 8 salt-packed anchovy fillets
4 hard-cooked eggs
½ red onion
12 to 15 chervil sprigs
3 to 4 ripe summer tomatoes
¼ to ⅓ cup Niçoise olives

PINCH the ends from ¼ pound *haricots verts* and wash ½ pound tiny new potatoes. Blanch the shelled fava beans in abundant boiling salted water for 2 to 3 minutes. Drain them, but reserve the water. Blanch the green beans in the same water until they are bright green and crisp but tender, 2 to 3 minutes. Remove, drain, but reserve the water, and let cool. Boil the potatoes in the same water until they are just done, 4 to 7 minutes. Remove, drain, but reserve the water, and let cool to room temperature.

Trim 3 to 4 artichokes to their hearts, remove their chokes, and cut the hearts into quarters. Put them in a bowl of cold water with the juice of ½ lemon. Squeeze the other half into the boiling water and add the lemon rinds. Blanch the artichoke hearts until they are just done, 2 to 4 minutes. Remove, drain, and toss while they are still warm with a little of the vinaigrette. Wash and seed 1 red bell pepper and cut into thin slices.

Toss the pepper in a little vinaigrette. Toss the green beans in some vinaigrette. Quarter the potatoes and toss them in some vinaigrette.

TO COMPOSE THE SALAD:

RINSE 6 to 8 salt-packed anchovies well and cut the fillets in half lengthwise. The 4 eggs should be boiled just long enough so that the yolk is still a little soft and bright orange. Slice ½ red onion in paper-thin slices. Toss 12 to 15 chervil sprigs with the artichoke hearts. Cut 3 to 4 summer tomatoes into wedges and toss them with a little vinaigrette.

Arrange the vegetables in groups or in a nice but unfussy pattern on a salad platter. Toss the tuna with some vinaigrette and put it in the center of the platter. Arrange the eggs, anchovy fillets, and ¼ to ⅓ cup Niçoise olives on the salad, and drizzle the whole with the remaining vinaigrette.

Mexican Garlic Soup

Serves 6

3 to 4 heads fresh red Mexican garlic
about 1 cup virgin olive oil
2 sprigs thyme
1½ quarts hot rich chicken stock
Salt and pepper
Cayenne
12 garlic croutons made from peasant bread
½ cup freshly grated Parmesan cheese
6 basil leaves

PEEL the cloves of 3 heads fresh Mexican garlic (use 4 heads if they are small). Reserve 2 or 3 cloves. Stew the cloves in 1 cup virgin olive oil in a heavy-bottomed soup pan over low heat until the garlic is very tender, almost melted. This will take about 20 minutes; add 2 sprigs of thyme after 10 minutes. The garlic must not take on the slightest color. Cover the pot and keep the heat very low.

When the garlic is done, pour off all but 2 or 3 tablespoons of the oil and remove the thyme. (The oil may be used for a marinade.) Add 1½ quarts hot rich chicken stock. Cook the soup over low heat for 15 to 20 minutes. Strain through a fine sieve and discard the garlic. Season with salt and pepper and a pinch of cayenne. Heat the soup for 5 minutes until it is very hot but not simmering.

While the soup is cooking, cut 12 croutons from peasant bread, each about 2 by 3 inches and ½ inch thick. Rub with some of the oil used to stew the garlic and bake at 375°F. for 15 minutes or so. The croutons should be well done and crunchy through. Rub with cut garlic while they are still warm.

To serve, put two croutons in each warm soup plate and sprinkle ½ cup grated Parmesan equally over the croutons. Ladle the hot soup over the croutons and garnish each bowl with a fresh basil leaf.

Charcoal-Grilled Veal with Mustard Herb Butter

Serves 6

FOR THE MUSTARD HERB BUTTER:

6 tablespoons unsalted butter
2 tablespoons Dijon mustard
1 shallot
8 to 10 sprigs Italian parsley
8 to 10 chives
Black pepper

MAKE the mustard herb butter first. Soften 6 tablespoons butter and mix well with 2 tablespoons Dijon mustard. Dice 1 shallot very fine and mince 8 to 10 parsley sprigs, enough to equal 2 tablespoons. Cut 8 to 10 chives very fine, enough to equal 2 tablespoons. Mix the shallot and herbs into the butter. Add rather coarse ground black pepper to taste.

THE VEAL:

6 ¼-pound cutlets from a leg of veal
about ¼ cup light olive oil
Salt and pepper
Garnish: 6 ¼-inch lemon slices, cut from a peeled lemon

TRIM 6 ¼-pound veal cutlets of any connective tissue and tendons. Pound the cutlets between lightly oiled parchment paper to about ¼ inch thick. Lightly oil the cutlets again and season with a little salt and pepper.

Prepare a medium-hot charcoal fire of any wood charcoal. Put the cutlets on the grill for 20 seconds and give each a quarter turn to make crisscross grill marks. Grill for 20 seconds, baste with olive oil, and turn the cutlets over. Repeat the quarter turns after 20 seconds and grill for another 20 seconds. The cutlets will be done in about 1½ minutes. Remove to warm serving plates and put about a tablespoon of the mustard butter on each cutlet. Garnish with the lemon slices.

Straw Potato Pancakes

Serves 6

2 pounds russet potatoes
about 8 tablespoons unsalted butter
Salt to taste

PEEL 2 pounds of russet potatoes and grate them coarsely. Rinse them, but do not soak them. Dry the potatoes very well.

Melt about ½ tablespoon butter in a 7- or 8-inch omelet or crêpe pan over medium heat. When the butter is bubbling, add about ¾ cup grated potatoes and press them with a spatula into a thin layer. The edges of the pancake must be even. Cook for 3 minutes, brushing the edges with a little soft butter so that they do not brown before the center is done.

When the pancake holds its shape and slides as a single mass, flip it to the other side and cook for about 3 minutes. Both sides should be a rich golden brown. This recipe makes six pancakes. They can be kept warm in the oven on a baking tray. (Zucchini may be substituted for half of the potatoes. Scrub and trim the zucchini, but leave the peel on. Grate coarsely, rinse, and dry very well. Mix the zucchini with the grated potatoes and cook the pancakes in the same way.)

Artichoke Tart
Charcoal-Grilled Duck Breast
Potato and Wild Mushroom Gratin
*Raspberries and Crème Fraîche

This menu combines three rich but complementary dishes. It also contrasts the rather complex artichoke tart with the simplicity of the rapidly cooked duck breast. I often think of dishes in a menu that way: I like the contrast of following a dish that involves a number of procedures with a simple piece of fruit or a salad.

SUGGESTED WINES: Serve a Stony Hill Gewürztraminer with the tart, and an old Beaulieu Vineyards Private Reserve Cabernet Sauvignon with the duck.

Artichoke Tart

Serves 6

¼ recipe puff pastry (see page 147)
6 large artichokes
1 lemon
4 tablespoons unsalted butter
1 shallot
10 to 12 sprigs Italian parsley
10 to 12 sprigs chervil
2 sprigs tarragon
1 tablespoon light olive oil
1 egg yolk
1 teaspoon Dijon mustard
Salt and pepper
⅓ cup heavy cream

FORM the tart shell according to instructions and refrigerate it for at least 30 minutes.

To prepare the filling, trim 6 large artichokes to the hearts and remove the chokes. Slice the hearts ⅛ inch thick and put the slices in a bowl with cold water and the juice and rind of half of a lemon.

Make an herb butter by mixing 3 tablespoons softened butter with 1 shallot diced finely, and 10 to 12 sprigs Italian parsley, 10 to 12 sprigs chervil, and 2 sprigs tarragon finely minced together.

Leave 18 to 20 center artichoke slices in the lemon water and pat the rest dry with tea towels. Sauté the dry slices over medium heat in 1 tablespoon butter and 1 tablespoon olive oil for 4 to 5 minutes. Toss the artichokes while they are still warm in the herb butter and season with salt and pepper and lemon juice.

Remove the reserved artichokes and lemon rind from the water, salt the water lightly and bring it to a boil. Blanch the reserved artichokes in the water for 2 to 3 minutes. Drain them and pat them dry.

Spread the sautéed artichokes evenly in the prepared tart shell and arrange the blanched artichokes in a pattern on top. Pour any remaining herb butter over the artichokes. Put a flan ring over the tart to help it keep its shape. Bake the tart in a preheated 400°F. oven for 15 minutes and remove the flan ring from the tart. Reduce the oven to 350°F. Leave the oven door ajar for 1 minute to lower the temperature.

Make a custard by stirring 1 lightly beaten egg yolk, 1 teaspoon Dijon mustard, and salt and pepper into ⅓ cup heavy cream. Take the tart out of the oven, pour the custard mixture over the artichokes, and cover with a 10-inch round of buttered parchment paper. Bake the tart at 350°F. for 30 to 35 minutes, until the custard is set and golden brown. Remove the tart to a cake rack and let it stand for 20 minutes before cutting.

Charcoal-Grilled Duck Breast

Serves 6

The breasts from 3 ducks of 4 to 5 pounds each
about ⅓ cup duck fat
Salt and pepper
½ cup duck *demi-glace* (see page 76)
¼ cup wild mushroom liquor (see below)

BONE the breasts from 3 ducks and remove the skin and veins. Scrape off any fat from the skin and save it for another use. Sauté the skin in a heavy pan in 1 tablespoon duck fat over medium heat until it is completely crisp, about 20 minutes. Chop the skin very fine and set aside.

Prepare a medium-hot wood charcoal fire. Pound the duck breasts to ¼ inch thick and season them on both sides with salt and pepper. Brush the breasts on both sides with duck fat and put them on the grill. Grill each side for 3 minutes and place on warm serving plates.

To make the sauce, reduce ½ cup duck *demi-glace* and ¼ cup wild mushroom liquor together over high heat to about ⅔ cup. Pour some sauce over each duck breast and sprinkle each with the crisp duck skin.

Potato and Wild Mushroom Gratin

Serves 6

1½ pounds new red potatoes, about equal size
1½ ounces dried wild mushrooms (boletus mushrooms, chanterelles, or morels)
4 tablespoons unsalted butter
2 to 3 tablespoons heavy cream
about ½ teaspoon minced garlic
Salt and pepper

PEEL 1½ pounds new red potatoes and slice them evenly ¼ inch thick. Put the potatoes in cold water and change the water three times at 10-minute intervals.

Soak 1½ ounces dried wild mushrooms in 1¼ cups very hot water for about 20 minutes. Pick over the mushrooms for grit, rinse them, and chop them coarsely. Strain the mushroom liquor through rinsed triple cheesecloth in a fine sieve and set aside. Sauté the mushrooms in 2 tablespoons butter for 5 or 6 minutes. Halfway through the cooking, stir in 2 to 3 tablespoons heavy cream, ½ teaspoon minced garlic, ½ cup mushroom liquor, and salt and pepper to taste.

Dry the potatoes well with tea towels and arrange a layer of them in a lightly buttered earthenware casserole about 9 inches in diameter and 2 inches deep. Salt the potatoes lightly and spoon some of the mushroom mixture over them. Continue layering, ending with a layer of potatoes. Dot the potatoes with 2 tablespoons butter and bake in a preheated 425°F. oven for 15 to 20 minutes, until the potatoes are a deep golden brown.

UNCOMPLICATED MENUS

❧

The ultimate in simplicity is good homemade bread, generously brushed with olive oil, grilled over the charcoal, and then rubbed liberally with fresh garlic. Salads, too, just picked fresh from the garden replete with unique flavors and fragrances, are perfect in their simplicity. My obsession with salads must have had its beginnings in the costume my mother created for me to wear to the local park's party and contest in New Jersey when I was three and a half. Dressed as the queen of the garden, I was adorned with the fruits and vegetables from my parents' Victory garden. Radish bracelets on my wrists and strawberries strung about my neck, I wore a lettuce-leaf skirt atop my bathing suit, garlands of red and green peppers wound about my ankles, and a crown of asparagus atop my head completing the illusion of a small bundle of produce! How fond is the memory of bringing home a prize for this ensemble!

A sense of renewal comes upon me each time I work with incredibly fresh and sweetly scented ingredients for a salad. In fact, I would rather make salads than almost any other dish. Cooks sometimes mistakenly attempt to make foods taste and look like something other than what they actually are, without perceiving that there can be no greater accomplishment than the composition of a salad or any dish that results in a naturally genuine symmetry of taste, texture, aroma, and appearance. In a sense, what one does *not* do to ingredients is as important as what one does do.

The basic simplicity of a salad depends for its success on the correct oil and vinegar, as well as a harmonious blend of lettuces. Combining the right olive oil and vinegar in proper proportions with the splendid little garden lettuces in precisely the correct manner can create a virtually perfect balance, analogous to the balance of nature in many ways. My goal is to emulate the harmony of the garden in the kitchen, and at the dining table. A light hand with the oil and a delicate, but sufficient, touch from the vinegar bottle or barrel isn't difficult to achieve when inspiration and incentive come from the salad greens as they are washed.

Much of my knowledge of the many varieties of lettuces comes from the time I spent visiting my friends in the south of France near Nice, for it was there that I discovered that incomparable mixture of lettuces called *mesclun,* from the Niçois *"mescla,"* meaning to mix. This Provençal dialect word refers to a mixed-up wild assemblage of greens and vegetables. Outdoor market-places in Provence display *mesclun* in profusion, a melange of the first tender young leaves which appear in the garden. *Mesclun* can be an extraordinary lettuce mixture: rocket, much like the rugola (arugula) found in Italian markets; chervil; *mâche,* or lamb's lettuce; and oak leaf. On occasion, baby curly endive (chicory) or young dandelion greens find their way into the medley, depending solely upon the grower's personal preferences combined with the reality of whatever else might send up shoots in the spot where *mesclun* grows. How well I remember buying armloads of *mesclun*, as my friend Martine exclaimed, "But, Alice, you are not buying to feed the restaurant!" The commingling of colors and textures, and the contrasting flavors of those diminutive lettuces tempted me to eat the salad right from the sink as I washed the greens. And that's when salads always taste the best to me: straight from the kitchen sink. I always eat salads, even those served at the dining-room table, with my fingers. However, the appeal of beautiful salad ingredients is such that I simply can't stop myself from devouring those tempting little greens long before they make their way to the table.

As you can well imagine, a simple salad has often constituted a meal for me, or has been combined in a menu with an ungarnished piece of grilled meat and a good bottle of wine. On my days away from the restaurant, I find that I want food that is very straightforward and clean-tasting. For many years at a very highly regarded San Francisco restaurant, I never ordered anything other than a limestone lettuce salad, a grilled, aged filet of beef with no garnishing whatsoever on the plate—absolutely nothing else—and a wonderful old bottle of wine from their cellar. Pure and simple.

Pure and simple are synonymous with picnics, too, which can provide wonderful opportunities for the preparation of simple, yet satisfying, meals. I once made a picnic lunch for a friend to take on the plane back home to Nice: roasted red peppers in olive oil, garnished with chopped garlic and sweet basil; young radishes and sweet carrots from the garden, as well as a tub of sweet butter; small pieces of leftover roast pigeon with rocket lettuces; tiny olives and goat cheese in a marinade with thyme branches; hard-cooked eggs; a dry sausage with cornichons and mustard; a few *madeleines* and some beautifully ripe and juicy nectarines and cherries. There was more involved in achieving the correct combination of foods than in the actual cooking.

The unfortunately widespread misconception that cooking that isn't com-plicated isn't cooking has sometimes proven to be a trap for me. In cooking classes we once gave at the restaurant, I was face to face with people's expectations of intricately involved and lengthy recipes. I sometimes felt foolish saying that good cooking meant having the freshest ingredients you could find, and then doing as little as possible to them; it seemed so obvious. Not wanting the class participants to be disappointed, I nonetheless realized that I had to be true to myself. I found that it required a tremendous interchange of information and lots of experience in order to convey what it takes to make simple foods succeed. One night, looking at the guests in the dining room as they ate slices from perfect, tiny melons, I began to wonder if perhaps the food had failed to live up to their expectations and that they had, horrifyingly, all come expecting to have *filet mignon en croûte;* instead, all they saw before them was a beautifully faultless piece of melon. Anyone could have chosen a perfect melon, but unfortunately most people don't take the time or make an effort to choose carefully and understand what that potentially sublime fruit should be. It is not simply a matter of going down to the local supermarket and buying the imperfect, below-average, or even mediocre melon, and then serving that. It involves the intimate knowledge that comes from having eaten hundreds of melons, and having learned precisely what they're about.

I would like the cooking at Chez Panisse to be perceived as straightforward and basically unsauced because I believe that is a very healthful way of cooking and eating. I find it to be more visually and aesthetically pleasing than the heavier "classic" *haute cuisine* which abounds in many French restaurants in this country. Just as the food of Provence is about the sunny hillsides abloom with purple flowers and the sweet scent of lavender, Chez Panisse's food is meant to be a reflection of the bounty of this Northern California environment. We try to interfere as little as possible with the transition of good and pure ingredients from their origins to the tables at Chez Panisse.

Baked Goat Cheese with Garden Salad
Carrot and Shallot Soup with Chervil Cream
Charcoal-Grilled Chicken with Garlic Purée
*Cherries and Almond Cookies

I think this menu has an earthy taste from the goat cheese to the garlic purée. It is very easy to prepare and serve: the chicken goes on the grill when the goat cheese comes out of the oven.

SUGGESTED WINES: A young, fresh white wine to begin, and a medium-bodied dry red with the chicken.

Baked Goat Cheese with Garden Salad

Serves 4

3 to 4 2½-inch–diameter rounds of fresh goat cheese, each about ½ inch
   thick
about ¾ cup virgin olive oil
3 to 4 sprigs fresh thyme
1 teaspoon dried thyme
1 cup fine dry bread crumbs
2 to 3 tablespoons red wine vinegar
Salt and pepper to taste
16 garlic croutons (see page 95)
about 4 handfuls garden lettuces (rocket, lamb's lettuce, small oak leaf
   and red leaf lettuces, chervil)

MARINATE the goat cheese rounds in ¼ cup of the olive oil with
the sprigs of fresh thyme for a day. Mix the dried thyme with the
cup of fine bread crumbs.

Prepare the vinaigrette by whisking the remaining ½ cup of olive oil into
the 2 to 3 tablespoons of vinegar until the vinaigrette is balanced, and season
with salt and pepper. Wash and dry the lettuces. Make the garlic croutons.

To bake the goat cheese, take the rounds out of the olive oil marinade and
then dip them in the bread crumbs. Put the cheese on a lightly oiled baking
dish and bake in a preheated 400°F. oven for about 6 minutes, until the cheese
is lightly bubbling and golden brown.

Meanwhile, toss the lettuces with enough vinaigrette to lightly coat them
and arrange them on round salad plates. Place the cheese in the center of the
plates with the browner side up, and arrange the croutons around the cheese.

Carrot and Shallot Soup with Chervil Cream

Serves 4

4 large shallots
3 tablespoons unsalted butter
2½ to 3 pounds tender sweet carrots, enough to equal 6 cups roughly
  chopped
1½ to 2 quarts chicken stock, enough to barely cover the carrots
Salt and pepper to taste
½ cup heavy cream
2 to 3 tablespoons minced chervil

MINCE the 4 shallots fine and melt them in 3 tablespoons butter in a heavy soup pot over low heat. While they are cooking, peel and roughly chop the carrots. Add the carrots to the shallots and sweat them together for about 10 minutes. Stir, and add just enough chicken stock to barely cover and cook until the carrots are just tender. Purée the soup through the medium grid of a food mill or briefly in a blender.

To serve, heat the soup for 5 minutes over low heat, but do not allow to simmer. Season to taste. Barely whip the heavy cream and flavor it with 2 to 3 tablespoons of minced chervil and salt and pepper to taste. Serve the soup in hot bowls and float a little whipped cream on top.

Charcoal-Grilled Chicken with Garlic Purée

Serves 4

1 frying chicken, about 3 pounds
2 heads garlic
½ bottle red wine
2 to 3 sprigs fresh thyme or 1 teaspoon dried thyme
1 cup virgin olive oil
Salt and pepper to taste

CUT the chicken into serving pieces; peel 8 to 10 cloves of the garlic and chop them roughly. Marinate the chicken in ½ bottle red wine with the chopped garlic and 2 or 3 sprigs fresh thyme for 2 to 4 hours in the refrigerator.

Spread the remaining cloves of garlic, with the skins on, in a small baking dish in one layer and cover with the cup of olive oil. Sprinkle with salt and pepper and bake in a preheated 300°F. oven for 1½ hours or until the garlic is completely soft. Purée the garlic through a food mill when it is done. Discard the skins and reserve the purée.

About an hour before cooking the chicken, remove it from the refrigerator. Prepare a medium-low charcoal fire. When the fire is ready, remove the chicken from the marinade, pat the pieces dry, and salt and pepper them. Cook the chicken on the grill slowly for about 35 minutes, turning frequently. The chicken should be nicely browned, but a bit rare and juicy. Spread the garlic purée over the chicken and heat it in a 375°F. oven for 5 minutes. Serve the chicken on a platter with oven-roasted potatoes, garnished with watercress and lemon wedges.

Shrimp Grilled on Rock Salt
Roasted Eggplant Soup with Red Pepper Garnish
Baked Leg of Lamb with Wilted Escarole Vinaigrette
*Fresh Figs and Mint

This menu is meant to be light but still savory. Cooking the shrimp in their shells on rock salt contains the flavors. Timing is facilitated by preparing the soup in advance; and the leg of lamb need not be hot when served with a salad. These elements come together in a menu that seems to fit September best.

SUGGESTED WINES: Cassis Blanc with the shrimp, and a Domaine de Beaurenard Châteauneuf-du-Pape with the lamb and eggplant.

Shrimp Grilled on Rock Salt

Serves 6

about 2½ pounds rock salt
8 tablespoons unsalted butter
about 1 tablespoon cracked black pepper
18 fresh large shrimp in their shells
Optional: 2 lemons

CHOOSE a very heavy pan with a lid, large enough to hold the shrimp comfortably. An enameled cast-iron casserole 2 to 3 inches deep is very good. Spread a 1-inch layer of rock salt in the pan, put the lid on, and heat for 30 to 40 minutes in a preheated 400°F. oven.

Soften 8 tablespoons butter and mix in about a tablespoon of black pepper cracked medium-coarse. Put the butter in a small saucepan.

Put 18 fresh large shrimp on the heated rock salt, cover and bake for about 2 minutes. Meanwhile, heat the butter over low heat until it just melts. Turn the shrimp over, cover, and bake for another 2 minutes, until the shrimp have turned pink and are sizzling.

After the shrimp have been turned, pour about a tablespoon of melted butter on each of six warm serving plates. When the shrimp are done, put three shrimp on each plate in the butter and serve very hot. Instead of the butter you may prefer to serve them with lemon wedges.

Roasted Eggplant Soup with Red Pepper Garnish

Serves 6

2 pounds eggplant
1 medium red onion
2 to 3 cloves garlic
4 tablespoons light olive oil
Salt and pepper
about 1 quart chicken stock
1 small red pepper
⅓ cup whipping cream

PREPARE a medium-hot wood charcoal fire. Grill 2 pounds of egg-plant, turning frequently, until the skin is scorched. Cool and remove the blackened tough outer skin. Cut the peeled eggplant into 1-inch cubes. Dice 1 medium red onion and roughly chop 2 to 3 garlic cloves. Stew the eggplant with the onion and garlic in 4 tablespoons light olive oil over low heat for 15 to 20 minutes, until the vegetables are very soft. Season with salt and pepper and just cover with chicken stock. Cook for 10 minutes, covered, over low heat.

While the vegetables are stewing, grill a small red pepper over the fire, then put it in a plastic bag to steam; after 5 minutes, remove it and peel off the blackened skin. Discard the seeds and stem. Dice the pepper and pound it to a paste in a mortar. Reserve the paste for the garnish.

Purée the soup in a blender. Return it to a soup pot and heat until very hot but not simmering.

Prepare the garnish by lightly whipping ⅓ cup heavy cream with the red pepper purée. The cream should be in very soft peaks.

Ladle the soup into very hot soup plates and garnish each plate with about 2 tablespoons of the red pepper cream.

Baked Leg of Lamb with Wilted Escarole Vinaigrette

Serves 6

1 5- to 6-pound whole leg of lamb

TRIM a 5- to 6-pound whole leg of lamb of as much fat as possible.

FOR THE MARINADE:

2 onions
6 to 8 cloves garlic
6 to 8 sprigs thyme
6 to 8 sprigs oregano
1 bottle strong white wine (Chardonnay or white Burgundy)
1 cup virgin olive oil

MAKE a marinade by slicing 2 onions and lightly crushing 6 to 8 cloves of garlic. Bruise 6 to 8 sprigs of thyme and 6 to 8 sprigs of oregano and put them with the garlic and onions in a shallow dish large enough to hold the lamb. Pour in 1 bottle strong white wine and 1 cup virgin olive oil and rub the marinade all over the lamb. Marinate in a cool place for 6 to 8 hours or overnight and turn the lamb frequently.

TO BAKE:

1½ teaspoons salt
2 teaspoons coarsely ground black pepper

PREHEAT the oven to 450°F. and remove the lamb from the marinade about 2 hours before it is to be served. Pat the lamb dry and set aside. Remove the leaves from the thyme and oregano and mince them finely with the garlic from the marinade. Add about 1½ teaspoons salt and 2 teaspoons coarsely ground black pepper to the herbs and make a rather stiff paste with a little of the marinade. Rub the paste all over the lamb and place it on a rack over a shallow pan in the oven. Bake for 15 minutes and reduce heat to 350°F. Turn the lamb after 30 minutes and bake for another 30 minutes. Turn again and bake for 15 minutes. The lamb will be cooked rare after a total of 1 hour and 15 minutes. Remove the lamb from the oven and let it rest for 15 minutes.

THE WILTED ESCAROLE VINAIGRETTE:

1½ to 2 pounds escarole
½ cup virgin olive oil
3 tablespoons red wine vinegar, or to taste
Salt and pepper

WASH and trim 1½ to 2 pounds escarole; the larger amount will be necessary if there are many tough outer leaves. Cut the escarole into about ¾ inch strips and leave some water clinging to the leaves. Just before carving the lamb, heat ½ cup virgin olive oil in a sauté pan over low heat until it is very warm, but not hot. Add the escarole to the pan all at once and cover. Wilt the escarole for about 2 minutes, until it is a bright deep green. Remove the cover and stir in 3 tablespoons or more of red wine vinegar. Season with salt and pepper.

Carve the lamb into ⅜ inch slices and reserve the juices. Put three pieces of lamb on each of six warm serving plates and drizzle with the carving juices. Put an equal amount of wilted escarole on each plate, and pour the remaining vinaigrette over the lamb and the escarole.

La Bouillabaisse Chez Panisse
*Mesclun *Salad*
Tender Tart à la Alice B. Toklas

Bouillabaisse is not a simple dish, but with incredibly fresh fish it can be straightforward, clean, and pure. And once it is served, the cooking is over.

This tart recipe came about because I could not make the Alice B. Toklas recipe work for me. There always seemed to be too much pastry and not enough filling. I made some adjustments and added a little citrus zest, and now this is the version of her recipe that I use.

SUGGESTED WINES: Drink a light, chilled Provençal rosé such as Bandol.

La Bouillabaisse Chez Panisse

Many ingredients are needed to make a wonderful bouillabaisse; however, the ingredients are easy to obtain and some of the preparation may be done in advance. There are two important things to remember in making a bouillabaisse: the fish and shellfish must be absolutely fresh, and the saffron and Pernod should be added with a light hand. The rouille *in this recipe is a spicy Provençal sauce.*

Serves 8 to 10

THE FISH AND SHELLFISH:

about 8 pounds whole very fresh rockfish (rock cod, snapper, sea bass, halibut)
a whole ocean perch or anglerfish, about 2 pounds
3½ dozen clams
1½ dozen mussels

FILLET the fish and cut the fillets into even-sized pieces about 2 inches long and 1 inch thick. The thickness should be equal for all pieces; the length can vary. Reserve the scraps for the *fumet.* Clean and scrub the clams and mussels.

FOR THE MARINADE:

about ½ cup virgin olive oil
about 2 cups dry white wine
2 sprigs fresh thyme
2 sprigs fresh fennel tops
6 sprigs parsley
3 cloves garlic, peeled
2 tablespoons Pernod
Pinch saffron

MARINATE the pieces of fish in about ½ cup olive oil and 2 cups white wine with 2 sprigs fresh thyme, 2 sprigs fresh fennel tops, 6 sprigs parsley, 3 whole cloves garlic, 2 tablespoons Pernod and a pinch of saffron. Cover and refrigerate the fish if the bouillabaisse will not be cooked within 2 hours.

FOR THE *FUMET:*

The well-cleaned bones, heads, and trimmings of all the fish
2 carrots
1 leek
1 medium yellow onion
2 medium tomatoes
6 mushrooms
⅓ cup virgin olive oil
2 cloves garlic, unpeeled
Bouquet garni: 6 sprigs parsley; 1 teaspoon fennel seeds; 2 bay leaves; ½
     teaspoon dried tarragon; ½ teaspoon dried thyme; 10 to 12 black
     peppercorns; 6 to 8 coriander seeds
2 cups dry white wine
6 mussels
6 clams
Peel of 1 small orange, with no white pith
2 tablespoons Pernod
Pinch saffron
Pinch cayenne

CLEAN and peel the carrots, leek, onion, tomatoes, and mushrooms. Chop the vegetables coarsely. Be sure that there are no bloody parts left on the fish bones and that the gills have been removed. Heat ⅓ cup olive oil in a heavy 12-quart stock pot and gently cook the vegetables, the 2 cloves of garlic, and the fish bones and scraps for 10 to 12 minutes.

Make a bouquet garni in cheesecloth of 6 sprigs parsley, 1 teaspoon fennel seeds, 2 bay leaves, ½ teaspoon dried tarragon, ½ teaspoon dried thyme, 10 to 12 black peppercorns, and 6 to 8 coriander seeds. Add it to the stock pot, along with 2 cups of white wine and cold water to cover. Finish the *fumet* by adding 6 mussels and 6 clams, the orange peel, 2 tablespoons Pernod, and a pinch of saffron and cayenne. Bring the *fumet* to a boil, reduce the heat immediately, skim the *fumet* often, and simmer for about 30 minutes.

Let the *fumet* stand off the heat for 15 minutes, then strain it. If the *fumet* is being made in advance, let it cool to room temperature, then cover and refrigerate. You will have to warm it before adding it to the broth.

FOR THE *ROUILLE:*

1 medium sweet red pepper
1 ripe tomato
1 slice good white bread, crusts removed
¼ cup strained *fumet*
Pinch of saffron and cayenne
3 egg yolks
5 to 8 cloves well-crushed garlic
¾ cup virgin olive oil
¾ cup light olive oil
Salt, pepper, saffron, and cayenne to taste

ROAST the red pepper over a grill or flame. When the skin is black, remove the pepper from the heat and put it in a plastic or paper bag to steam for 4 or 5 minutes. When the pepper is cool enough to handle, scrape the skin from it and discard the seeds and stem. Grill or roast a ripe tomato. When it has cooled, remove its seeds.

Soak the slice of bread in the *fumet* with a pinch of saffron and cayenne until it is very soft. Beat 3 egg yolks together with the bread and the garlic. Proceed to make a mayonnaise in the usual way with the two kinds of olive oil mixed together, keeping it rather thick. Make a purée of the roasted pepper and the grilled tomato in a mortar, and stir the purée into the mayonnaise. Season the *rouille* with salt, pepper, saffron, and cayenne to taste.

THE GARLIC CROUTONS:

24 slices of baguette, about ⅜ inch thick
about ½ cup virgin olive oil
2 to 3 cloves garlic, cut in half

BRUSH the baguette slices lightly with the virgin olive oil and bake at 400°F. for 5 minutes, or until the croutons are golden brown. Rub them with the cut garlic while they are still warm.

THE HERB GARNISH:

about ¼ cup minced parsley
10 to 12 basil leaves

HAVE the garnishes ready before cooking the broth.

THE VEGETABLES AND SEASONING FOR THE BROTH:

2 leeks, white part only
2 medium onions
4 large, very ripe tomatoes, peeled, seeded, and diced
¼ cup virgin olive oil
1 bay leaf
Pinch saffron
Salt and pepper to taste
The warm strained *fumet*
3 cloves minced garlic
1 sprig fresh fennel
1 sprig parsley
Peel of ½ small orange, with no white pith
1 cup white wine
Pernod and saffron to taste
The shellfish and fish

TO make the broth, clean and peel the leeks and onions and cut them into medium dice. Peel, seed, and dice 4 large tomatoes. Sauté the leeks and onions in ¼ cup olive oil with a bay leaf, a pinch of saffron, and salt and pepper to taste in a large heavy pan for 10 minutes over medium heat. Add the warm strained *fumet*, 3 cloves minced garlic, 1 sprig fresh fennel, 1 sprig parsley, the orange peel, the diced tomatoes, 1 cup white wine, and Pernod and saffron to taste. Add the clams and mussels, then cover and steam them for 1 to 2 minutes, until they begin to open. Add the fish from the marinade, larger pieces first, and cook for 3 to 4 minutes, until the fish and shellfish are just done. Do not stir the broth, or the fish will break. Remove the fish and shellfish to bowls. Bring the broth to a boil and correct the seasoning with whatever is necessary. This may be more oil, wine, Pernod, saffron, cayenne, or salt. Ladle the broth over the fish and garnish with the *rouille,* herbs, and croutons.

Tender Tart à la Alice B. Toklas

Serves 8 to 10

PASTRY:

8 tablespoons butter
1 cup all-purpose flour
1 tablespoon sugar
3 to 4 drops each almond and vanilla extracts
1 tablespoon water

PREPARE the pastry first. Cut 8 tablespoons butter into bits and let soften slightly. Mix 1 cup flour with 1 tablespoon sugar in a bowl. Cut the butter into the flour mixture with a pastry blender or knives until it resembles very coarse meal. Mix 3 to 4 drops each almond and vanilla flavoring with 1 tablespoon cold water and quickly stir the mixture into the butter and flour. Gather the dough into a ball and flatten it slightly. Cover it with plastic wrap and chill for at least 1 hour.

Allow the dough to stand at room temperature until it is malleable. Divide it in two sections, one part twice as large as the other. Put the smaller section in plastic wrap and chill.

Press the larger section into a tart ring 8 inches wide and 1½ inches deep and with a removable bottom. Press the dough evenly and gently to form a crust about ⅛ inch thick, and rising about ⅛ inch above the top edge of the ring. Cover the shell lightly with plastic wrap and chill in the freezer for at least 1 hour.

Preheat the oven to 375°F. Remove the tart shell and the unformed dough from the refrigerator. Place the tart shell on a rack in the lower third of the oven. Bake for 15 to 20 minutes, until a rich golden brown. Prick the shell gently two or three times as it begins to puff in the oven. Cool on a cake rack. Let the unbaked dough stand at room temperature until it is malleable.

THE FILLING:

6 ounces shelled hazelnuts
2 eggs
¾ cup sugar
Zest of 1 lemon or tangerine
¼ teaspoon vanilla flavoring

ROAST 6 ounces shelled hazelnuts in a preheated 350°F. oven for 10 to 15 minutes, until they are a rich deep brown. Spread the hazelnuts on a tea towel and rub them vigorously to remove as much of the skin as possible. Grind them in batches in a nut grinder or blender to a fine meal. Measure 1 cup of nut meal.

Whisk 2 eggs with ¾ cup sugar until the sugar just dissolves but the eggs are still liquid. Stir in the zest of 1 lemon or tangerine and ¼ teaspoon vanilla. Blend in the hazelnut meal and pour the filling into the baked tart shell.

Roll out the unbaked dough to a 8½-inch circle. Slit the dough with a small sharp knife in a pinwheel design and lay the crust gently over the tart. Crimp the edges to seal well.

FOR THE GLAZE:

1 egg yolk
1 tablespoon heavy cream

BEAT the egg yolk lightly with 1 tablespoon heavy cream and brush the glaze lightly over the unbaked top crust. Bake the tart on a rack in the lower third of a preheated 350°F. oven for 20 to 25 minutes, until the top is a rich golden brown, and begins to puff. Let the tart stand at room temperature for 1 hour or longer before cutting and serving.

Pasta with Smoked Trout and Golden Caviar
Chicken Breasts Escoffier
*Green Bean Salad with Shallots and Chervil
*Apricot Soufflé

Since these utterly simple chicken breasts Escoffier have been a favorite dish at the restaurant, I have had to place them on many menus. I think it is appropriate to begin with something creamy and exotic because the chicken breasts are crisp and uncomplicated. Once the pasta is rolled out, all the preparation is easy.

SUGGESTED WINES: Champagne with the pasta, and an old Bordeaux with the chicken.

Pasta with Smoked Trout and Golden Caviar

Serves 2

½ pound fresh pasta dough
2 ounces smoked trout
1 cup heavy cream
Salt and pepper to taste
2 tablespoons golden caviar

ROLL ½ pound fresh pasta dough as thin as possible and cut it into fettuccine noodles. Flour the noodles lightly, spread them on a baking sheet, cover with a tea towel, and refrigerate until ready to cook.

Flake 2 ounces smoked trout and set aside. Bring a large pot of salted water to a boil. Meanwhile, in a large sauté pan, reduce 1 cup heavy cream slightly over medium heat. Cook the fettuccine *al dente,* about 40 to 60 seconds. Drain. Off the heat, toss the fettuccine and the flaked trout in the cream. Season lightly with salt and pepper. Put equal mounds of pasta on two warm serving dishes and garnish each with a tablespoon of golden caviar.

Chicken Breasts Escoffier

Serves 2

1 whole large chicken breast, about ¾ pound
Salt and pepper
12 tablespoons clarified unsalted butter
1 cup fine fresh bread crumbs

SKIN and bone the chicken breast, and cut it in half. Remove the tendons and any fat from the two single breasts. Salt and pepper the breasts and fold the tenderloins to the side of each breast so that the meat is evenly thick.

Dip the breasts in a flat dish with 6 tablespoons of the clarified butter to coat both sides. Pat the breasts in the bread crumbs to form a crust. Let the breasts stand for 10 minutes.

Heat 3 tablespoons clarified butter in a heavy cast-iron pan over medium heat. When the butter is hot, put the breasts in the pan, season with salt and pepper, and reduce the heat to medium-low. Sauté gently for 5 minutes, turn, and sauté on the other side for 5 minutes. The crust should be a rich golden brown.

Heat 2 or 3 tablespoons clarified butter in a small saucepan. Put the chicken breasts on two warm serving plates and pour some of the butter over each chicken breast. Serve with briefly sautéed cherry tomatoes.

A PICNIC

Charcoal-Grilled Chicken Wings with Lemon and Pepper
Goat Cheese and Lentil Salad
Fennel and Red Onion Salad Vinaigrette
*Pears with Niçoise Olives
*Radishes and Sweet Butter
*Baguettes
Pat's Biscotti

I always think of picnics as easy. There isn't any of the pressure of last-minute timing and preparation; everything is ready to eat and you get to sit down with your friends. It is important to provide contrasting textures and flavors that still complement each other in any combination, because on a picnic everything tends to get consumed in a rather haphazard way.

Pat's biscotti are irresistible. She used to make them every Saturday night for the staff to take home for the weekend; but most were consumed at the restaurant before they had time to cool.

SUGGESTED WINES: Any good, light chilled red or rosé.

Charcoal-Grilled Chicken Wings with Lemon and Pepper

Serves 6

3 lemons
6 to 8 cloves garlic
about 1 tablespoon black peppercorns
18 chicken wings
½ cup virgin olive oil
Salt

THINLY slice 3 lemons and slightly flatten 6 to 8 cloves unpeeled garlic. Using a mortar and pestle, crack about 1 tablespoon black peppercorns. Toss 18 chicken wings with ½ cup olive oil in a shallow dish and mix in the lemon slices, garlic, and pepper. Marinate the chicken wings at cool room temperature for 4 to 5 hours, turning them five or six times.

Prepare a medium-hot wood charcoal fire. With a sharp paring knife, make a small horizontal cut in the skin of the large muscle of each wing, about halfway between the joints. Work the tips of each small part of the wings firmly into the incisions. Pat the wings free of excess marinade and salt them lightly.

Put the wings on the grill with the cut sides up and baste lightly with the marinade. Grill the wings for 4 minutes, then turn them and baste again. Grill for 3 to 4 minutes and check for doneness by pressing the fleshy part of the wings lightly with a finger. The wings are done when the flesh is firm yet springy. Remove them to a rack to cool.

Goat Cheese and Lentil Salad

Serves 6 to 8

2 cups French lentils (small green lentils imported from France)
1 teaspoon salt
10 to 12 sprigs Italian parsley
12 to 15 sprigs basil
6 to 8 cloves garlic
1 carrot
1 red onion
1 celery rib
1 to 1½ cups virgin olive oil
8 ounces goat cheese
½ cup snipped chives
⅓ to ½ cup strong red wine vinegar
Ground black pepper
Salt
Garnish: 1 or 2 ripe summer tomatoes if available; 8 to 10 basil leaves

PICK over 2 cups French lentils and rinse them. Barely cover the lentils with water in a saucepan. Add 1 teaspoon salt. Make a bouquet garni by tying 6 to 8 sprigs Italian parsley, some of the basil, and 3 to 4 cloves garlic unpeeled and slightly crushed, in cheesecloth. Add the bouquet garni to the lentils and bring them to a boil, then reduce the heat to a simmer.

Simmer the lentils for 10 minutes. Cut 1 peeled carrot, 1 red onion, and 1 celery rib into fine dice. Add the vegetables to the lentils and simmer for 10 to 15 minutes, until the lentils are tender but *al dente.* If necessary, add hot water, ¼ cup at a time, to keep the lentils from sticking. There should be very little liquid when the lentils are done.

When the lentils are cooked, discard the bouquet garni, toss them with ⅓ cup olive oil, and spread them on baking sheets to cool to room temperature. If the goat cheese tastes very strong, trim the outer rind to the chalk-white center. Crumble the cheese coarsely into a large bowl. Finely mince the remaining stemmed parsley and peeled garlic cloves.

Add the lentils and vegetables to the bowl with the cheese along with the minced parsley, garlic and ½ cup snipped chives. Add ½ cup olive oil, ⅓ cup red wine vinegar, and an ample amount of freshly ground black pepper. Toss well and taste for balance and salt. Cover the salad and refrigerate for at least 2 hours.

Remove the salad from the refrigerator about 1 hour before serving and taste again for balance in the vinaigrette; you may need more vinegar, oil, salt or pepper. Keep the salad cool but not on ice while going to the picnic. Just before serving, garnish the salad with summer tomatoes cut into wedges and 8 to 10 basil leaves cut into very fine strips.

Fennel and Red Onion Salad Vinaigrette

Serves 6

6 bulbs fennel, 2 to 2½ inches in diameter
1 large red onion
½ to ¾ cup virgin olive oil
2 to 3 tablespoons red wine vinegar
Salt and pepper

TRIM the tops, butt ends, and outer leaves from 6 bulbs of fennel. Slice the fennel into ⅛-inch slices lengthwise. Peel 1 large red onion, cut it in half lengthwise, then cut it into thin slices crosswise.

Mix ½ cup virgin olive oil with 2 tablespoons red wine vinegar and salt and pepper. Toss the fennel and onion with the vinaigrette and marinate at cool room temperature for 1 hour. Taste the salad and add more oil and vinegar if necessary. Keep the salad cool but not iced on the way to the picnic.

Pat's Biscotti

6 eggs
2½ cups sugar
½ pound unsalted butter, melted and cooled almost to room temperature
1½ teaspoons anise seed
6 ounces chopped nuts (almonds, walnuts, or hazelnuts)
6 ounces raisins
½ teaspoon vanilla
2¼ pounds all-purpose flour
1½ teaspoons baking powder
Pinch of salt

SEPARATE 6 eggs and beat the egg yolks with 1¼ cups sugar until they are pale lemon-colored and the sugar has dissolved. Beat the egg whites stiff and fold in 1¼ cups sugar a little at a time. Fold the egg whites into the egg-yolk mixture and then add ½ pound melted butter. Lightly blend in 1½ teaspoons anise seed, 6 ounces chopped nuts, and 6 ounces of raisins. Stir in ½ teaspoon vanilla. Mix 2¼ pounds flour with 1½ teaspoons baking powder and a pinch of salt. Fold the flour into the egg mixture one quarter at a time. It will become stiff at the end and require a wooden spoon.

Roll the dough lightly into cylinders about 1½ inches in diameter and 8 to 10 inches long. Put the cylinders on lightly buttered baking sheets and bake in a preheated 350°F. oven for 15 to 20 minutes, until they are lightly brown on top. Remove the cylinders from the baking sheets and cut them into cookies about ¾ inch wide at a 45-degree angle. Return the cookies to the baking sheets, with the cut surfaces down. Bake for 5 to 10 minutes, until they are lightly brown and the edges are crisp.

THEMES AND VARIATIONS

Dining in other restaurants often provides the incentive for visualizing menus from a different perspective than usual and suggests novel means of approaching a familiar ingredient. One day I went to my favorite Japanese restaurant and discovered a wonderful use for red caviar and quail eggs from their sushi. Back at Chez Panisse, I adapted the combination of ingredients by serving red caviar and a quail egg yolk atop a crouton, and by creating a dish of creamed quail eggs with red caviar.

A Zen vegetarian restaurant frequently produces dishes that make me visualize vegetables as something other than entrée accompaniments. Unexpected combinations of vegetables in soups, and hyssop and borage garnishes —instead of the ubiquitous parsley or watercress—emerge from its kitchen, and I always return from such an outing with a renewed sense of enthusiasm and excitement about the versatility of vegetables.

Dinners at Chinese restaurants have given me unusual variations for duck, squab, chicken, and asparagus: squab wrapped in lettuce leaves, or a sauté of chicken breast tenderloins, or briefly cooked asparagus served vinegared, sweet and cold. The charcoal-grilled and stuffed grape leaves at a Vietnamese restaurant conjured up a number of potential variations. And the barbecued oysters I love so much were the direct result of a Sunday afternoon drive along the coast and a stop at a local oyster house. Miserably overcooked oysters were served with a canned tomato sauce, but the idea was good when it was translated into properly barbecued oysters with a fresh herb butter. A Provençal hors d'oeuvre and a lunch entrée were both developed after I ate skewered grilled beef hearts at a Spanish restaurant in San Francisco. Undoubtedly the most successful of these transformations is the calzone we serve in the upstairs café at the restaurant; its origins lie in an Italian restaurant where we eat on Sundays. No matter where I dine, I am always absorbing ideas and inspirations for use at Chez Panisse.

A friend inspired me with her description of a Japanese dinner she had eaten in Kyoto. A freshly killed fish, right from the tank, was filleted and sliced very thin for a first-course sashimi. Later in the meal came the bottom half of the fish, marinated and broiled, and the meal's end brought a return of the fish in the form of the fish bones, deep-fried, hot and crunchy, and reconstructed in the shape of the fish! This kind of perception, the ability to see an ingredient in a myriad of ways, enables you to take the greatest advantage of seasonal abundance. With a flexible and experimental attitude toward familiar foods, you will remain interested and excited by the foods themselves.

LOBSTER, SPRING LAMB, AND ARTICHOKES

Lobster Mousse Vinaigrette with Garden Salad
Risotto with Artichokes and Spring Lamb Kidneys
Spring Lamb Ragoût
*Strawberries with Crème Fraîche

Hors d'Oeuvres Variés
Lobster in Cabbage Leaves with Roasted Peppers
Charcoal-Grilled Spring Lamb
White Vegetable Purée
*Dry Monterey Jack Cheese

Deep-Fried Artichoke Hearts with Herbs
Pasta with Lobster and Asparagus
Stuffed Shoulder of Spring Lamb with Grilled Leeks
*Fresh Cherries and Ripe Italian Fontina Cheese

I chose these three ingredients for these menus because they appear at the same time of the year and they're familiar to most people. And I wanted to include the most successful dishes using them that we've served at the restaurant. But as menus, they may have become complicated to the diner's rather than to the cook's advantage.

SUGGESTED WINES: Artichokes tend to conflict with wine where they are the dominant element in a dish. Lobster seems to call for a rich, full-bodied white wine. And spring lamb goes well with a young, fruity wine like a Zinfandel if it's not too heavy.

Lobster Mousse Vinaigrette with Garden Salad

Serves 8

FOR THE MOUSSE:

10 ounces very fresh fish (sole, trout, or halibut)
6 ounces fresh scallops
1 egg
1 egg white
1 tablespoon softened butter
½ cup heavy cream
¼ cup lobster bisque reduction (see page 203)
Salt and cayenne to taste
about ½ cup lobster tail meat

REMOVE all bones and bits of skin from 10 ounces of sole, trout, or halibut fillets. Trim 6 ounces of scallops. Dice fish and scallops into ½ inch cubes. Grind them through the finest screen of a meat grinder, or chop with an on and off motion in a food processor with a steel blade. Put the mixture through the grinder a second time, or scrape the sides of the processor bowl and chop the fish until it is almost a purée. Force the fish through a very fine sieve.

Put the fish in a large bowl over ice and work in 1 egg and 1 egg white for 5 to 10 minutes with a wooden spoon. Add 1 tablespoon butter, ½ cup heavy cream, and ¼ cup lobster reduction. Season with salt and cayenne. Continue to work the mixture for 5 to 10 minutes. The longer the mixture is worked, the lighter the mousse will be. When the mixture is light, fold in ½ cup lobster tail meat, cut into small pieces. Cover the mixture and chill it thoroughly.

To check the mousse for seasoning and cooking time, fill a buttered 3-ounce ovenproof mold or ramekin with mousse. Chill the mold, and place it in a simmering bain-marie. Bake the mousse in a preheated 375°F. oven for 15 minutes and check for doneness with a toothpick inserted in the center. The mousse should be set but not completely dry. Taste it and correct the seasoning in the chilled mousse if necessary. Butter and fill seven more 3-ounce molds, put them in the bain-marie, and bake until done. Remove them from the water when they are done and set aside.

THE VINAIGRETTE FOR THE MOUSSE:

½ cup lobster bisque reduction (see page 203)
2 to 3 tablespoons tarragon vinegar
¼ cup light olive oil
¼ cup virgin olive oil
Lemon juice to taste
Salt and pepper to taste

MAKE a vinaigrette for the mousse by first tasting the lobster bisque reduction to make sure that it has a very concentrated flavor. If it does not, reduce it further. Mix the bisque reduction with 2 tablespoons tarragon vinegar. Whisk in ¼ cup light olive oil and ¼ cup virgin olive oil. Flavor with lemon juice to taste and add more tarragon vinegar if necessary. Season with pepper and salt if necessary (the bisque may be salty).

THE VINAIGRETTE FOR THE SALAD:

4 handfuls garden lettuces
½ cup virgin olive oil
¼ cup sherry vinegar
1 shallot
Salt and pepper

WASH the garden lettuces, dry them, and set them aside. Make a vinaigrette by mixing well ½ cup virgin olive oil, about ¼ cup sherry vinegar, 1 finely diced shallot, and salt and pepper to taste. Toss the lettuce with the vinaigrette and arrange on salad plates. Unmold the warm mousse in the center of each plate and drizzle with the lobster bisque vinaigrette.

Risotto with Artichokes and Spring Lamb Kidneys

Serves 8

2 medium onions
about ¾ cup light olive oil
½ pound unsalted butter
1 sprig fresh thyme
1 bay leaf
3 cloves garlic
3 cups Italian Arborio rice
1 to 1½ quarts light poultry stock
12 small artichokes, about 2 inches in diameter
Vinegar or lemon juice
½ pound spring lamb kidneys
Salt and pepper
1 tablespoon minced parsley

TO cook the rice, finely chop 2 onions and sweat them over low heat in a heavy pot with 4 tablespoons light olive oil and 4 tablespoons butter. Add 1 sprig fresh thyme, 1 bay leaf, and 2 cloves minced garlic; cook for 10 to 15 minutes, until the onions are very soft. Add 3 cups Arborio rice and stir continually over low heat for 5 minutes, until the rice is evenly coated with the fat and onions. Have the stock at a simmer and pour in enough of it to just cover the rice. When the broth is almost completely absorbed, add more simmering stock to just cover the rice, and stir. Repeat this process a third time and cook until the rice is *al dente,* but not crunchy —a total of 15 to 20 minutes depending on the variety of rice. The broth should not be totally absorbed with the last addition, resulting in a saucy texture. Remove the pot from the flame, remove the garlic cloves and herbs. Taste for seasoning, and correct if necessary. Add a good lump of sweet butter. Cover and let rest for 5 minutes.

While the risotto is cooking, trim 12 small artichokes to their hearts and remove the chokes. Cut the hearts into sixths and put them in a bowl with cold water and a little vinegar or lemon juice. Trim ½ pound spring lamb kidneys and cut them into slices about ⅜ inch thick. Mince the remaining clove garlic. Drain the artichoke hearts, pat dry, blanch briefly in salted water, and sauté in 3 tablespoons olive oil over medium heat for 3 to 4 minutes, until they are *al dente.* Stir in half of the minced garlic during the last minute of cooking, and season with salt and pepper. Sauté the lamb kidney slices in 3 tablespoons olive oil over medium heat for 2 to 3 minutes. Stir in the rest of the minced garlic during the last minute of cooking and season with salt and pepper. At the last minute, toss with 1 tablespoon minced parsley.

Time the cooking of the risotto, the artichoke hearts, and the kidneys in such a way that they are all ready at the same time. Serve the risotto on a large platter garnished with the artichokes and the kidneys.

Spring Lamb Ragoût

Serves 8

THE MEAT AND MARINADE:

3 to 4 pounds boned and trimmed spring lamb from various cuts (the legs, loins, and tenderloins)
3 medium onions
1 cup virgin olive oil
2½ cups white wine
10 to 12 parsley sprigs
4 to 5 thyme sprigs

CUT 3 to 4 pounds boned and trimmed lamb into 1-inch cubes. Slice 3 onions. Marinate the lamb with the onions, 1 cup olive oil, 2½ cups white wine, 10 to 12 parsley sprigs, and 4 to 5 thyme sprigs, for 3 to 4 hours at room temperature or loosely covered in the refrigerator overnight. Bring the lamb to room temperature for 3 to 4 hours if it has been refrigerated.

THE LAMB STOCK:

The bones and trimmings from 1 spring lamb
½ cup white wine
2 medium onions
2 medium carrots
2 medium celery ribs
Bouquet garni: 6 to 8 parsley sprigs, 4 to 5 thyme sprigs; 2 bay leaves; 2 shallots; 10 to 15 black peppercorns
2 medium tomatoes, if good ones are available

BROWN the bones and trimmings in a 450°F. oven for 25 to 30 minutes, until they are well-browned. Deglaze the roasting pan with ½ cup white wine and put the bones and pan juices in a stock pot. Roughly chop 2 onions, 2 carrots, and 2 celery ribs and add them to the pot. Add a bouquet garni of 6 to 8 parsley sprigs, 4 to 5 thyme sprigs, 2 bay leaves, 2 roughly chopped shallots, and 10 to 15 black peppercorns. Add 2 tomatoes, if available, roughly chopped, and barely cover the meat and vegetables with cold water. Bring the stock to a boil and reduce it to a strong simmer. Skim the surface frequently for 2 hours, and occasionally for another 2 hours. Strain the stock and reserve 1 cup of it. Reduce the rest to a *demi-glace*.

THE VEGETABLE ACCOMPANIMENT:

2 to 2½ pounds of the tenderest spring vegetables (possibilities include
   turnips, potatoes, carrots, asparagus, peas or snow peas, and pearl
   onions)
4 tablespoons unsalted butter
1 cup lamb stock
½ cup water

PEEL and trim 2 to 2½ pounds of spring vegetables. Cut the turnips,
potatoes, carrots and asparagus tips into uniform pieces. Blanch the
vegetables separately until they are *al dente,* refresh, drain, and dry. Peel the
pearl onions and cook, uncovered, over low heat with 4 tablespoons butter,
1 cup lamb stock, and ½ cup water for 15 to 20 minutes. The liquid should
be reduced to a glaze and the onions completely cooked. Keep the vegetables
in a warm place.

FINISHING THE RAGOÛT:

The marinated lamb
Salt and pepper
4 tablespoons light olive oil
½ cup white wine
about 1½ cups lamb *demi-glace*
4 tablespoons unsalted butter
Garnish: 4 sprigs Italian parsley
           4 sprigs thyme

DRY the pieces of marinated lamb and season them with salt and
pepper. Sauté in 4 tablespoons light olive oil over high heat for 5 to
6 minutes, turning the meat for even browning. The lamb should be pink
inside and well-browned on the outside. Transfer the lamb to a warm pan
and deglaze the browning pan with ½ cup white wine. Add 1½ cups lamb
demi-glace and reduce if necessary. Correct the seasoning and heat the sauce
thoroughly, but do not boil. Finish the sauce with about 4 tablespoons butter
cut into bits and whisked in.

Arrange the meat on a warm serving platter surrounded with the vegetables. Pour the sauce over the meat and garnish with 4 sprigs each Italian
parsley and thyme, stemmed and minced.

Hors d'Oeuvres Variés

Serves 6

Artichoke Hearts with Melted Goat Cheese

6 large artichokes
Tarragon vinegar
about ½ cup virgin olive oil
¾ pound fresh goat cheese
1 clove garlic
3 sprigs thyme
Pepper to taste
2 to 4 tablespoons heavy cream
⅓ cup fresh bread crumbs

TRIM 6 large artichokes completely of leaves, stems, and chokes. Cook the artichoke hearts in boiling salted water and some tarragon vinegar for 8 to 12 minutes depending on the size of the hearts. Test for doneness with the point of a sharp knife; the hearts should be cooked *al dente*. Drain the artichoke hearts and marinate them while still warm in ½ cup virgin olive oil.

Trim the rind from ¾ pound goat cheese and mix the cheese with 1 clove minced garlic, 3 sprigs stemmed and minced thyme, pepper to taste, and 2 to 4 tablespoons heavy cream. (The amount of cream will depend on the saltiness of the cheese.) Put the artichoke hearts in a lightly oiled earthenware baking dish. Mound the mixture on them and sprinkle with ⅓ cup bread crumbs. Drizzle the artichokes with a little olive oil and bake them in a preheated 450°F. oven until the crumbs are completely browned and the cheese just begins to melt, about 10 minutes.

Beets with Walnut Orange Vinaigrette

1½ pounds fresh beets, about 1½ to 2 inches in diameter
2 tablespoons orange zest
½ cup virgin olive oil
½ cup raspberry vinegar
1 tablespoon walnut oil
Salt and pepper

WASH and trim the tops and tails from 1½ pounds beets. Put them in a baking pan with about ¾ cup water and bake in a preheated 350°F. oven until they are just tender, about 45 minutes. Let them cool, peel them, and cut them into thin slices.

To make the vinaigrette, mix together 2 tablespoons orange zest, ½ cup virgin olive oil, ½ cup fruit vinegar, about 1 tablespoon of walnut oil, and salt and pepper to taste. Toss the beets in the vinaigrette.

Lamb's Lettuce and Rocket Salad

4 handfuls lamb's lettuce and rocket
½ cup virgin olive oil
3 tablespoons red wine vinegar
1 teaspoon Dijon mustard
Salt and pepper
Optional: 12 hard-cooked quail eggs (see page 19)

WASH 4 handfuls lamb's-lettuce and rocket and dry well. Make a vinaigrette of ½ cup virgin olive oil, 3 tablespoons red wine vinegar, or to taste, 1 teaspoon Dijon mustard, and salt and pepper to taste. Dress the greens with some of the vinaigrette.

To serve the hors d'oeuvres, arrange the greens on salad plates and garnish with the warm artichoke hearts, the beets, and hard-cooked quail eggs, if available.

Lobster in Cabbage Leaves with Roasted Peppers

Serves 6

THE CABBAGE:

1 head savoy cabbage, about 1½ pounds

CUT out the cone-shaped heart of a firm green savoy cabbage. Remove the outer leaves and blanch the whole cabbage in boiling salted water for 2 to 3 minutes. Drain. When the cabbage is cool enough to handle, separate the leaves and blanch them for 1 to 2 minutes. Drain them and dry them well. Cut out the large ribs of 12 leaves and trim them into rectangles about 5 inches by 3 inches. Set aside.

TO COOK THE LOBSTER:

3 lively lobsters, 1 to 1½ pounds each
½ cup coarse sea salt
2 bay leaves
4 sprigs thyme
1 lemon
10 to 12 black peppercorns

PREPARE a *court-bouillon* of 8 to 10 quarts water, ½ cup coarse sea salt, 2 bay leaves, 4 thyme sprigs, 1 sliced lemon, and 10 to 12 black peppercorns. Bring the *court-bouillon* to a rapid boil and cook the lobsters in it for about 3 to 4 minutes. Remove the lobsters. Strain and reserve the *court-bouillon.* When the lobsters are cool enough to handle, remove the meat from the tails and claws and reserve it. Remove the gravelly stomach sac and discard it; reserve the shells and the coral, if any.

THE LOBSTER BISQUE:

The reserved shells (and coral) from the cooked lobster
2 tablespoons olive oil
¼ pound unsalted butter
2 medium carrots
2 medium onions
1 medium leek
1 celery rib
3 shallots
2 tablespoons Armagnac or Cognac
1 cup white wine
3 medium tomatoes

HEAT 2 tablespoons olive oil over medium-high heat and sauté the shells of the lobsters for 3 minutes. Reduce the heat to medium and add ¼ pound butter (and the reserved coral). Cook over very low heat until the butter melts. Trim and dice finely 2 carrots, 2 onions, 1 leek, 1 celery rib, and 3 shallots. Add the vegetables to the pan and cook over medium heat for 5 minutes. Increase the heat and flame with 2 tablespoons Armagnac or Cognac. Add 1 cup white wine, 3 chopped tomatoes, and water to barely cover. Simmer for 30 minutes. Break the shells in a blender and force the shells and sauce through a very fine sieve. Let the sauce rest for 5 minutes to allow the butter to rise to the surface. Skim the butter and reserve it.

TO ASSEMBLE THE LOBSTER PACKAGES:

The prepared cabbage leaves
The reserved lobster meat
The reserved lobster butter
12 chervil sprigs
The strained *court-bouillon*

ALLOW one half of a claw and one quarter of a tail for each package. Lay the 12 cabbage leaves flat on a worktable. Place the lobster meat, red side down, in the lower center of the leaves. Drizzle some lobster butter over each package and put a sprig of chervil on top of each. Fold the bottom of each leaf over the lobster, then fold in the sides and roll forward over the top of the leaf to make a tightly closed package. Steam the packages for 8 to 10 minutes over the simmering *court-bouillon.*

THE SAUCE AND THE GARNISH:

The lobster bisque
½ pound unsalted butter
1 small red pepper, roasted, peeled, and cut into ¼-inch dice
12 chervil sprigs

REDUCE the lobster bisque by half over high heat and whisk in ½ pound butter, cut into bits and softened. Remove the sauce from the heat.

Place the lobster packages on warm plates and spoon the sauce over them. Garnish with the diced peppers and chervil.

Charcoal-Grilled Spring Lamb

Serves 6 to 8

1 spring lamb, dressed weight of about 30 pounds
3 to 4 cups virgin olive oil
6 to 8 thyme sprigs
6 to 8 marjoram sprigs
6 to 8 oregano sprigs
3 to 4 shallots

BUTCHER the lamb into the following cuts: the legs, the loin section, the rack, the shoulders, and the neck. The whole lamb will serve about 25 people. Marinate 6 to 8 pounds of lamb, choosing a mixture of cuts—one leg, one rack, half the loin, one shoulder, etc. Leave the bones in and allow about 1 pound per person. (The marinade may be increased by 2½ times to marinate the whole butchered lamb.) There should be an abundance of herbs in the marinade and enough olive oil to coat each piece of lamb well. Cover the pieces of lamb with 3 to 4 cups of olive oil, 6 to 8 sprigs each of thyme, marjoram, and oregano, and 3 to 4 sliced shallots. Marinate the meat at room temperature for 3 to 4 hours or loosely covered and refrigerated overnight. If the lamb has been refrigerated, allow it to stand at room temperature for 3 to 4 hours.

Prepare a large charcoal fire and allow it to burn down to an even, medium-hot fire. Put the lamb over it according to the thickness of the pieces. The legs will take about twice as long as the rack. The shoulders and loin take about one and a half times as long as the rack. The internal temperature of the rare lamb may be between 125° and 130°F., according to taste. Turn the lamb and baste it frequently with the marinade. As each piece is done, let it rest to collect the juices.

To serve the lamb, slice some of each piece for each serving and spoon some of the collected juices over the meat.

White Vegetable Purée

Serves 6

2 potatoes
3 pounds celery root
10 medium turnips
3 cloves garlic
4 medium leeks
Bouquet garni: 4 thyme sprigs; 1 bay leaf; 2 cloves garlic; 6 to 8 parsley
    sprigs; 10 to 15 black peppercorns
¼ pound unsalted butter
about ½ cup heavy cream
Salt and white pepper

PEEL 2 potatoes, a celery root of about 3 pounds, 10 medium turnips, and 3 cloves of garlic. Trim all the green from 4 leeks and wash them well. Chop the vegetables roughly and make a bouquet garni of 4 thyme sprigs, 1 bay leaf, 2 cloves garlic, 6 to 8 parsley sprigs, and 10 to 15 black peppercorns. Put the vegetables and the bouquet garni in a pot with lightly salted water to barely cover. Cook, covered, over medium heat for about 15 minutes, until the vegetables are very tender.

Remove the bouquet garni, drain the vegetables, and purée them through a food mill. Put the purée in a bain-marie or double boiler over very low heat, stir in ¼ pound butter, cut into bits, and about ½ cup heavy cream, and season with salt and white pepper.

ॐ

Deep-Fried Artichoke Hearts with Herbs

Serves 6

THE BATTER:

1¾ cups all-purpose flour
¼ teaspoon salt
2 cups warm water
¼ cup olive oil
2 egg whites (to be added later)

MEASURE the flour with the salt into a bowl and make a well in the center. Mix the water with the oil and pour about half of the mixture into the well. Gently incorporate the flour into the water with a whisk, stirring in one direction only. Add thé rest of the water mixture gradually. When the batter is smooth, strain it through a large, very fine sieve, and let it rest for 2 to 3 hours.

THE ARTICHOKE HEARTS:

18 baby artichokes
Juice of 1 lemon

TRIM the artichokes, removing the tough outer leaves, but leaving about an inch of leaves and stems. Cut the artichokes in half and remove the chokes. Squeeze the juice of 1 lemon into a bowl of cold water and put the artichokes in it as they are trimmed.

THE HERBS:

2 handfuls mixed salad herbs (Italian parsley, rocket, dandelion greens, and a few sprigs of marjoram and chives)

CLEAN and stem the salad herbs. Chop half of the herbs coarsely, put them in a bowl, and cover with a damp tea towel. Reserve the rest of the herbs for the garnish.

ADDITIONAL GARNISH:

1 to 2 lemons
½ cup freshly grated Parmesan cheese

TO fry the artichokes, heat 1 quart peanut oil in a wok. Beat 2 egg whites to soft peaks and fold them into the batter. Drain the artichoke hearts and dry them well. The batter can stand at room temperature for about 25 minutes. When the oil is at 350°F., dip the artichokes into the batter and gently drop them into the oil. Let the batter set for 20 to 30 seconds, then turn the artichokes continually until they are golden brown, about 3 minutes. Fry them in small batches, and allow the oil to return to 350°F. before frying the next batch.

Drain the deep-fried artichokes briefly on paper towels and serve sprinkled with the chopped herbs and about ½ cup freshly grated Parmesan cheese. Garnish the platter with the whole herbs and lemon wedges.

Pasta with Lobster and Asparagus

Serves 6

1¼ pounds fresh pasta cut into very thin noodles *(tagliolini)*

FOR THE LOBSTER BISQUE:

2 medium carrots
2 medium onions
2 medium celery ribs
1 lemon
Bouquet garni: 8 to 10 parsley sprigs; 2 bay leaves; 4 thyme sprigs; 10 to
    12 black peppercorns
2½ cups white wine
1 tablespoon coarse sea salt
2 or 3 1- to 1½-pound lobsters
1 small sweet red pepper
3 tablespoons olive oil
1 tablespoon grappa or Cognac
Cayenne pepper to taste

PREPARE the pasta, then make the *court-bouillon* to cook the lobsters. Roughly chop 1 onion, 1 carrot, and 1 celery rib, and slice 1 lemon. Make a bouquet garni of 8 to 10 parsley sprigs, 2 bay leaves, 4 thyme sprigs, and 10 to 12 black peppercorns. Put these ingredients in a large pot with 2 cups of the white wine, 1 tablespoon coarse sea salt, and 8 to 10 quarts water. Bring the *court-bouillon* to a boil and add the lobsters. Cook for 8 to 10 minutes if they weigh 1½ pounds, or for 6 to 8 minutes if they weigh 1 pound. Pick up the lobsters and let them cool. Strain the *court-bouillon* and set aside. Shell the lobster tails and claws; remove and discard the gravelly stomach sacs. Reserve the coral (if any) and the shells.

Finely dice 1 carrot, 1 onion, 1 celery rib, and ½ small sweet red pepper. Sauté the lobster shells in 3 tablespoons olive oil over high heat for 2 minutes. Flame the shells with 1 tablespoon grappa and reduce the heat. Add the diced vegetables, the remaining ½ cup white wine, and a pinch of cayenne. Add about ½ cup of the strained *court-bouillon* and water to cover. Taste for salt and add a little more *court-bouillon* if necessary. Simmer the mixture for 30 minutes, then put it in a blender to break up the shells. Force the bisque through a very fine sieve into a saucepan and reduce it to about 2 cups. (Whisk in the reserved coral.)

FOR THE SAUCE:

1¼ pounds thin asparagus
1 carrot
1 onion
1 celery rib
3 tablespoons unsalted butter
4 thyme sprigs
1 bay leaf
Salt and pepper
6 to 8 Italian parsley sprigs
16 to 18 chervil sprigs
1 cup heavy cream
1 cup lobster bisque
The lobster meat, cut into small pieces
1 to 2 teaspoons grappa or Cognac

BEGIN the sauce by trimming the tips, about 1½ inches long, from 1¼ pounds asparagus. Blanch the tips in boiling salted water for 20 to 30 seconds. Drain the asparagus and spread on a towel to cool.

Dice, then mince 1 carrot, 1 onion, and 1 celery rib, and cook them in 3 tablespoons butter over medium-low heat with 2 of the thyme sprigs, 1 bay leaf, and salt and pepper to taste. Cook for 5 to 7 minutes, remove the herbs, and set the vegetables aside.

Stem 2 thyme sprigs, 6 to 8 Italian parsley sprigs, and 8 or 9 chervil sprigs, and mince the herbs. Reduce 1 cup heavy cream slightly over medium heat and stir in 1 cup reduced lobster bisque. Add the cooked vegetables, the minced herbs, the lobster meat, the blanched asparagus tips, and grappa to taste.

Cook the *tagliolini* in rapidly boiling salted water for about 30 seconds, or until they are *al dente*. Drain the *tagliolini*, toss in the sauce, and season with salt and pepper. Serve in warmed pasta plates and garnish with the remaining chervil.

Stuffed Shoulder of Spring Lamb with Grilled Leeks

Serves 6

2 shoulders from a spring lamb of about 30 pounds dressed weight

BONE the shoulders from a spring lamb and trim them of fat and connective tissue.

FOR THE MARINADE:

1 cup virgin olive oil
2 cups white wine
10 to 12 parsley sprigs
4 to 5 thyme sprigs
4 to 5 marjoram sprigs
4 to 5 oregano sprigs
3 shallots
3 cloves garlic

MIX all the ingredients. Put the meat in the marinade and leave it for 3 to 4 hours at room temperature or covered and refrigerated overnight. If the lamb has been refrigerated, allow it to stand at room temperature for 2 or 3 hours before cooking it.

FOR THE STUFFING:

about ¾ pound lamb kidneys
¼ cup virgin olive oil
Salt and pepper
2½ cups day-old bread, cut into ¼-inch cubes
4 sprigs each of parsley and thyme
2 sprigs marjoram
4 cloves garlic

TRIM ¾ pound of lamb kidneys and rinse them well in cold water. Cut the kidneys into ⅜-inch dice. Sauté the kidneys in ¼ cup virgin olive oil over medium heat for 2 or 3 minutes. Season with salt and pepper and mix with 2½ cups diced bread, 4 sprigs each parsley and thyme, and 2 sprigs marjoram, stemmed and roughly chopped, and 4 cloves garlic chopped fine. Let the stuffing cool and season it with salt and pepper.

FOR THE ROASTING:

The marinated shoulders
The stuffing
Salt and pepper
¼ cup virgin olive oil
2 carrots
2 onions
2 celery ribs
½ cup white wine
½ cup water

SPREAD out the meat and salt it lightly, then cover it with the stuffing. Roll the shoulders and tie them securely. Salt and pepper the roasts and brown them for 10 minutes over medium-high heat in ¼ cup of virgin olive oil. Deglaze the browning pan with 2 or 3 tablespoons white wine. Cut 2 carrots, 2 onions, and 2 celery ribs into ½ inch cubes and spread the vegetables on a roasting pan. Put the shoulders on the vegetables and drizzle them with the deglazing juices, and the rest of the wine. Pour ½ cup of water around the vegetables. Roast the shoulders in a preheated 425°F. oven for 35 to 40 minutes, basting frequently.

Remove the roast to a platter to collect the juices. Skim off all but 1 tablespoon of the fat from the roasting pan. Put the vegetables and pan juices through a fine sieve, and reduce if necessary. Stir in the juices that have collected around the roasts. Slice and serve with the roasting sauce.

Charcoal-Grilled Leeks

Serves 6

6 to 12 leeks, depending on size (smaller leeks are better)
3 to 4 tablespoons virgin olive oil
½ cup heavy cream
4 tablespoons unsalted butter
1 tablespoon Dijon mustard
Salt and pepper

TRIM the leeks of the root and all but 1½ inches green stem. Slit them lengthwise to within ½ inch of the root end, leaving them whole, and rinse well under cold water. Tie the leeks securely in bundles; put the smaller leeks in the center of the bundles. Blanch the bundles in boiling salted water until just tender. Refresh under cold water and squeeze the leeks thoroughly. Open up the bundles and brush the leeks generously with virgin olive oil. Grill over a low charcoal fire for 3 to 4 minutes. Turn and grill on the other side for 2 to 3 minutes. Baste frequently.

While the leeks are grilling, make a mustard butter. Heat ½ cup cream over high heat until it foams. Stir in 4 tablespoons butter, softened to room temperature and cut into bits. Remove from the heat when the butter has been incorporated, whisk in about 1 tablespoon Dijon mustard, and season with salt and pepper. Pour over the leeks and serve with the lamb.

GREEN BEANS, QUAIL, AND SALMON

Charcoal-Grilled Quail with Shallots and Parsley
Warm Green Bean Salad with Rocket and Garden Lettuces
Salmon Baked with Anchovy Butter
Red Potato and Red Onion Gratin
*Red Apples and Wisconsin Blue Cheese

Cured Grilled Salmon Vinaigrette
Buckwheat Pasta with Rocket and Goat Cheese
Sautéed Quail Served with Mushroom Toasts
*Pears with Raw Milk Vacherin

Warm Green Beans and Beets with Aïoli
Poached Salmon with Fresh Basil and Olive Butters
Marinated Quail Grilled with Sausages and Bay Leaves
Fresh Pasta with Beet and Spinach Greens
*Ripe Figs with Goat Cheese

The three ingredients interwoven in these menus have appeared repeatedly on the Chez Panisse menus over the years. I think I was spoiled by the tender-green-bean salads you used to find at almost any little restaurant in France. We began at the restaurant by buying about three cases of Blue Lake beans in order to glean one small bowlful of the undersized ones to put in the salad. Now we have found seeds for the tiny French varieties, and friends with gardens have planted them for us. Someone in Mexico had the same idea, and small tender beans appear in California markets from the early spring; undoubtedly they can be found in specialty markets in larger cities. Every once in a while at the peak of the season, a Kentucky Wonder bean will taste like the tender sweet bean it should be.

I'm not sure what to say about the commercially available quail. It is largely a matter of making something quite tasteless taste like what you imagine it should taste like. I want that flavor of wild quail, so I turn to the grill and the flavors of wild mushrooms and strong herbs.

The flavor of salmon, on the other hand, has a pronounced and special character that changes as the season progresses. We always try and buy whole fish with the head on so that its freshness is obvious in its bloody gills and shiny eyes and skin. It is possible to use just part of the fish fresh and cure or smoke the rest.

SUGGESTED WINES: Crisp white Rhône wines would complement some of the green bean and salmon recipes; but lighter-bodied red wines are always a possibility with salmon, too. The quail dishes listed in these menus most often suggest an earthier red wine—a Nuits-St.-Georges or a Châteauneuf-du-Pape.

Charcoal-Grilled Quail with Shallots and Parsley

Serves 6

1 cup dry white wine
¾ cup duck fat
6 quail
4 shallots
6 cloves garlic, slightly crushed
10 juniper berries, slightly crushed
3 bay leaves
20 to 25 sprigs Italian parsley
2 cups fresh bread crumbs
Salt and pepper
1 lemon

MAKE a marinade by mixing 1 cup dry white wine with ½ cup duck fat which has been melted gently over low heat. Put the wine and fat in a shallow dish large enough to hold 6 quail. Peel and slice 3 of the shallots ¼ inch thick. Put the quail in the dish and add the sliced shallots, 6 cloves crushed garlic, 10 crushed juniper berries, and 3 bay leaves, and 10 to 12 sprigs Italian parsley. Mix everything together well, cover and set in a cool place for several hours or overnight. Turn the quail four or five times.

Toss 2 cups fresh bread crumbs with about ¼ cup of duck fat. The crumbs should be moist but not soggy. Spread them about ⅜ inch thick on a baking sheet and bake in a preheated 375°F. oven for about 10 minutes, or until they are a rich golden brown. Keep in a warm place to serve with the quail.

Prepare a medium fire of mesquite or other wood charcoal. Remove the quail from the marinade, split them down the back and remove the backbone, salt and pepper on both sides, and put them on a platter. Mince the remaining shallot, stem 10 to 12 sprigs of Italian parsley, and cut a lemon into 6 wedges.

To grill the quail, put them breast down on the grill for 2 to 3 minutes and brush the open side with some marinade. Turn them, cook 2 to 3 minutes, and brush the breast with marinade. Turn again and brush with marinade. Cook for 1 to 2 minutes. The quail are done when the breasts feel springy yet firm when pressed with a finger.

Divide the bread crumbs between six warm serving plates. Put the quail on top of the crumbs and sprinkle about 1 teaspoon of diced shallot on each quail. Put 2 or 3 parsley leaves on top of each quail. Garnish the plates with the remaining parsley and the lemon wedges.

Warm Green Bean Salad with Rocket and Garden Lettuces

Serves 6

6 handfuls mixed garden lettuces and rocket (include small red leaf
   lettuce for color)
½ pound *haricots verts*
1¼ cups shelled walnut halves
1½ tablespoons finely diced shallots
¾ cup virgin olive oil
¼ to ⅓ cup Balsamic vinegar
Salt and pepper
¼ cup Niçoise olives

WASH and dry the mixed garden lettuces and rocket. Pinch the ends
from ½ pound haricots verts. Spread 1¼ cups walnut halves on a
baking tray and bake in a preheated 350°F. oven for 10 to 15 minutes until
they are well-toasted. Remove from the oven and set aside.

Make the vinaigrette by combining 1½ tablespoons finely diced shallots,
¾ cup olive oil, about ¼ cup Balsamic vinegar, and salt and pepper to taste.

Blanch the beans for 2 to 3 minutes in plenty of boiling salted water, or
until they are crisp but tender and bright green. Drain the beans.

Toss the warm beans, the greens, the walnuts, and ¼ cup Niçoise olives
in enough vinaigrette to coat lightly but thoroughly. Arrange the salad on
slightly warm plates and serve.

Salmon Baked with Anchovy Butter

Serves 6

6 salt-packed anchovy fillets
8 tablespoons unsalted butter
Juice of ½ lemon
1 to 1½ teaspoons freshly ground black pepper
2 pounds fresh salmon fillet

TO make the butter, bone and rinse 6 anchovy fillets and dry them well.
(Use only salt-packed anchovies, available at Italian delicatessens.)
Pound the anchovies to a smooth paste in a mortar. Mix the paste by hand
with 8 tablespoons butter cut into bits and softened to room temperature.
Work in the juice of ½ lemon and 1 to 1½ teaspoons freshly ground black
pepper.

Cut 2 pounds of salmon fillet into six pieces, each about ½ inch wide. Put the salmon on a lightly oiled baking sheet and spread each piece with about 1½ tablespoons anchovy butter. Bake in a preheated 400°F. oven for 4 to 5 minutes, until the salmon is just cooked. The salmon is done when it feels springy yet firm when pressed with a finger.

Serve the salmon on warm plates with a red-potato and red-onion gratin.

Red Potato and Red Onion Gratin

Serves 6

2 pounds red potatoes, about equal size
3 medium red onions
¼ cup and 2 tablespoons light olive oil
2 to 3 sprigs thyme
Salt and pepper
2 tablespoons unsalted butter

PEEL the potatoes and slice them ¼ inch thick into a bowl with plenty of cold water. Keep them covered by 1 inch of water, changing the water as it becomes starchy. The number of changes depends on the potatoes; three to four times is usual.

Peel the onions and slice them ¼ inch thick. Cook them in 3 tablespoons olive oil with 2 to 3 sprigs thyme over very low heat. Cover the pan, but stir occasionally. The onions should be sweet, slightly softened, and still crunchy after 10 minutes. Remove from the heat, uncover, and set aside.

Rinse the potatoes in a colander and pat them very dry between tea towels. Toss them in the remaining olive oil.

Layer a lightly oiled shallow 2- to 3-quart earthenware casserole with potatoes slightly overlapping in concentric circles, and salt and pepper lightly. Remove the thyme from the onions and strew some of them lightly over the layer of potatoes. Continue layering and seasoning the potatoes. End with a layer of potatoes.

Dot with 2 tablespoons softened butter and bake in a preheated 425°F. oven for 25 to 30 minutes until the potatoes are a deep golden brown.

Cured Grilled Salmon Vinaigrette

Serves 6

1 whole fillet of salmon, about 2 pounds
¼ cup coarse salt
6 3-inch tarragon sprigs

LAY a 2-pound fillet of salmon skin side down, and sprinkle with ¼ cup coarse salt. Place 6 sprigs of tarragon on top of the salt. Put the salmon skin side up in a lightly oiled dish and cover with a damp tea towel. Refrigerate for 1 day.

FOR THE VINAIGRETTE:

1 shallot
10 to 12 chives
12 to 14 sprigs chervil
¾ cup light olive oil
Juice of 1 lemon, or to taste
Salt and pepper
1 cucumber (Japanese, if available)

TO make the vinaigrette, dice 1 shallot very finely and mince 10 to 12 chives. Remove the leaves from 12 to 14 sprigs of chervil. Mix the shallot and herbs with ⅔ cup of the olive oil and lemon juice to taste. Season with salt and pepper. Wash the cucumber and cut it into thin slices.

Take the salmon out of the refrigerator ½ hour before serving. Remove the salt and tarragon from the salmon and peel off the skin. Prepare a wood charcoal fire. Brush the salmon lightly with olive oil on both sides and put it on a hot grill for 2 to 3 minutes on each side, until it feels firm and springy when pressed with a finger. It should be quite rare in the center.

Toss the cucumber slices with the vinaigrette and divide them on six serving plates. Cut the grilled salmon into thin slices and serve it with the cucumber salad.

Buckwheat Pasta with Rocket and Goat Cheese

Serves 6

FOR THE PASTA:

1½ cups all-purpose flour
½ cup buckwheat flour
¾ teaspoon salt
2 eggs
1 to 2 tablespoons water

MIX 1½ cups all-purpose flour with ½ cup buckwheat flour and ¾ teaspoon salt in a bowl. Make a well in the flour. Lightly beat 2 eggs with 1 tablespoon water and add to the well. Incorporate the eggs into the flour, adding another tablespoon of water if the dough is dry. Knead the dough vigorously for 20 minutes, cover it with plastic wrap, and let it rest for 30 minutes.

Divide the dough in half and roll each half through all the settings on a pasta machine to the next to thinnest setting. Flour the dough and cut the pasta by hand into *pappardelle* noodles, each about 1¼ inches wide and 2¼ inches long. Flour them lightly and lay them on baking sheets in one layer. Cover the noodles with tea towels and refrigerate until ready to cook.

FOR THE SAUCE:

2 cups heavy cream
3 ounces very fresh goat cheese, crumbled
about ½ pound *haricots verts*
about 2 handfuls rocket
Salt and black pepper

BRING plenty of salted water to boil for the pasta and the beans. Meanwhile, reduce 2 cups heavy cream slightly over medium heat in a large saucepan. Whisk 3 ounces crumbled goat cheese into the cream and set aside.

Blanch the beans for 2 or 3 minutes or until they are crisp but still tender. Remove the beans and drain them. Carefully add the *pappardelle* to the boiling water and cook them just past *al dente*. Drain the pasta and toss it in the sauce, along with about 2 handfuls rocket leaves, the beans, and salt and black pepper to taste. Serve the pasta on a warm platter.

Sautéed Quail Served with Mushroom Toasts

Serves 6

12 quail

FOR THE MARINADE:

1½ cups Madeira
3 shallots
10 juniper berries
8 to 10 black peppercorns
8 to 10 sprigs Italian parsley

MARINATE 12 quail overnight in a cool place in 1½ cups Madeira, 3 sliced shallots, 10 lightly crushed juniper berries, 8 to 10 black peppercorns, and 8 to 10 sprigs Italian parsley. Turn the quail several times during the marination.

FOR THE MUSHROOM TOASTS:

1 ounce dried wild mushrooms (boletus, chanterelles, or morels)
½ cup hot water
½ pound fresh mushrooms
2 shallots
Salt and pepper
4 tablespoons unsalted butter
6 thin slices *pain de mie* (see page 233), crust removed
about ⅓ cup clarified butter

SOAK 1 ounce dried wild mushrooms in ½ cup hot water for 30 minutes. Strain the mushroom liquor through dampened triple cheesecloth. Rinse the mushrooms and pick over for grit. Mince ½ pound fresh mushrooms with the wild mushrooms. Mince 2 shallots and mix with the mushrooms. Season the *duxelles* with salt and pepper, and sauté over medium heat in 4 tablespoons butter for 15 to 20 minutes. Add the mushroom liquor little by little during the cooking. The mushroom mixture should not be too juicy when it has finished cooking. Cover and set aside.

Cut 6 thin slices *pain de mie* diagonally in half and brush both sides of the bread lightly with clarified butter. Bake in a preheated 350°F. oven for 10 minutes, until the toasts are golden brown. Remove from the baking tray and set aside.

TO SAUTÉ THE QUAIL:

1 cup fresh bread crumbs
about ½ cup duck fat
Salt and pepper
2 or 3 tablespoons Madeira
1 cup quail, pigeon, or duck *demi-glace* (see page 76)
3 tablespoons unsalted butter

TOSS 1 cup fresh bread crumbs with ¼ cup duck fat and spread the mixture about ½ inch thick in a baking dish. Bake in a preheated 350°F. oven for 15 to 20 minutes, until the crumbs are a rich golden brown. Remove from the oven and keep in a warm place.

Remove the quail from the marinade, pat them dry, and salt and pepper them. Sauté the quail in ¼ cup duck fat over medium heat for 10 to 12 minutes, turning the quail for even browning. When the quail are done, remove them to a platter and keep them warm.

Pour the fat from the pan and deglaze with 2 or 3 tablespoons good Madeira. Add 1 cup quail, pigeon, or duck *demi-glace* and reduce the sauce slightly. Strain the sauce into a clean pan and keep warm over very low heat.

To serve, spread the *duxelles* on the toasts and put two toasts on each plate. Finish the sauce by swirling in 3 tablespoons of butter. Place the quail on the toasts and pour the sauce over. Sprinkle with the prepared bread crumbs.

Warm Green Beans and Beets with Aïoli

Serves 6

FOR THE AÏOLI:

2 large egg yolks (organic if available)
1½ cups light olive oil
3 to 4 cloves young very fresh garlic
Salt

MAKE the aïoli by beating 2 egg yolks well with a whisk. Add about ⅓ cup light olive oil drop by drop, whisking continually. Add another ⅓ cup oil, teaspoon by teaspoon, whisking continually. Using a mortar and pestle, mash 3 peeled cloves of garlic well and whisk the garlic paste into the mayonnaise. Salt to taste, keeping in mind that half of the oil remains to be added. Whisk in the rest of the oil about a tablespoon at a time. Season the aïoli, adding another mashed garlic clove and salt if necessary.

THE BEETS AND THE BEANS:

6 small red beets
6 small golden beets
½ pound *haricots verts*

PUT 6 small red beets and 6 small golden beets in a shallow baking dish with about ⅓ cup water and bake in a preheated 300°F. oven for 30 to 40 minutes, until the beets are tender. Remove them from the baking dish and allow to cool.

Pinch the ends from ½ pound *haricots verts* and blanch in plenty of boiling salted water for 2 to 3 minutes, until the beans are tender but crisp and bright green. Drain.

Peel the red and golden beets and slice them into rounds. Arrange the vegetables on serving plates and garnish with the aïoli.

Poached Salmon with Fresh Basil and Olive Butters

Serves 6

2 pounds whole salmon fillet

CUT 2 pounds salmon fillet into six equal pieces.

FOR THE *COURT-BOUILLON*:

1 carrot
1 onion
½ celery rib
1 bay leaf
½ teaspoon fennel seeds
6 to 8 black peppercorns
2 teaspoons sea salt
2 cups white wine
about 2 cups water

PEEL 1 carrot and 1 onion and chop them coarsely with ½ rib of celery. Mix the vegetables with 1 bay leaf, ½ teaspoon fennel seeds, 6 to 8 black peppercorns, 2 teaspoons sea salt, 2 cups white wine, and 2 cups water. Bring the *court-bouillon* to a boil, reduce heat, cover, and simmer for 15 to 20 minutes. Strain the *court-bouillon* and taste for salt; it should be rather salty.

FOR THE FRESH BASIL BUTTER:

1 cup basil leaves
8 tablespoons softened unsalted butter
¼ cup strained *court-bouillon*
Scant tablespoon lemon juice

MINCE 1 cup basil leaves and pound to a rough paste using a mortar and pestle. Mix 8 tablespoons softened butter into the basil by hand and set aside. Reduce ¼ cup *court-bouillon* and 1 scant tablespoon of lemon juice in a small sauce pan to a glaze of about 1 tablespoon.

FOR THE OLIVE BUTTER:

½ cup pitted Niçoise olives
1 salt-packed anchovy fillet
½ teaspoon minced garlic
4 tablespoons softened unsalted butter

USING a mortar and pestle, make a paste of ½ cup pitted Niçoise olives, 1 salt-packed anchovy fillet, rinsed, and ½ teaspoon minced garlic. Work in 4 tablespoons softened butter by hand. Set the butter in a cool place.

TO COOK AND SERVE THE SALMON:

POACH the salmon in simmering *court-bouillon* until just done, about 3 to 4 minutes. The salmon is done when it feels firm yet springy when pressed with a finger. Meanwhile, whisk the basil butter into the glaze of reduced juices over low heat until it forms an emulsion, about 2 minutes.

To serve, drain the fillets briefly on a tea towel. Spread the basil butter in the center of six warm serving plates. Put a salmon fillet on each plate and spread about 2 teaspoons of olive butter over the fillet.

Marinated Quail Grilled with Sausages and Bay Leaves

Serves 6

3 shallots
10 lightly crushed juniper berries
12 to 16 sprigs parsley
16 fresh bay leaves
10 to 12 black peppercorns
⅓ cup duck fat
1½ cups port
12 quail
¾ pound Toulouse sausage
½ ounce dried boletus or chanterelle mushrooms
½ cup hot water
6 tablespoons unsalted butter
12 pieces French bread, ½ inch thick and about 1½ inches square

PEEL and slice 3 shallots and lightly crush 10 juniper berries. Mix the shallots and juniper berries with 12 to 16 sprigs parsley, 6 to 8 bay leaves, 10 to 12 black peppercorns, and ⅓ cup duck fat in a dish large enough to hold the quail. Stir in 1½ cups port and toss the quail in the marinade. Marinate the quail in a cool place overnight or up to 12 hours, turning the quail four to five times during this time.

Start a medium-hot fire of wood charcoal. Prepare ¾ pound Toulouse sausage for the grill by blanching it in lots of boiling water for 5 minutes. Remove the sausage to drain and cool. Soak ½ ounce dried wild mushrooms in ½ cup hot water for 10 minutes. Strain through rinsed triple cheesecloth and add the liquor to the quail marinade. Check the mushrooms carefully for grit, and mince them finely. Mix the mushrooms by hand with 6 tablespoons softened butter. Cut 12 pieces of French bread, each about ½ inch thick and 1½ inches square. Cut the cooled sausage into 12 equal pieces. Soften the remaining bay leaves for 15 minutes in the quail marinade.

To grill the quail and sausages, first stuff each quail with an equal amount of mushroom butter. Wedge the pieces of French bread into the cavity of each quail to keep the butter in. Thread a bay leaf onto each of 4 skewers. Thread a quail crosswise onto each skewer; thread a piece of sausage through the skin next to each quail. Thread a bay leaf next to the sausage and repeat the procedure, ending with a bay leaf. There will be 3 quail and 3 pieces of sausage on each skewer. Brush the quail and sausages liberally with the marinade and put on the grill. Turn the skewers five or six times and brush with marinade frequently for 10 to 12 minutes. The quail should be completely cooked; they are better a little on the done side.

Put 2 quail and 2 pieces of sausage on each of six warm serving plates. Serve with fresh pasta with beet and spinach greens.

Fresh Pasta with Beet and Spinach Greens

Serves 6

1 pound fresh pasta dough
1 pound mixed tender beet greens and spinach leaves
4 tablespoons unsalted butter
½ to 1 teaspoon minced garlic
Salt and pepper

ROLL 1 pound fresh pasta through the thinnest setting of a hand-turned pasta machine. Divide the pasta sheet into 12-inch lengths, flour each length very lightly and roll each loosely four times. Cut the pasta through the short side of the rolls into ½-inch strips. Toss the cut pasta well to prevent sticking and spread it on a very lightly floured baking sheet. Cover with a tea towel and refrigerate.

Clean and stem 1 pound mixed young beet greens and spinach leaves. Cut the greens into ½ inch strips and dry well. Bring plenty of salted water to boil to cook the pasta.

Put the greens in a pan with 4 tablespoons melted butter and ½ to 1 teaspoon minced garlic over low heat. Cover and cook until the greens just wilt, about 1 minute. Meanwhile, cook the pasta in boiling water until it is *al dente,* about 30 seconds. Drain the pasta and toss it with the greens and butter. Season with salt and pepper.

BREADS

It is a mystery that the simple, homey process involving yeast, flour, and water is rarely duplicated commercially in a delicious and proper way. It is difficult to understand why there are so few good bread bakeries, and I must ask, Why is this so? My criterion for good bread is simple: it must stand by itself, perhaps with only the addition of a little sweet butter. Good bread has a look, a smell, and a texture that tells you it is "handmade." This means, at the very least, that the bread will have a final shaping by hand which produces the charming irregularities that seduce you immediately. The aromas and flavors of breadmaking depend on the purity and quality of the ingredients, for although preservatives and yeast nutrients may hasten the process, they will diminish the result. Given the wholesomeness of honest ingredients and a good recipe, the bread needs *time*—time in which to develop a texture and a crust that will give it depth and interest. When the bread is forced to rise too quickly, the flour and yeast are not given an opportunity to develop the special qualities which I associate with good bread.

These recipes are all the result of lengthy experimentation and work by an instinctive baker, Steve Sullivan of Chez Panisse, who has been inspired by Elizabeth David's *English Breads and Yeast Cookery* and, of course, by Marcel Pagnol's film *La Femme du Boulanger.* At long last, we are making all our own bread for the restaurant, and I rejoice in that. The following insights are those which I have gleaned directly from the baker himself.

The two most formidable obstacles to successful home baking are inexperience and lack of time; the only way around them is the practical experience of repetition. It is only through persistent experimentation that the hours and hours required for baking will be reduced to twenty minutes to begin with, five more minutes in an hour or so, five more a bit later, and three quarters of an hour spent in the kitchen during the actual baking time, a total of less than an hour of true working time, for the forty-five minutes spent in the area during the baking could be devoted to other things in between checking the bread.

However, it is only through repeated effort that a bread recipe will cease to be anything other than a list of ingredients and hackneyed instructions to "knead until satiny smooth." The transformation of printed words from vagueness to clarity and comprehension is the most important step in the development of your baking skills, for it indicates that you have attained an understanding of the ingredients and the process which will allow you to use any recipe to bake successfully.

The first step toward understanding is the choice of *one* recipe on which to concentrate. Jumping from recipe to recipe will only slow down the comprehension process and the learning that comes with it. From the beginning, use only the proper ingredients: an unbleached flour which is cream-colored, not white, and which clumps together when squeezed firmly in your hand; which is approximately 13 percent gluten or protein; and which is stone-ground, if possible, as this type of slow grinding leaves the wheat more chemically intact than do the high-speed steel rollers used in more modern grinding processes. The necessity for this particular kind of flour cannot be overemphasized, because unless the whole-grain flours—barley, buckwheat, and wheat—are stone-ground and absolutely fresh, they will contribute nothing more than their color to the bread. In yeast, there is neither a choice nor any need for one. Fresh and dried yeasts are of the same strain, and both produce the required carbon dioxide.

When you have baked the one recipe of personal choice, using the fresh stone-ground flour and either yeast, over and over again, until you have achieved exactly the results you desire, *then,* and only then, should you alter it to bake other breads that interest you: add whole-grain flours, or take them out of the recipe; use sourdough starters. Do whatever intrigues you, just so long as you can relate it back to your original recipe. In all cases, you will find that there is a basic weight ratio of flour to water, 1½–2:1, and of salt to flour, ¼–½ ounce per pound. You will also find that concentrating on one recipe and its variations will teach you a bit about the other recipes you may try later. For example, the inevitable stickiness of a rye dough will not alarm you because it will be quite different from the all-white dough that was sticky because it was too wet; as you knead a whole-wheat dough you will realize that it is becoming *less* workable, rather than more so, because the bran in full-wheat dough will chop the gluten fibers into shorter and shorter lengths if you give it more than the shortest possible working time needed to mix the flour.

In fact, it is in the mixing stage of breadmaking that the greatest number of problems can occur, very nearly all of them reversible, despite fears to the contrary! A baker will often use water that is warmer than necessary. Water that *feels* warm is 95–100 degrees, but a long kneading can raise the temperature of the dough 10 degrees, and the recommended "warm place" can bring these dough temperatures past the 115 degrees at which yeast dies; or the dough can be brought to such a state of activity that it is unmanageably lively. All bread-baking operations, including rising, are best carried out at 70–80 degrees. If the day is quite warm, use cool water to start the yeast and the dough will be far more manageable. Kneaded, most breads should have a resiliency like that of your relaxed inner thigh. If the dough seems too dense or tough, let it stand for 15 minutes, then chop it into small pieces on the counter. Put a little water into a bowl, and add the dough bits one at a time. The increased surface area will allow the dough to partially absorb the water, and further kneading or mixing will complete your bread dough's salvation.

Always remember to taste a pinch of your dough after mixing it so that an omission of salt will not go uncorrected. An inadvertent lack of salt will result in a frothy, wildly active dough and clammy, lumpy bread. The salt can be added to the dough by simply dissolving the salt in a little *hot* water, and adding the water as described above.

It is indeed possible to overmix dough by machine, so that the dough feels distinctly warm, loses its elasticity, and begins to collapse into a grainy mass. In all but the most severe cases, this error can be remedied by letting the dough rest for a few minutes and then very gently kneading in more flour *by hand*.

One of the most common problems in hand-working of bread dough is the reluctance to add all of the flour called for in the recipe because the amount, initially, may seem to be too much. Failure to add sufficient flour will result in a dough that is too soft to properly support its shape, yet too tense to accept more than a pinch or so of flour at a time, resulting in the tedious frustration of overworking the dough. Check the recipe early on to make certain that the proportion of flour to water is very close to the usual 1½–2:1, and then add *all* the flour and mix as directed.

In letting your bread rise, avoid the "warm place" or "low oven" often suggested. As long as the dough and the room temperature are above 65–70 degrees, the yeast will perform.

The understanding of the forming and baking of loaves is gained only through the experience and knowledge of repetition. There is simply no other way for you to acquire the knack of instinctively knowing how much work or kneading is required before the dough must rest and relax. Likewise, you must tap dozens of loaves until, out of the myriad of "hollow sounds," the proper one will automatically catch your ear. Along with repeated effort, a notebook is definitely worthwhile, for in it you can record your observations surrounding each step of the bake. This will enable you to trace any difficulties back to their source in order to determine which factors and choices aided or hindered you in your efforts to bake the very best possible bread.

Chez Panisse Bread

8 baguettes

3¼ pounds all-purpose flour (or bread flour with 12%–13% gluten)
5 teaspoons salt
3 tablespoons dry yeast
4 cups water (70–80°F.)

MIX 3¼ pounds all-purpose flour with 5 teaspoons salt. In a large mixing bowl, dissolve 3 tablespoons dry yeast in 4 cups lukewarm water. Add the flour mixture, a cup at a time, whisking it smooth until it is thick enough to require mixing with a wooden spoon or paddle. The last cup or so of flour will have to be kneaded in. Turn the mass of dough, which will be shaggy, onto a floured surface and knead hard and rhythmically for 5 to 10 minutes, until the dough is smooth and elastic. Allow the dough to rise once in a large, covered bowl; punch down, and refrigerate, covered, overnight. The dough should be refrigerated in a container that allows for its triple expansion.

Let the dough stand at room temperature for 3 or 4 hours, until it is warm and rising. Punch down the dough and divide it into eight 10-ounce balls. Pound the air from the balls and roll them into baguette shape. This you should do in two stages. Press each ball into a roughly square, bubble-free sheet, and fold toward yourself, from the top, until you have a cylinder an inch or so in diameter and 6 to 8 inches long. Allow the dough to rest for 3 to 5 minutes. Then, placing your fingers (not your palms) on the dough, press moderately and roll back and forth, gradually moving your hands apart until the loaf you are shaping is 12 inches (or the width of your pan) long. Don't push too hard or stretch too fast or you'll tear the loaves.

Put the dough on baking sheets which have been lined with bakers' parchment and lightly floured. Cover the dough with light cloths and leave it in a warm place where there is no air movement for about 1½ hours, until the dough has doubled in size and a finger impression remains when the dough is poked lightly.

Slash the loaves or snip them into a wheat-stalk shape, and spray them thoroughly with a light mist. Put the loaves into a preheated 475°F. oven on the middle rack and immediately lower the heat to 425°F. once the loaves are baking. (Ideally, line the lower shelf with thick tiles and bake the loaves directly on them, using an oven temperature of 425°F. all the way through.) Spray very quickly after 2 minutes. Spray again quickly after 5 minutes, and again after another 5 minutes. After the final spraying the loaves should be glossy and beginning to brown. Turn the baking sheets around if necessary for even browning. The baguettes will be done in 15 to 20 minutes, when they are evenly brown and sound hollow when rapped.

Rye Bread

2 loaves

2 tablespoons dry yeast
½ cup water
2 cups sparkling hard cider or beer
1¼ pounds all-purpose flour
¾ pound rye flour
1 tablespoon salt

SOFTEN 2 tablespoons yeast in ½ cup warm water in a large mixing bowl and stir in 2 cups sparkling hard cider or beer. Mix 1¼ pounds all-purpose flour with ¾ pound rye flour and 1 tablespoon salt. Whisk the flour into the liquid, a cup at a time, until the dough is too thick to continue. Stir in the remaining flour, a cup at a time, until the dough comes together in a solid, sticky mass. Turn the dough onto a floured surface and begin kneading. Use a gentler motion than in kneading a white-bread dough, so that the dough stretches less. The dough will probably remain sticky throughout the kneading, but do not add more flour. After 3 to 4 minutes the dough will have a limp, silky elasticity. Put the dough in a container that allows for triple expansion, cover, and refrigerate overnight.

Allow 3 to 4 hours for the dough to come to room temperature. Work out all air from the dough, then shape it into 1-pound balls or baguettes. Let the dough rise to slightly less than double in bulk, as the bread is better dense than light. Bake in a preheated 400°F. oven for 35 to 40 minutes, until the loaves are a deep ruddy brown.

Walnut *Fougasse*

(An adaptation of a Madeleine Kamman recipe)

3–4 loaves

4 teaspoons salt
2¾ pounds all-purpose flour
2 tablespoons dry yeast
3 cups water
2 cups chopped walnuts
1½ cups walnut oil
1 tablespoon coarse sea salt

STIR 4 teaspoons salt into 2¾ pounds all-purpose flour. Soften 2 table-spoons yeast in 3 cups water. Whisk the flour, a cup at a time, into the water until the mixture is very thick. Stir in 2 cups chopped walnuts and ½ cup walnut oil with a wooden paddle and mix thoroughly. Continue stirring in the flour with a wooden paddle until the dough mass holds its shape. Turn the dough onto a floured surface and knead the remaining cup or so of flour into it. Knead the dough well for 5 minutes and let it rise for about 1½ hours in a covered bowl, until double in bulk.

Pour ½ cup walnut oil over the dough and knead it in thoroughly. Let the dough rise again until double in bulk. Pour the final ½ cup walnut oil over the dough and knead in. Let the dough rest for 5 to 10 minutes.

A *fougasse* is a flat, irregular loaf, originally baked directly on the hearth, and now enjoyed for the variety of crust textures possible in a single loaf. In France the shape will often be that of a ladder, or a tree—or even a flat, abstract loaf, whimsically poked and stretched.

To shape your *fougasse,* divide the dough into three or four portions. Work all the air from the dough, piece by piece. The bread is best suited to small-diameter loaves, as the oil softens the dough considerably, causing it to spread rather than rise up. Press the dough into an oval or rectangle ¾ to 1 inch thick; the diameter or length may vary, but it is important to keep the thickness even. Put the dough on baking sheets lined with bakers' parchment and well dusted with flour. Let rest for 3 minutes, then slash, prod, and stretch the dough into whatever shape you like. Cover with barely damp tea towels and let rise until double in bulk. Brush the loaves lightly with walnut oil and sprinkle with a small amount of coarse sea salt.

Bake the loaves in a preheated 425°F. oven for 30 to 35 minutes, until they are an even walnut brown and sound hollow when sharply thumped. The bread is better slightly underdone, as the crust thickens rapidly in the final minutes of baking.

Peasant Bread

4 round loaves

3 cups water
½ cup sourdough starter
½ pound whole-wheat flour
2 tablespoons and 1 teaspoon dry yeast
1½ pounds white unbleached all-purpose flour
¼ pound barley flour
¼ pound rye flour
4 teaspoons salt

PREPARE the "sponge" the night before baking. Mix 3 cups water, ½ cup sourdough starter, and ½ pound whole-wheat flour thoroughly with a whisk and leave it, covered, at room temperature overnight.

The next day, add 2 tablespoons and 1 teaspoon yeast to the sponge and stir. Let the yeast dissolve. Mix 1½ pounds unbleached all-purpose flour with ¼ pound barley flour, ¼ pound rye flour, and 4 teaspoons salt. When the yeast has dissolved, whisk the flour in, a cup at a time, until the dough is smooth and too thick to whisk. Incorporate the rest of the flour, a cup at a time, with a wooden paddle. When the dough forms a shaggy mass, turn it onto a floured surface and knead for 5 to 10 minutes, until it is smooth and elastic. Leave it in a container, covered, until it doubles in bulk, between 1 and 1½ hours.

Divide the dough into four equal parts and work the air from each portion, one at a time. Form each portion into a ball and place on baking sheets lined with bakers' parchment. Cover the loaves lightly and let them rise until double in bulk. Slash the tops, spray lightly with water, and bake in a preheated 400°F. oven for 40 to 45 minutes. The loaves are done when they are an even dark-brown color and make a hard hollow sound when rapped.

Pain de Mie

2 loaves

1 tablespoon dry yeast
2 teaspoons sugar
2½ cups warm milk
¼ pound unsalted butter, at room temperature
1½ pounds all-purpose flour
2½ teaspoons salt
Optional: ¼ pound barley flour, for flavor
Extra flour for dusting

THE *"mie"* of a loaf is the crumb: everything within, but not including, the crust. Because this bread is baked in a covered pan, it has a very thin crust, and even that is often trimmed away for its most frequent uses in canapés or as croutons.

Dissolve 1 tablespoon yeast and 2 teaspoons sugar in 2½ cups warm milk. After 5 minutes add ¼ pound softened butter and whisk occasionally to melt the butter. Mix 1½ pounds all-purpose flour and ¼ pound barley flour very well with 2½ teaspoons salt. Whisk the flour into the milk, a cup at a time, until the mixture is too thick to whisk. Stir in the rest of the flour with a wooden paddle, a cup at a time, and turn onto a floured surface when the flour has been incorporated. Knead the dough for 7 to 10 minutes, until it is smooth. Use quick, sharp kneading movements and dust liberally with flour, as this dough is prone to stick. Let the dough rise until double in bulk in a lightly buttered and covered bowl.

Punch down the dough and work all air from it. Cut off two portions weighing 22 ounces each. (Cover the remaining dough and reserve to make bread sticks—see below.) Butter two 14-inch rectangular pullman baking pans very well on top, sides and bottom. If pullman pans are not available, butter two 9- by 5-inch metal bread pans and one side of two metal baking sheets which completely cover the bread pans. Pat the dough evenly into the pans; it should fill about one third of the pans. Cover with plastic wrap and let rise until the dough fills three quarters of the pans. Cover the pullman pans with their lids or the bread pans with the baking sheets, buttered side down; weight the baking sheets with small metal ovenproof pans.

Preheat the oven to 400°F. Bake the bread in pullman pans for 25 minutes. Remove the lids and bake for another 15 minutes or so, until all sides are a deep golden brown and the bread is solid to the touch.

If you are using the metal bread pans, bake for 35 minutes and remove the weighted baking sheets. Continue baking for 15 to 20 minutes, until all sides are a deep golden brown and the bread is solid to the touch.

To make bread sticks, divide the remaining dough into 10 to 12 portions, and roll each portion into sticks about 1 inch in diameter. Let the dough rest for 5 minutes, then roll the sticks to about ½ inch in diameter. Put the sticks on baking sheets lined with bakers' parchment and bake in a preheated 375°F. oven for 30 to 35 minutes.

Brioche

4 tablespoons dry yeast
½ cup water
½ cup sugar
2 teaspoons salt
½ cup warm milk
6 egg yolks and 3 whole eggs
about 4 cups unbleached flour
1 cup unsalted butter, at room temperature

DISSOLVE 4 tablespoons dry yeast in ½ cup warm water. Put the softened yeast in a large bowl and mix well with ½ cup sugar, 2 teaspoons salt, ½ cup warm milk, and 6 egg yolks and 3 whole eggs. Add 3 cups flour and stir in with 1 cup softened butter. Turn the dough onto a floured surface and knead well for at least 10 minutes, adding flour as necessary. The dough should form a glossy ball with no stickiness. Place it in a bowl and allow it to double in bulk at room temperature, for about 1½ hours. Punch it down, return it to the bowl, and refrigerate overnight. The slow rise in the refrigerator creates a very good texture.

Remove the dough and let it warm up to room temperature. Punch it down and roll it into desired shape. Let it rise until almost double in bulk and bake in a 450°F. oven for 10 minutes, more or less depending on its shape.

Marion's Cornmeal Graham Bread

2 medium loaves

1 package dry yeast
½ cup warm water
3 tablespoons butter
2 cups buttermilk, slightly warmed
1½ teaspoons salt
2 tablespoons sugar
2 cups graham flour
3 cups all-purpose flour
1 cup yellow cornmeal

SPRINKLE the yeast over the water in a large bowl, stir to dissolve and let stand for several minutes. Add the butter, buttermilk, salt, sugar, and the graham flour and beat vigorously for a minute. Add enough of the all-purpose flour to make the dough come away from the side of the bowl and collect around the spoon. Add the cornmeal and stir to blend. Turn the dough onto a lightly floured board and knead for a minute or two and then let rest for 10 minutes. Adding just enough flour so that the dough is not sticky, resume kneading until the dough is smooth and elastic.

Put the dough in a large greased bowl, cover and let rise until double in bulk. Punch down and shape into two loaves. Place in greased loaf pans, cover, and let rise to the top of the pans. Bake in a preheated 375°F. oven for about 45 minutes or until done. Remove from pans and cool on racks.

MEMORABLE MENUS

❧

The following menus are highlights of the last ten years at Chez Panisse and illustrate the range of menu ideas inspired by our many friends. I have tried to explain something about each menu as I recall it—the problems we encountered and the successes we achieved in the kitchen and in the dining room.

Many of these menus were conceived and executed by Jeremiah Tower, who was the chef at the restaurant during its formative years. He developed the idea of regional dinners celebrating the food of provincial France (Brittany, Périgord, Champagne, Burgundy, Alsace, etc.), Morocco, Louisiana, and ultimately, our own region of Northern California; his innovative and adventurous menus gave the restaurant its reputation for ambitious experimentation and exploration.

A TOAST TO GREAT WINES AND GREAT FRIENDS

Country-style Pastry Tart Filled with Roquefort Cheese and Cream
1967, 1972, 1973 Ridge Monte Bello Chardonnay

*Lulu Peyraud's Bouillabaisse of Salt Cod with Garlic, Saffron, Tomatoes,
Basil, and Olive Oil*
1971 Ridge Eisele Cabernet Sauvignon
1971, 1974 Ridge Monte Bello Cabernet Sauvignon

*Charcoal-Grilled Rack and Saddle of Spring Lamb Served with a Leek
Compote with Fresh Mint and a Sauce Made with Ridge Zinfandel*
1968, 1970 Ridge Jimsomare Zinfandel
1970 Ridge Geyserville Zinfandel
1970 Ridge Occidental Zinfandel

Cheeses
1971, 1974 Ridge York Creek Petite Sirah

Coffee
1971 Ridge Lodi Zinfandel Essence

This dinner was inspired by the birthdays of various friends and the fourth anniversary of a dinner group which chooses special wines for monthly celebrations. The meal was built around the wines, and this was the first time we made Lulu's salt cod bouillabaisse. This menu is another example of foods and wines that worked well together: the bouillabaisse was surprisingly good with the Cabernets.

THE DINNER VERNON MADE FOR ME

California Caviar on Croutons

Various Raw Fish Prepared Japanese Style with Garnishes

Marinated Raw Beef Salad with Julienned Scallions and Vinaigrette Dressing

Richard Olney's Chicken Baked in Sealed Crocks with Garlic Cloves and Herbs de Provence and Served with Charcoal-Grilled French Bread

Cheeses

Fresh Strawberry Ice Cream

This dinner was made privately by a friend who knew me very well, so he chose dishes that had very clean and unusual tastes. On the one hand, it was elegant; on the other, it was extremely earthy. When he prepared this meal for my birthday, we had a 1929 Margaux Blanc with the raw beef salad and a 1968 Mayacamas Late Harvest Zinfandel with the cheese. The raw beef salad and the Margaux Blanc remains one of my very favorite wine and food marriages.

DINNER FOR FRED ON HIS BIRTHDAY

Poached Salmon Cheeks with Shallots and Sweet Butter

Salt-Water Trout with Deep-Fried Parsley

Charcoal-Grilled Brochette of Capon Hearts and Livers

Spit-Roasted Capon Stuffed to Taste Like Suckling Pig

Goat Cheese Croutons and Lettuces

Many-Layered Sherbet Cake

Another dinner for someone with a jaded palate that needed to be satisfied on his birthday! Since we were cooking this for a small number of people, we managed to get enough of the salmon cheeks. The spit-roasted capon is an adaptation of a Giuliano Bugialli recipe that tastes like wild boar.

A DINNER FOR RIDGE WINERY
(A Menu Inspired by Restaurant Girardet)

Onion Tart with a Puff Pastry Crust
1967 Hanzell Chardonnay

Maine Lobster Steamed in Cabbage Leaves and Served with Black Caviar and
Red Peppers in a Butter Sauce
1974 Ridge Monte Bello Chardonnay
1976 Ridge Monte Bello Chardonnay

Chicken Steamed with Black Truffles under the Skin and Served
with a Leek Confit
1959 Château Léoville-Barton
1967 Ridge Monte Bello Cabernet Sauvignon
1962 Château Lynch-Bages
1965 Ridge Monte Bello Cabernet Sauvignon
1968 Draper-Maytag Chilean Cabernet Sauvignon, Longeri Vineyards

An Assortment of Swiss Cheeses
1967 Ridge Jimsomare Zinfandel
1968 Ridge Picchetti Zinfandel

Orange Gratin
1962 Château Guiraud

A recent gastronomic tour of Europe provided the incentive for a week of menus from my favorite restaurants there. This dinner, the Ridge Winery's Board of Directors Meeting, is held annually at Chez Panisse. This provides a most interesting opportunity for comparing and contrasting wines that have been especially chosen to complement one another, as well as the menu. The orange gratin was made with Seville oranges and gratinéed with a bit of crème anglaise.

THE THIRD ANNUAL GARLIC FESTIVAL CONTINUES

Vegetables with Five Garlic Sauces

Hunan Chinese Garlic Cakes

Italian Tortellini Served with Garlic, Olive Oil, and Oregano

Charcoal-Grilled Mexican Fish Dish with Dried Chiles and Garlic

Fresh Quail Stuffed with Whole Garlics Baked in Grape Leaves

Moroccan Eggplant Salad

Wine-Spiced Garlic Sherbets

Trying to come up with a week of completely different garlic dishes for the annual "Garlic Gala" is always a challenge, and this brought us eventually to the dishes of China, Italy, Mexico, and Morocco. The most memorable aspect of this meal for me was the garlic sherbets, which were made with red fruits macerated with red wine and garlic cloves and with white fruits macerated with white wine and garlic cloves to create a very fruity beginning flavor to the sherbet and a lovely garlic aftertaste.

A DINNER HONORING MR. AND MRS. HENRY MORRIS

Fresh Drake's Bay Oysters on the Half Shell

Brittany-Style Buckwheat Crêpes Filled with Goat Cheese and Chard and Served with Crème Fraîche

Marinated Loin of Pork Braised with Cider and Served with Glazed Apples

Salad and Cheeses

Fresh Fruits

Andrew Hoyem, a well-known San Francisco printer, designed this printer's dinner to honor Mr. and Mrs. Morris. We chose the dishes of Brittany with accompanying wines from that region.

DÎNER DES SPECIALITÉS BOURGUIGNONNES

Salade de Queues d'Écrevisses et d'Haricots Verts

Saucisson à l'Aïl en Brioche

Cochon de Lait à la Façon de Bourgogne

Fromages

Mousse au Miel

This was a dinner of Burgundian specialties which worked extremely well, each course complementing and supporting others.

ROYAL THOMAS GUERNSEY III BIRTHDAY DINNER

Buckwheat Blini Served with Butter and California Black Caviar

*Poached Fresh Salmon Served with a Sauce Royal Enriched with a Fish
Fumet and Lobster and Served with Dilled New Potatoes*

Watercress and Orange Salad Dressed with Walnut Oil and Sherry Vinegar

Lindsey's Chocolate Cake à la Mode

A birthday celebration for the president of Chez Panisse. This was an
excessively rich meal, but it was short enough so that it did not really
overwhelm anyone, an important factor to consider in planning a menu of
a number of heavy, intense dishes.

AN ADAPTATION OF A DINNER FROM LA RÉSERVE DE BEAULIEU

"Vagabond" Raw Vegetable Salad with Avocados, Grated Carrots, Finely Minced Mushrooms, Lettuce Hearts, and Fresh Herbs

Fried Fresh Oysters and Mussels with a Tartar Sauce

Rack of Lamb Grilled over Charcoal and Served with Small Stuffed Vegetables Niçoise

Fresh Strawberry Soufflés

This was one of the most memorable dinners at the restaurant in terms of successful accomplishment of the dishes and the reception it received in the dining room. We intended to serve a little *friture* of lots of tiny fried fish, but we were unable to get anything fresh except the oysters and the mussels, which we cooked in a very light batter. The vegetables were sliced and arranged, then sprinkled with a very fine mince of mushrooms, and dressed. All the vegetables were from the garden: eggplant, yellow and green squash, and small tomatoes.

AN AMERICAN SUMMER MAINE LOBSTER DINNER

Smithfield Ham with Figs and Melons

Corn Soup with Green Peppers

Live Maine Lobster Steamed and Served with Butter

Rhubarb Pie à la Mode

At one point or another, especially during the summer, I always wish that I lived on the East Coast rather than on the West Coast. I wish that I were going up to New Hampshire for the weekend instead of sitting here in the summer fog! This is a menu to satisfy those longings.

DINNER FOR GERALD ASHER'S BIRTHDAY

Lebanese Salad Made with Cracked Wheat, Onions, Parsley, Tomatoes, and a Vinaigrette Dressing

Fresh Fish Poached in a Fish Stock and Served with Garlic Whisked into the Broth and Garnished with Croutons

Leg of Lamb Roasted and Served with Flageolets Cooked with Onions, Lamb Stock, and Tomatoes

Salad of Various Lettuces Dressed with Walnut Oil

Plum Tarte

Knowing that this patron of Chez Panisse liked Provençal foods, particularly leg of lamb, we designed a menu around those preferences. I do believe the tabouleh salad is one of the most refreshing beginnings possible for a meal and is not at all filling if made properly with enough lemon and parsley.

A WHITE TRUFFLE DINNER

Gratin of Cardoons with Cream and White Truffles

Brochette of Fresh Fish with a Shallot Butter

*Chicken Breasts Stuffed under the Skin with White Truffles, Sautéed and
Served with a Cream Sauce and Watercress*

Salad

Fresh Fruits

Each year when the white truffles arrive, we try to use them in every
conceivable manner. The cardoon dish is an Escoffier idea for a gratin of
cardoons with cream and white truffles; the cardoons are cooked, then gratinéed with a little cream and with white truffles grated all over the top. There
is an exciting quality about the dish because of the combination of the bitter
taste of the cardoons and the rich taste of the aromatic white truffles.

DINNER FOR LINDA'S BIRTHDAY

Lobster Salad with Caviar Michel Guérard

Marinated Rack of Lamb with Fresh Chestnut Purée

Ripe Cheeses

Poires Suduiraut

For some reason, I always associate lobster with November birthdays, so I chose to make this adaptation of a Michel Guérard salad. The very simple rack of lamb with the rich chestnut purée was intended to complement a very special bottle of Château Montrose. Once again, I served cheeses rather than a salad so my guests could continue with the pleasures of wine through that course. I knew they planned to have a wonderful old bottle of Sauternes for dessert, so we poached Comice pears in Château Suduiraut, then made a pastry cream with crushed almond macaroons in the praline, and finally reduced the poaching liquids from the pears to make a glaze.

A BIRTHDAY DINNER FOR THE BEST PALATE
WE KNOW

Fresh Seafood on a Bed of Seaweed, Including Oysters, Crayfish, Clams, and Squid
1959 Montrachet, Bertrand de Monceny
1959 Puligny-Montrachet, Pierre Ponnelle

Provençal Vegetable Soup Infused with Garlic and Fresh Basil
1975 Ernest Priess Gewürztraminer, Cuvée Particulière

Marinated Lamb Hearts and Kidneys on Rosemary Branches, Charcoal-Grilled and Served with Shoestring Potatoes
1971 Joseph Swan Zinfandel
1972 Joseph Swan Zinfandel, Lots 1 and 2

Salad

Cheeses
1961 Charles Krug Pinot Noir
1964 Martin Ray Pinot Noir

Tarte Tatin
1953 Schloss Eltz Trockenbeerenauslese

In this case, the foods were successful because they didn't interfere at all with extraordinary wines. Each one followed the other in a perfectly planned procession of flavors and aromas. This was a birthday celebration for a friend of the restaurant.

BRITTANY REGIONAL DINNER

Oysters on the Half-Shell

Mussel Crêpes

Roast Duckling with Baby Peas

Watercress Salad

Pont L'Evêque Cheese

Traditional Brittany Almond Cake with Almond Paste and Crème Chantilly

Jeremiah Tower proposed and prepared this dinner, one of the first celebrations of a particular region at Chez Panisse. The meal included a cheese from the region of Brittany, and mussels in an extremely light Mornay sauce, wrapped inside a buckwheat crêpe. In Brittany I had enjoyed a similar presentation, with tiny mussels lavished over the entire crêpe.

NEW YEAR'S EVE DINNER

Fresh California Caviar

Beef and Veal Consommé Garnished with Fresh Alsatian Goose Liver Pâté

Spit-Roasted Young Wild Boar Served with a Chestnut Purée

Watercress Salad

Various Cheeses

Fruit Tartlets

What a memorable dinner this was! I don't think I'll ever forget the spit we had to rig up in front of the restaurant in the courtyard, to accommodate the two wild boar we spit-roasted. The rains came that night, which necessitated our erecting a tent over the entire front yard of Chez Panisse. The sight of us in what resembled a Moroccan den of iniquity, smoke pouring from the boars as we tried to baste them, must have been an amazing scene to behold! We had to run from the hastily assembled grill in the front, through the rain, to get back into the restaurant with the food.

ALSATIAN REGIONAL DINNER

Pig's Ears Breaded and Grilled with a Mustard Sauce

Alsatian Vinaigrette Salads

Live Garrapata Trout Cooked in a Court-Bouillon and Served with a Butter Sauce

Munster Cheese

Tart of Dried Fruit with a Coffee Cream

This is another of our regional dinners planned and prepared by Jeremiah Tower, who was then cooking at Chez Panisse. We had never served pig's ears at the restaurant before, and carrying that off was very amusing. A friend who never liked to eat anything except very plain food happened to come in that night, and before I had a chance to tell him what the dish was, he had eaten it, believing it to be veal scallopini. When he finally learned it was pig's ears, he was horrified!

The trout were kept alive in the kitchen by using aeration tanks; we killed them as we needed them for the *truite au bleu,* gutting them through the neck. As far as I am concerned, the only way to eat trout is to kill it and then throw it right into the pan. This was certainly a successful if slightly bizarre meal!

GERTRUDE STEIN DINNER

Mushroom Sandwiches

Sole Mousse with Virgin Sauce

Gigot de la Clinique

Wild Rice Salad

A Tender Tart

Cream Perfect Love

This was surely one of the most favorably received dinners we ever had at Chez Panisse. Jeremiah Tower conceived this dinner, and the menu was written by him and by the poet Michael Palmer in the spirit of the one hundredth anniversary of Gertrude Stein's birth. I won't ever forget the Gigot de la Clinique because it took everyone at the restaurant at least a week of using syringes to shoot the tangerine juice and brandy into the legs of the lamb. It was worth the effort, for the effect was a very roasty, nearly caramelized outer coating, and a very juicy interior.

LOUISIANA CREOLE REGIONAL DINNER

Oysters Rockefeller

Crab Filé Gumbo

Chicken Breast with Ham Sauce Béarnaise

Ice According to the Whim of the Pastry Chef

Monterey Prawns Served in a Vol-au-Vent with an Herb Cream Sauce

Salad of Dandelions and Cabbage

Fresh Peach Ice Cream

Filbert Cookies with Black Coffee

We have used the various components of this menu many times over, particularly the Oysters Rockefeller. This regional celebration was also the beginning of a long series of gumbos at Chez Panisse, made in a lighter style than the traditional New Orleans gumbo.

The poultry dish consisted of a sautéed and boned chicken breast on a crouton spread with a *duxelles* made up partially of wild mushrooms; a slice of prosciutto was placed over the breast, then the entire dish was garnished with a piquant Béarnaise sauce.

NORTHERN CALIFORNIA REGIONAL DINNER

Tomales Bay Bluepoint Oysters on Ice
1973 Schramsberg Cuvée de Gamay

Cream of Fresh Corn Soup, Mendocino Style, with Crayfish Butter

Big Sur Garrapata Creek Smoked Trout Steamed over California Bay Leaves
1973 Mount Eden Chardonnay

Monterey Bay Prawns Sautéed with Garlic, Parsley, and Butter

Preserved California-Grown Geese from Sebastopol
1970 Beaulieu Cabernet Sauvignon, Private Reserve

Vela Dry Monterey Jack Cheese from Sonoma
1974 Ridge Fiddletown Zinfandel

Fresh Caramelized Figs
1974 Harbor Mission Del Sol

*Walnuts, Almonds, and Mountain Pears from the San Francisco
Farmers' Market*

This regional dinner, conceived and prepared by Jeremiah Tower, marked a turning point in the restaurant's focus. This was the first time we made a really concerted effort to serve the ingredients available to us here in the Northern California area, and it truly set a precedent which has been followed since then. It was an extremely well composed and executed meal, and was successful from the point of the reception it received. I can say that with some authority, since I actually sat in the dining room and ate this meal, a rare experience for me at my own restaurant!

PÉRIGORD REGIONAL DINNER

Pâté of Carp and Foie Gras

Soup of Fresh Sorrel and Parsley

Ragoût of Goose with Morels

Walnut and Chicory Salad

Caramelized Chestnut Cake with a Rum Cream and Nuts

Again, this was a menu which involved wonderful ideas for a dinner, but which was extremely difficult to prepare for a large number of people. When we began cooking, we had only the vaguest idea of what a carp stuffed with foie gras might be! As I recall, we were not able to get either the carp or the foie gras!

A CHAMPAGNE DINNER

White Sausage of Rabbit Breaded and Grilled

Fresh Trout Poached in Champagne

Sweetbreads in a Brioche Pastry with a Champagne Sauce

Salad with Various Fresh Greens

Special Cheeses from the Champagne Region of France

Fresh Comice Pear and Black Currant Sherbets

This was a remarkable dinner from the customers' point of view, for we have often been asked to repeat this menu. At the time of the original dinner, I believe that its appeal was related to a certain complexity of the menu as well as a genuine richness of flavor that was balanced by the champagne so as not to overwhelm. I well remember the two wonderful sherbets at the meal's end: we had managed to find some black currants and there were bits of peel in the sherbet; the other one was a Comice pear sherbet which was splendid when combined with the black currant. It seems a trite pairing, but the two flavors are truly delicious together.

THE BANDOL WINE DINNER
(A Celebration of the Arrival of the 1971 Vintage from Domaine Tempier)

Fresh Delicacies from the Sea

A Bouillabaisse of Salt Cod Made with Garlic, White Wine, Tomatoes, Onions, Potatoes, Fresh Basil, Orange Rind, Olive Oil, and Fish Broth
1973 Bandol, Domaine Tempier

Fresh Quail Roasted Provençal Style with Branches of Fresh Thyme and Olive Oil Served with Wild Rice and Fresh Peas
1971 Bandol, Domaine Tempier, Cuvée Speciale
1972 Bandol, Domaine Tempier

Goat Cheeses from the South of France
1974 Bandol, Domaine Tempier

Figs Cooked with Honey and Bandol Wine Served with Crème Fraîche

This menu was composed to celebrate the arrival of the 1971 vintage of the Domaine Tempier wines. The look of the wild rice with the tiny green peas was a wonderful accompaniment to the quail. It was at this meal that we decided that crème fraîche is ideally suited for serving with stewed figs.

A "MAS DES SERRES" MENU

Spiced Veal and Chicken Sausage Served with Sorrel Purée

Slices of Duck Breast Served with a Fresh Peppercorn Sauce and Brown Potatoes

Provençal Mélange of Lettuces with a Berry Vinaigrette

Wild Honey Ice Cream

This menu was inspired by Mas des Serres, a restaurant just outside of St. Paul de Vence which is no longer in existence. On my last visit there, I was enchanted by the honey ice cream made from the lavender on the property, and tried to duplicate it at Chez Panisse. Mas des Serres was a very small and highly personal restaurant which I shall long remember.

A SAUTERNES DINNER

Culpepper, Virginia Ham Braised in Sauternes and Served with Prunes
Stuffed with Green Olives
1947 Château Caillou

Quenelles of Salmon with Crayfish Butter Sauce
1949 Château Climens
1949 Château Doisy-Daëne

Entrecôte of Beef Served with Potatoes Cooked in Butter and
Duck Fat with Mushrooms
1955, 1967 Château d'Yquem

Green Apples Filled with Berries and Served with Crème Fraîche
1959 Château Guiraud

Hot Deep-Dish Fruit Pie
1959 Château Suduiraut

Almond Cream Dessert
1922 Château d'Yquem

Caramelized Walnuts and Coffee

Jeremiah Tower's brilliant pairing of the entrecôte of beef with the Château d'Yquem resulted in a combination that married in an indescribably wonderful manner. And the sensation created by pairing the saltiness of the ham with the clean, light flavors of the Barsac, Château Caillou, was not one of overwhelming sweetness, but a perfectly balanced harmony. The entire concept of a meal with which one drinks Sauternes throughout is revolutionary in concept, but magnificent in effect.

A SOUTHERN RHÔNE DINNER

Tiny Grass Shrimp Cooked with Butter and Fresh Thyme
1978 Château du Trignon Côtes-du-Rhône Blanc

Fresh Anchovies Wrapped in Grape Leaves and Charcoal-Grilled
1977 Châteauneuf-du-Pape Blanc, Domaine du Vieux Télégraphe

Rabbit Liver and Garlic Mousse on a Crouton
1976 Lirac Rouge, Berard et Fils

*Young Rabbit Baked in a Sealed Crock with 40 Cloves of Garlic, Fresh
Rosemary, and Olive Oil*
1971 Châteauneuf-du-Pape, Domaine Beaurenard

Regional Cheeses and Fresh Fruit

This dinner was designed around the wines which Kermit Lynch imported
into this country, so we decided to do this rabbit variation on the chicken
recipe in Richard Olney's *Simple French Food.* Provençal food needs Provençal wines. When looking for the right wine to serve with a specific plate,
think regionally. I recall that the wines worked extremely well with the
foods.

A DINNER FOR THE BAUDELAIRIANS

*Le Crépuscule du Soir: Puff Pastry Filled with Black Caviar, Poached Quail
Eggs, and Cream*

Rêve Parisien: Timbale of Duck Liver with Black Pepper Aspic

Le Mort Joyeux: Whole Roast Stuffed Pigeon with Black Mushrooms

Les Bijoux: Salad of Endive and Pink Grapefruit

Les Promesses d'un Visage: Ice Creams with Sauces and Caramel

A society involved with the works of Charles Pierre Baudelaire, the
French poet, asked us to plan a Baudelairian dinner for them. After rereading
his poems, I wasn't quite sure what that might be, but I decided to use the
names of his poems and imagine what dish they might represent. We left the
head on the pigeon and served it on a platter so that it looked rather dead
with lots of black mushrooms surrounding it, and that was the "joyful dead."
I tried to make the salad resemble sparkling jewels, so that is why I chose
the pink grapefruit.

THE "THIS AIN'T NO SPRING CHICKEN" DINNER

Brain Fritters with Seville Oranges

Grilled Quail with Rosemary

Blanquette d'Agneau

Roast Baron of Spring Lamb

Salad of Garden Herbs and Lettuces

Canestraletti

We catered this dinner in Sacramento at Darrell Corti's home for his birthday celebration. I wanted to do the brain fritters with Seville oranges, but the reality of no Seville oranges necessitated doing them with a mixture of lemon and orange in which we marinated them, then rolled them in a little flour, and deep-fried them. The blanquette of spring lamb, a dish Darrell dreamed up, was amazingly good.

DINNER FOR LA FEMME DU BOULANGER

Garlic Mayonnaise Served with Radishes, Fresh Snails, and Cauliflower

Provençal Terrine Made with Pork, Rabbit, and Fresh Herbs

Fresh Rockfish Grilled over Vine Branches and Served with Fried Onions and Lemon

A Long-Simmered Beef Daube Made with Red Wine, Garlic, and Vegetables and Served with Pasta with Three Cheeses

Goat Cheeses

Fresh Fruits

In conjunction with the Pacific Film Archive's showing of Marcel Pagnol's film *La Femme du Boulanger,* we tried to select dishes for this menu that Pagnol himself might have eaten during the shooting, as recalled by Charles Blavette's *Ma Provence en Cuisine.* We discovered that it is very difficult to make the beef daube in large quantities; I think it would be wonderful made in small crocks for a limited number of guests.

DINNER OF FLOWERS

Artichokes Served with a Mustard-Flower Vinaigrette

Cream of Cauliflower Soup Garnished with Fresh Chervil and Parsley

Spit-Roasted Duck Served with Croutons Glazed with Quince Jelly and a Red Wine Duck Essence Sauce

Salad with Rocket Flowers and Violets

Fresh Fruits

Plum Blossom Ice Cream

This dinner was essentially an amusement for the flower shop around the corner from Chez Panisse which provides all the fresh flowers for the restaurant. I do believe we collected the plum blossoms from all the trees in Berkeley to make the ice cream!

A DINNER FOR OUR FRIENDS AT RIDGE

1971 Deutz Champagne, Cuvée William Deutz

Charcoal-Grilled Fish and Shellfish Served with a Ridge Wine Butter
1979 Ridge Monte Bello Chardonnay

Madeleine Kamman–Inspired Cabbage Soup with Roquefort Cheese
1973 Ridge Langtry Road Zinfandel
1973 Ridge Lytton Springs Zinfandel

Roast Leg of Suckling Pig Served with Wild Mushroom Pasta
1971, 1972, 1975 Ridge Monte Bello Cabernet Sauvignon
1971, 1972, 1975 Château Latour

Cheeses and Fresh Fruits

Dessert
1959 Château Suduiraut

The especially delicious part of this menu was the cabbage soup, which
we made with savoy cabbage; it was a rich cabbage soup, which we served
with grilled bread spread with Roquefort cheese, which, in combination with
the chosen wines, created a wonderful pairing of flavors.

SPECIALTIES FROM TOURRETTES FEATURING WINES FROM BANDOL

Little Tartlets Filled with Artichoke Purée and Onions, Tomatoes, and Olives

Pot of Bouillabaisse Cooked with Fresh Fish and Shellfish, Fennel, and Tomatoes, and Served with a Rouille

Chicken Stuffed under the Skin with a Garlic and Parsley Butter

Salad of Mesclun, Bitter Greens as Served in Nice, and Cheeses

Anise Soufflé

Fresh Fruits

This particular evening's menu was for the birthday of a friend who lived near Tourrettes in the south of France, so I decided to compose a menu of food from that exact spot. Since violets are raised in profusion in that area, we candied some for the anise soufflé.

AN INSPIRATION FROM RESTAURANT LUTÈCE

Sautéed Duck Livers and Sweetbreads Served with a Rocket Salad

Poached Salmon Served on a Bed of Onions and Scallions with a Beurre Blanc with Rose Peppercorns

Sautéed Loin of Lamb with Mustard Seeds Served with a Julienne of Carrots and Beans

Cheeses

Special Baked Fruits

This was an interesting menu to prepare because we had no idea how the dishes I enjoyed at Lutèce had been cooked. I was just guessing, so in the recipe for the lamb with mustard seeds, we sautéed the loins, then rolled them in mustard seeds, and then baked them in the oven just until cooked through. The mustard seeds added a very nice little crunch on the outside of the already trimmed loin. The duck livers and sweetbreads were a little difficult to accomplish because of the necessity for sautéeing them and having them ready simultaneously.

WE'RE GOING ON VACATION DINNER

Jay's Tomato Salad

White Corn on the Cob

Steamed Tomales Bay Mussels Served with Garlic Bread

Charcoal-Grilled Cajun Hot Sausage with Potato Salad

Homemade Ice Cream

The night before we closed the restaurant for a vacation of several weeks, we decided to prepare a meal we felt like eating—and hoped the public would feel like eating it, too! This particular menu happened to coincide with the visit of a French restaurant critic. In the midst of the meal I realized that the Cajun hot sausages were so hot I couldn't eat more than two bites of them, and I had nothing else to serve to our visitors. They truly did grin and bear it, but on the way out, their only comment was that it was all wonderful, but were the sausages supposed to be like that?!

BACK TO NEW ORLEANS FOR YOUR BIRTHDAY
(Celebrating the Birthday of David Goines)

Looziana-Style Boudin Blanc with Pickled Zucchini

Bleu Crab and Corn Bisque

Charcoal-Grilled Filet of Boeuf with Sauz Debris

Green Salad with Basil

Fresh Pêche Ice Creme

I had just been to New York, where I met Paul Prudhomme for the first time, and he cooked a special dinner there with the beef and the debris sauce. It was so fantastic that I asked him for the recipe. Right in the middle of preparing it at Chez Panisse, we had to call up Paul in New Orleans because the process seemed so unlikely: leaving the vegetables and the bones for the debris sauce in the oven until they are smoking and black! He assured us we were doing it the correct way!

A SPECIAL EVENT TO CELEBRATE ALLIUM SATIVUM, FILM, MUSIC, AND AND THE VERNAL EQUINOX

Galantines of Pigeon, Duck, and Quail, Filled with Layers of Meats, Livers, and Garlic Mosaics

Whole Baked Fish Served with a Garlic Puff Pastry and Lobster Butter Sauce

Spring Lamb with Three Garlic-Infused Vegetable Purées

Rocket Salad with Goose-Fat and Garlic-Rubbed Croutons

Poached Figs in Red Wine with Garlic-Shaped Meringues

It wasn't easy to plan an extravagant garlic dinner that would warrant the $100 price of each seat at this benefit, so we dreamed up the galantines in aspic as a special dish. They really took weeks to prepare. In the end, I think we may have missed the real point because the meal itself was almost too elaborate for the peasant appeal of garlic.

DINNER FOR A WINE TASTING

Oysters and Truffle Sausages
1966 Dom Ruinart Blanc de Blancs
1966 Taittinger Blanc de Blancs

Tart Filled with Fresh Sorrel, Cream, and Onions
1971, 1973 Chalone Pinot Blanc

Roast Duck Served with Duck Livers Sautéed with Grapes and a Rich Red Wine Sauce
1945, 1953, 1955, 1961 Château Calon-Ségur

Roquefort Cheese
1953 Chapelle-Chambertin, Pierre Ponnelle
1964 Martin Ray Pinot Noir

Blancmange
1959 Château Suduiraut

Coffee
1963 Sandeman Vintage Port, Avery's

The blancmange featured in this menu was the very first we ever made at Chez Panisse, but it was certainly worth the effort. As Richard Olney says, blancmange is the absolute perfect accompaniment for Sauternes.

A CHEF'S FÊTE

Seasonal Salad

Charcoal-Grilled Live Maine Lobster with a Lobster Butter

Fresh Pasta Served with a Sauce of Roast Squab and Squab Essences

Cheeses

Tangerines and Grapes

Homemade Ice Creams and Ices

This meal was prepared for a well-known chef who was coming from Paris. I was so intimidated by the idea of having him to dinner that we tried to choose the most predictable and vague menu, in case we needed to cover a multitude of errors. Everything went wrong that night: we undercooked the lobster in an effort not to overcook it—this was easy to do because it was underneath the seaweed on the grill, so it was difficult to tell when it was done. We then should have taken all the squab meat off the bones to toss with the sauce at the last minute, but I loved the look of the little birds on the pasta, so I compromised and the result was that the components didn't marry as well as they should have. However, when we repeated the dish later, we tossed the rare squab meat together with the rich sauce and then tossed in the pasta—it was splendid!

A DINNER TO HONOR THE WINES OF CHÂTEAUNEUF-DU-PAPE

Plateau de Coquillages
1978 Domaine du Vieux Télégraphe Blanc

Saucisse de Langue de Boeuf Farci aux Truffes
1977 Domaine du Vieux Télégraphe

Agneau de Lait Rôti
1974, 1976 Domaine de Beaurenard

Salade de Mesclun

Plateau des Fromages
1972 Domaine du Vieux Télégraphe

Gâteau Soufflé aux Pistaches
Muscat de Beaumes de Venise: Domaine de Durban

Richard Olney proposed the menu for this dinner. It included a complicated, reworded recipe for tongue from an old French cookbook which he described in great detail for us. I would say not only that it was the great success of the dinner, but that it was a perfect marriage with the wine chosen, the 1977 Domaine du Vieux Télégraphe.

SALVADOR DALI DISHES: AN EXOTIC DINNER FOR AN EXOTIC FRIEND

Leeks Baked in a Brioche Pastry

Jellied Salt Cod with Olives, Tarragon, and Garlic Served with a Sauce

Leg of Suckling Pig Marinated and Roasted and Served with Three Vegetable Purées

Cheeses and Fresh Fruits

We had such fun preparing this dinner! The pictures and recipes in Salvador Dali's *Les Dîners de Gala* leave a lot of room for adaptation and inspiration. We were not exactly certain how the salt cod had been intended, but our jelly didn't set in large quantities—it melted as soon as it hit the plates, but we had to serve it, anyway!

DINNER FOR A TRIPLE SCORPIO

An Array of Shellfish, Including Lobster, Grilled and Served with
Various Sauces
1973 Chalone Chardonnay
1973 Mount Eden Chardonnay

Special Small Salads of Warm Duck and Wild Cabbage

Entrecôte of Beef Baked in Rock Salt and Served with a Garlic, Anchovy, and
Olive Sauce
1957, 1961, 1964, 1967, 1970, 1975 Château Montrose

Cheeses and Fresh Fruits
1962 Charmes–Chambertin, Drouhin

Vacherin
1945 Château Lafaurie-Peyraguey

This was a birthday dinner for someone who eats at the restaurant every week, so we wanted to select dishes that were extremely esoteric but appealing. This dinner was composed of dark, savory flavors to appeal to the nature of a Scorpio.

NEW YEAR'S EVE 1980

Soufflé d'Oursins aux Caviar

Foie Gras en Gelée Michel Guérard

Timbale de Fruits de Mer

Rôti d'Oie aux Truffes

Salade de Mâche

Les Fromages

Bavarois Rubane

I loved the concept of this meal, for we had planned to decorate the dining room in an elegant turn-of-the-century fashion and compose a dinner to match. Jean-Pierre Moullé, the chef, had planned on having sea urchins as the first course, but ended up with baked oysters with a champagne butter. For the goose, he prepared the breast as a confit and the legs were roasted. He also had a wonderful fantasy about having frog's legs as the third course, and after calling all over Chinatown, we discovered that the ponds were frozen, so no one would go out collecting them. We wanted to use only the fresh, no frozen, but we could only manage to find about three frogs at an exorbitant price, so we changed the menu to accommodate what we could find!

CHÂTEAU L'EVANGILE DINNER

Fresh Oysters Wrapped in Spinach Leaves and Served with a Butter and
Yellow Caviar Sauce
1975 Chablis, Les Clos, Charton
1975 Chablis, Louis Max

Sautéed Duck Breast and Liver Served with Pommes Anna

Charcoal-Grilled Duck Leg Served with a Garden Lettuce Salad
1953, 1955, 1961, 1964, 1966 Château L'Evangile

Regional Cheeses
1959 Richebourg, Avery

Granita of Red Wine

Friends of the restaurant had a lovely selection of these wines. Since
Château L'Evangile happened to be a favorite of the chef's, we tried to think
of a menu that would complement the wines. The granita, made with a
Pomerol, proved once again that the wine you choose to cook with is very
important because, in this case, the use of that particular wine made a great
difference in the taste of the granita and provided a perfect finish to the meal.

A TROISGROS-INSPIRED DINNER

Layered Crêpe Cake Filled with Gruyère Cheese and Two Hams
with Cream

Ragoût of Six Fresh Fish with Fish Fumet, *White Wine, and Various*
Vegetables

Tenderloins of Veal Braised with White Wine, Pearl Onions, Salsify,
and Bacon

Salad

Fresh Fruits

This is one dinner from an entire week of menus using recipes that we had adapted from Pierre and Jean Troisgros. Unfortunately, I chose three overly complicated dishes for one evening's menu, so it was practically impossible for us to assemble the eight layers of the crepaze, the crêpe cake, as well as to cook to order the six separate types of fish, each with a different cooking time, not to mention the tenderloins of veal, which had to be carefully braised, and the pearl onions, which it took all night to peel! Any one of the dishes would have been sufficient in one dinner.

ZINFANDEL WEEK CHEZ PANISSE

Family-style dinner including a half-bottle of Nouveau Zinfandel made especially for Chez Panisse from 100 percent Napa Valley Zinfandel grapes by Walter Schug of Joseph Phelps Winery

TUESDAY:

Marinated Squid with Roasted Green and Red Peppers
Entrecôte Steak Grilled over the Grape Vine Branches, Served with a Sauce of Zinfandel with Shallots
Romaine Lettuce Salad with Anchovies and Croutons

WEDNESDAY:

Various Special Charcuterie, and Cardoons Served with Poached Marrow
Coq au Zinfandel—a Rich Chicken Dish Cooked with Zinfandel, Bacon, Mushrooms, and Pearl Onions, Served with Garlic Croutons
Spinach and Butter Lettuce with a Sieved-Egg Garnish

THURSDAY:

Duck Livers Sautéed with Sherry Vinegar and Walnut Oil, Shallots, and Parsley
Truffled Cervelas Sausage Poached in Zinfandel, Served with Braised Leeks and Potatoes
Chicory Lettuce Salad with Garlic Croutons

FRIDAY:

Mushrooms Stewed with Zinfandel, Garlic, and Olive Oil
A Confit of Duck, Served with a Flageolet Gratin
Various Lettuces with a Roquefort Cheese and Cream Dressing

SATURDAY:

French Onion Soup Gratinée with Croutons
Roast Suckling Pig from the Dal Porto Ranch Stuffed with Apples and Specially Prepared Fresh Sausages
Walnut, Watercress, and Belgian Endive Salad

This was a very successful week of straightforward, savory dishes that went very well with the fruity Zinfandel Nouveau. These were intended to be Paris bistro-style menus. My personal favorite was the meal with duck livers in sherry vinegar with walnut oil, and the truffled sausage poached in Zinfandel, with leeks and potatoes and chicory lettuce salad. This was a menu that was based on a dinner a friend cooked for me with whole foie gras and truffled sausages he had brought from Paris.

1979 NOUVEAU ZINFANDEL WEEK

TUESDAY:

Beef Marrow on Warm Toasts
Fresh Dungeness Crab Sautéed with Scallions and Spices
*Chicken poached with *Kunpods* (Bacon Dumplings) and Wild Mushrooms
Green Salad or Cheese
Fruits and Nuts

WEDNESDAY:

*Conserve of Wild Mushrooms
*Oysters Cooked with Muscadet and Fennel Butter
Cassoulet
Green Salad or Cheese
Fruits and Nuts

THURSDAY:

Charcoal-Grilled Leeks served with a Mustard Vinaigrette
Alpine Cheese Soufflé
Lamb Shanks Simmered with Provençal Herbs and Red Wine
Green Salad or Cheese
Fruits and Nuts

FRIDAY:

*Terrine of Rabbit with Hazelnuts and Chartreuse
  Warm Spinach Salad with Bacon and Garlic Croutons
*Charcoal-Grilled Filet of Beef Marinated to Taste like Venison
  Cheese
  Fruits and Nuts

SATURDAY:

Buckwheat Crêpes Filled with Wild Mushrooms
Charcoal-Grilled Fresh Fish with a Zinfandel Butter and Sorrel
*Oxtails Browned, Braised, and Served with a Five-Onion Sauce
Green Salad or Cheese
Fruits and Nuts

For the 1979 Zinfandel Festival the earthy and unusual dishes from Madeleine Kamman's special book *When French Women Cook* came to mind (here indicated with an asterisk). The most memorable dishes were the bacon dumplings (which we ended up making like soft *gougères* with bacon in them) and the oxtail stew (all the onion flavors in the five-onion sauce married perfectly). But we had great difficulty adjusting the proportions of the rabbit and hazelnut pâté recipe to make ten pâtés. Even more than most dishes, pâtés are best made one at a time, with great care.

NOTES ON INGREDIENTS

๑

CAVIAR

Fresh, lightly salted caviar is best, with the exception of Russian Beluga and pressed Russian caviar. California black caviar can be good in quality, but it is illegal to sell. The golden whitefish caviar from the Great Lakes has tiny eggs and is very good if not too old or soupy from defrosting.

Caviar should be slightly crunchy, and should never be sticky or gooey, with the obvious exception of pressed caviar, which is sticky by nature. The eggs should be clearly whole and separate, shiny, and should never have a fishy smell. Instead, good fresh caviar will taste of the sea in the same way that a good fresh oyster does, slightly salty and sweet. Salmon-egg caviar can be very easily made at home, and is especially good when freshly made.

FISH AND SHELLFISH

A truly fresh fish is one that has just been caught that day. It is important to know precisely how many hours the fish has been out of water, so search out a reliable and honest fish merchant. A fresh fish has bright-pink or red gills, clear eyes, a shiny appearance, a fresh clean aroma, and signs of rigor mortis. Unfortunately, fish may be kept fairly fresh-looking on ice for nearly a week, but the sparkle of fresh fish fades within a day. For these recipes, choose a fish for its freshness only and make substitutions when necessary.

Most fish change when they mature. In California, the salmon season is from mid-April to September. While the champagne-pink–colored fish with the silky texture are easily cooked in the spring, as the fish goes upstream later on in the season, it undergoes changes: the flesh appears more orange and the proper cooking of the salmon is more difficult. In the later season, it poses problems with cooking because it progresses very quickly from a raw to an overcooked state. Therefore, we poach the salmon in the spring, and tend to charcoal-grill it as the fish changes later in the season. Watch for similar changes in other fish.

The Dungeness crab season begins in October and lasts until March, but the crab changes as it goes through its seasonal cycle. It tastes best in the fall and through Christmas. Like other shellfish stored in tanks, it can change its flavor if it is kept too long outside its natural environment. Look for a hard shell and a heavy weight for its size.

Crayfish from the Sacramento River Delta are available on the West Coast from May until October. They will stay alive in burlap sacks with ice on top for several days, but the flavor changes and the crayfish may well eat the burlap sack they're stored in—or each other.

Live Maine lobsters are available during most of the year. We have found that the 2½-pound lobster is an ideal size, although the small 1-pound chicken lobsters are milder and less expensive. The lobster must be alive and kicking, the more the better. Spiny lobster *(langouste)* or Mexican West Coast lobster has a different and less rich taste than the Maine variety. These should always be purchased alive, a difficult thing to accomplish, since most are cooked immediately.

It is necessary to be extremely critical about mussels and clams. They are unpredictable in their tenderness, sandiness, and flavor. Good mussels and clams are usually a result of the combination of a good variety, a good fish source, and a certain degree of luck.

Oysters right from the water, eaten that same day, are ones that shrink back when opened and sparkle irresistibly. Oysters should be stored flat, with the top side up so that the liquid inside does not spill out, as this will eventually kill the shellfish. We are finding new varieties of oysters on the West Coast from the experiments at the Pigeon Point Shellfish Company.

There are many kinds of rockfish (striped bass in the East). Locally they are all called "Pacific red snapper," but they differ greatly in flavor and texture. The most widely available is the boccacio; it has soft white flesh with little flavor. The ones to look for are the fantailed rockfish, the black rockfish, the yellowtail, and the bolina, prized by the Chinese.

Familiarity with local fish and fishermen will provide the best fish on any coast.

MEATS

It is vitally important to your cooking that you always search out unadulterated meats that have been aged and stored correctly, as well as butchered properly and economically. We have been fortunate in finding farmers who have agreed to raise various animals for the restaurant. The taste of the animals raised to our specifications is remarkable, and the store-bought meats can in no way compare to these. Veal from calves that have neither been formula-fed nor received hormone injections is virtually impossible to find.

In referring to spring lamb, we are talking about a lamb whose live weight is approximately 55 pounds, and whose dressed weight with the head is about 25 pounds. Spring lambs are available in late February through April. The flesh is light in color, and there is very little fat, so little that it is not really necessary to trim the animal before cooking. The kidneys and livers have an especially delicate flavor. The neck and shoulder are tender and extremely flavorful. The lambs should be hung for at least 4 days before cooking, and can be held for 8 or 10 days. One spring lamb serves 25 to 30 people, if all parts of the lamb are used.

We have found that suckling pigs whose dressed weight is between 20 and 25 pounds have the same succulence and appealing texture as true suckling pigs that weigh only 10 to 15 pounds. The older, partially grain-fed pig has even more flavor, and it is possible to crisp the skin more easily. The larger animal is approximately 2½ feet in length, including the head. The kidneys are about 2 inches long and 1½ inches wide and have an incomparable flavor. The larger pig should serve 15 to 20 people. You should be able to order a fresh pig of approximately 30 pounds in Chinatown at most times of the year.

It is best to make sausages rather than purchase them. It is also better to buy salt-cured meats, like prosciutto, rather than the chemical-preservative–cured type.

INNARDS

Innards vary in size, shape, and even taste, from animal to animal of the same type. With the exception of liver, we have always had difficulty finding a source for fresh, not frozen innards.

Good fresh livers are shiny-looking with red blood that is firm and unclouded. Squab liver seems to have the most delicate and interesting flavor, but duck livers are readily available from Chinese poultry stores. The livers from suckling pig and spring lamb are exceptionally flavorful, as are those from any young, properly raised and fed animal. Any of the livers can be soaked overnight in milk to keep them fresh. Partially cooked foie gras in a block is being flown from France to the United States. It has a delicious flavor and texture, but should be used quickly. Avoid all tinned foie gras products.

Veal kidneys are most likely to be available fresh in butcher shops where they slaughter their own animals. The kidneys should be used quickly and trimmed completely before cooking. Lamb kidneys should be available with the whole loin, and they may be kept fresh in the fat until needed.

FATS

Rendering fats from the meats and poultry used in these recipes is a useful and tasty alternative to purchasing them from a delicatessen or specialty shop. At the restaurant we have found duck and goose fat to be the most successful and useful.

Goose fat is absolutely exceptionally flavored when fresh. It is difficult to find, but small, very expensive tins of it are often available in specialty stores and delicatessens. Regrettably, much of it in tins is slightly rancid. This fat should be enticing and inviting to the nose and the palate; if it isn't sweet and aromatic, it is probably old or has been improperly stored. Tinned goose fat arrives from France in the fall, so it is wise to purchase it then and store it in the refrigerator until needed.

POULTRY AND GAME BIRDS

In trying to obtain flavorful poultry and game, you are confronted with a number of obstacles: the limited number of available varieties and the difficulty of finding birds that have been raised on the right healthful food-stuffs without the use of hormones. A proper diet ensures the development of the flavor and texture unique to that particular bird.

Organically raised chickens are good, but the usual supermarket chicken needs a multitude of cooking disguises. For this reason, we use very little chicken at Chez Panisse.

We buy ducks from the Chinatown markets, as they seem to be the only ones available fresh. They do tend to have lean meat, with excessive subcutaneous fat deposits. Squab are also available in Chinatown and are of good quality.

A good goose is one from a good breed and good stock. We seem to be able to find good fresh geese only at Christmas time and in the late fall.

In the last few years various companies have cropped up that have been able to supply us with quail and other game birds on a regular basis. While their flavor is not remarkable, they do provide us with a certain variety.

DAIRY PRODUCTS

With the exception of a few pastry recipes, we use unsalted butter exclusively at Chez Panisse. I believe that it allows the flavors of the food to appear; salt can always be added later if necessary. Salted butter tends to be more watery and to have a lower butterfat content. Sweet butter must be kept frozen until ready for use, for in just one day its flavor can change. Even if it has not become rancid, it will lack the sweet freshness it should have. There are small dairy farms that can supply higher-quality products in limited quantities, and these are often preferable to the ultrapasteurized supermarket stock; it would be worth your while to investigate the available brands in your area. French butter, particularly butter from Normandy, is beginning to appear in some specialty shops. It has an unusually appealing flavor, but you must be cautious in purchasing it, for it can frequently arrive tasting a little old, even if it has been frozen. When sweet butter isn't perfect and sweet, it's a good idea to clarify it. Clarified sweet butter is excellent for use as a covering for crocks of pâté or for frying.

Investigate the available types of cream to determine which have added stabilizers so that you can avoid using them. These stabilizers prevent spoilage, and allow the cream to be used for an inordinately long period of time, long past the point when it should have been discarded because it no longer tastes fresh and sweet. Creams with a high water content can cause problems in cooking; creams with a high butterfat content are much preferable.

TRUFFLES

There is simply no substitute for fresh truffles. They should be used as close as possible to the time they are plucked from the ground. When truffles are canned or frozen, the texture changes completely, and the flavors are different. It is possible to use these truffles to make a truffle infusion with Madeira or Cognac to be used in a sauce, but you will not get the genuine truffle flavor.

It is important to examine each fresh truffle before you purchase them. They should be very firm, whole, and free of holes, which speed deterioration. The quality of fresh truffles seems to depend largely on where they come from and the pungency of the particular harvest—a factor that changes from year to year—rather than the size of the truffles themselves.

Fresh truffles are extremely perishable and dislike changes in temperature and environment. We have found that it is better to store the fresh truffles the way the store does from which they are purchased. This usually means that they are wrapped individually in cloth, then sealed in a container and kept in a cool spot, or buried in dry rice in a container and kept at wine-cellar temperature. They should be stored separated from one another. Considering the travel time from Europe, fresh truffles may remain fresh for only a few days or they may last for over a week, but they should be eaten as soon as possible after their arrival.

Black truffles seem to last a bit longer than fresh white truffles. We have found that the most successful way of using them is with eggs or potatoes, and they are more aromatic when cooked slightly. Fresh black truffles are available twice a year, just before Christmas and at the end of January. The best way of storing them is to wrap them individually in paper towels and then store them in a cool place; change the paper towels every few hours, as they absorb the moisture, preventing it from getting to the truffles and making them slippery and damp.

White truffles are brought in from Italy and are extremely perishable. They are available from early October through early January. Fresh white truffles should be sliced thin (I recommend a potato peeler) and served raw. These are best stored in rice, a method that also perfumes the rice.

Minute quantities of truffles are found along the Gulf Coast in Texas. The *Tuber texense* is very similar to the white summer truffle, *Tuber aestivum,* and seems to become more aromatic each year. They keep best in the dirt in which they were found, in a sealed container in the wine cellar.

RICE

After many experiments with rice, we have discovered that the most delicious rice dishes demand the use of Arborio rice from Italy, available in Italian delicatessens, or the perfumed Indian Basmati rice. Both are expensive, but well worth the investment.

VEGETABLES AND FRUITS

The best way to find high-quality fruits and vegetables with a genuine intensity of flavor is to grow your own. The cultivation of a small plot of ground, or containers on an apartment porch, or even a few clay pots has become a virtual necessity for good cooking. Our chef, Jean-Pierre Moullé, has helped us realize a major goal of the restaurant by planning, landscaping, planting, and caring for a garden of our own, which is located in the sharply sloping backyard of a couple who frequently eat at the restaurant. The effect on our menus has been astonishing, and we are no longer completely at the mercy of the wholesale produce suppliers.

The main Chez Panisse garden is terraced in an asymmetrical area, approximately 75 feet wide by 90 feet in length, and is perched on a 27-degree slope high atop the Berkeley hills. Because of the garden's location in a microclimate, the summer temperature is ten degrees higher than in the rest of the city, while the winter temperature is about ten degrees cooler. But whatever the particular topography or climate, it is possible to plan a garden and adapt it to a unique situation. And it is amazing to see how much produce can emerge from even a very small garden area.

In the Chez Panisse garden, terraced beds of herbs, vegetables, and flowers, interspersed with fruit trees, are connected by a winding pathway bordered with granite rocks and flowers. The garden is drip-irrigated and has a full southwestern exposure. The crops in each bed are rotated; however, all the beds are allowed to rest for several weeks between crops while compost is turned into the soil before any replanting is done. We maintain compost piles with organic garbage from the restaurant, such as outer lettuce leaves, which might otherwise be discarded.

Since the garden was first planted only in March of 1980, it hardly seems possible that we have gathered such lavish harvests of unusual lettuces and herbs such as French tarragon, three kinds of sage, chervil, lemon and English thyme, angelica, red basis, burnet, flat-leaf Italian parsley, lovage, hyssop, winter savory, and borage. In the future we hope to harvest tiny *fraises des bois,* berries for the tarts, yellow tomatoes for salads, and perhaps thin French green beans. Two other Berkeley gardens cultivated by our cooks supplement our main one, and friends in Napa and Sacramento, Marin, and the Chino Ranch in Solano Beach sometimes supply us with excellent organically grown produce. A good source of unusual vegetable and herb seeds is the J. A. Demonchaux Company, 225 Jackson Street, Topeka, Kansas 66603.

OIL

It is somewhat difficult to select and store oil correctly: it requires a cool place and a tight stopper or cap at all times. Because most varieties are adversely affected by heat or extremely long storage, you will often find that the oil on store shelves is slightly rancid because it has not been restocked and rotated frequently enough. Walnut and hazelnut oils are pressed in the fall, and ideally should be used shortly after that time. Because there has been a decrease in interest in picking olives and producing superior oil, the supply and quality of olive oil continue to diminish, while the price continues to rise. After you open oil, you should store it in a cool place. Good oil has a clean, fruity aroma and a pleasantly fruity flavor with no off or waxy aftertastes.

There are a number of different grades of olive oil. Oil classified as extra virgin or virgin oil is extracted by mechanical means only, and no heat or chemicals are used. The fruit is first mashed to a paste, then hydraulically pressed, and the oil and water are centrifugally separated. Extra virgin olive oil contains less than 1 percent oleic acidity. (The finest olive oils are those with the lowest oleic acidity, as acidity is an index of spoilage.) At Chez Panisse we prefer Puget extra virgin olive oil; although none of the Puget oils blend well with lemon for vinaigrettes, we find that they are good with garlic. It is a generally available oil, in both extra virgin and virgin grades; if it is not available, use one of the Italian virgin oils. Especially good olive oils often have a greenish cast.

We also use the Olio Extra Vergine d'Oliva della Fattoria de Santa Cristina from the Antinori Chianti estate of the same name. This oil changes from year to year, and its quality is highly dependent on the quality of the olives each year. There is more variation here in the quality than with the French. A bitter or hot aftertaste is not unexpected. Most extra virgin olive oils are of high quality, but they do have different nuances, flavors, and colors. You can often find them in specialty wine shops.

I find that American olive oil is very inconsistent in quality and flavor. Most of the time it has a strong olive flavor that could overwhelm a dish.

Among Spanish olive oils, I prefer the Union, Sivrana extra virgin. It is difficult to find. While this oil does not have the finesse of the French and Italian extra virgin olive oil, it is a good all-purpose oil. (The Spanish extra virgin olive oil does have the lowest oleic acid content—less than ½ percent.)

The olive oil designated as "pure" is produced from successive pressings of the olives and from treatment of the olives with hot water to encourage release of the oil. This oil is often harsher-tasting, although light-bodied, and it may be used for blending. It is normally very light in color, but it lacks the finesse and sensual appeal of the finer oils. We do use Sasso Italian Pure Olive Oil because it tastes real and of olives. Other light oils may have off flavors and aftertastes. Watch for slight rancidity in this medium grade of olive oils.

VINEGAR

The best vinegar available is homemade from good wine. Vinegars available in most supermarkets are produced industrially and adulterated with old garlic and herbs. We use French vinegar (red wine and champagne), and bulk French wine vinegar. All are quite sharp and aged in wood. Many of the domestic wine vinegars are harsher and less flavorful, although you should investigate any local brands that might be acceptable.

Spanish sherry wine vinegars have a distinctive and special taste that marries well with nut oils and certain sauces. We use both La Bodega brand and Fernandez Old Sherry Wine Vinegar.

Aceto Balsamico is a very special vinegar from Modena, Italy. It is sweet and rich and blends well with most oils. There are different brands and makers, and each has his own formula for aging the vinegar between fifteen and twenty years. They are expensive, but well worth the investment.

Fruit vinegars can give an extremely special adjustment to sauces by providing the acidity of vinegar with the flavor of the fruit. They are expensive to purchase, but fragrant fruit and good quality wine vinegar can be combined, two parts fruit to one part vinegar, to produce an excellent fruit vinegar. Simply macerate the fruit and vinegar together, strain, bottle, and store.

STOCKS

Making stock daily is basic to the restaurant kitchen, so I feel it necessary to emphasize here the importance of fresh and well-made stocks to the dishes in this cookbook. At the restaurant we use a great many reductions of stock which produce a much deeper and more complex sauce by using an essence of the stock, and then perhaps whisking in some butter to bind at the end. I have learned that any stocks, these included, taste best when freshly made, so I would advise against freezing unless absolutely necessary. Far preferable to freezing is the technique of reducing the stocks to a *demi-glace,* and then refrigerating it. Fish stocks should be made fresh because they can begin to taste old overnight.

When making stock for these or any other recipes, you should use the various parts of the animal that you have cut off for the different dishes. If these parts are not fatty, and there is some bone there to provide the gelatinous quality needed, you can make a little *jus,* which could later be reduced and used in the sauce for the presentation, if you really feel the need for a sauce. If it appears that you will have no bones left over, then you will have to buy an extra little beast or bones to make the sauce. Thus, making a chicken reduction may require purchasing an extra chicken, unless you have been fortunate enough to have purchased one with head and legs intact. You can also make a little lamb *jus* in the same way you would for the birds. Pork trimmings, too, can be used, although I personally find them to be a bit on the strongly flavored side—with the exception of suckling-pig trimmings. For lamb stock we prefer white wine because red wine produces an overly assertive flavor.

BIBLIOGRAPHY

Adams, Charlotte, *The Four Seasons Cookbook*. New York: Holt, Rinehart and Winston, 1971.

Androuet, Pierre, *The Complete Encyclopedia of French Cheeses*. New York: Harper's Magazine Press, Harper and Row, 1973.

Araldo, Josephine, *Cooking with Josephine*. San Francisco: Strawberry Hill Press, 1977.

————, *Sounds from Josephine's Kitchen*. San Francisco: Strawberry Hill Press, 1978.

Baker, Charles, *The Esquire Culinary Companion*. New York: Crown, 1959.

Beard, James. *Delights and Prejudices*. London: Victor Gollancz, 1964.

————, *Menus for Entertaining*. New York: Delacorte, 1965.

————, *The New James Beard*. New York: Knopf, 1981.

La Belle France: A Gourmet's Guide to the French Provinces. Preface by André Maurois of the Académie Française. New York: Golden Press, 1964.

La Mère Besson, *Ma Cuisine Provençale*. Paris: Albin Michel, 1977.

Bianchini, F., and Corbetta, F. *The Complete Book of Fruits and Vegetables*. New York: Crown, 1975.

Biarnes, Monique, *La Cuisine Sénégalaise*. Dakar: Société Africaine d'Édition, 1972.

Blavette, Charles, *Ma Provence en Cuisine*. Paris: Éditions France Empire, 1961.

Boni, Ada, *Italian Regional Cooking*. New York: Bonanza Books, 1969.

Boulestin, X. Marcel, *Recipes of Boulestin*. New York: St. Martin's Press, 1971.

Brillat-Savarin, Jean-Anthelme, *The Physiology of Taste*. Translated by M.F.K. Fisher. New York: Knopf, 1971.

Broadbent, Michael, *The Great Vintage Wine Book*. New York: Knopf, 1980.

Brown, Edward Espe, *The Tassajara Bread Book*. Boulder, Colo.: Shambhala, 1970.

Bugialli, Giuliano, *The Fine Art of Italian Cooking*. New York: Times Books, 1977.

Castans, Raymond, *Il Était Une Fois . . . Marcel Pagnol*. Paris: Julliard, 1978.

Chapel, Alain, *La Cuisine C'est Beaucoup Plus que des Recettes*. Paris: Robert Laffont, 1978.

Chiang, Cecelia Sun Yun, *The Mandarin Way.* As told to Allan Carr. Boston: Atlantic Monthly Press Book, 1974.

Child, Julia, Bertholle, Louisette, and Beck, Simone, *Mastering the Art of French Cooking, Volume One.* New York: Knopf, 1961.

Child, Julia, and Beck, Simone, *Mastering the Art of French Cooking, Volume Two.* New York: Knopf, 1970.

Claiborne, Craig, *Craig Claiborne's Favorites from the New York Times.* New York: Times Books, 1978.

Conil, Jean, *Gastronomic Tour de France.* London: George Allen and Unwin, 1959.

Courtine, Robert, *Feasts of a Militant Gastronome.* New York: William Morrow, 1974.

————, *Madame Maigret's Recipes.* New York: Harcourt Brace Jovanovich, 1975.

————, *Les Vacances dans Votre Assiette.* Paris: Fayard, 1970.

Craddock, Harry, *The Savoy Cocktail Book.* New York: Richard R. Smith, 1930.

Croze, Austin de, *Les Plats Regionaux de France—1400 Succulentes Recettes Traditionelles de Toutes les Provinces Françaises.* France: Daniel Morcrette, 1977.

Curnonsky, *Cuisine et Vins de France.* Paris: Librairie Larousse, 1953.

————, *Traditional Recipes of the Provinces of France.* New York: Doubleday, 1961.

Dali, Salvador, *Les Dîners de Gala.* New York: Felicie, 1973.

————, *The Wines of Gala.* New York: Harry N. Abrams, 1978.

David, Elizabeth, *Classics: Mediterranean Food, French Country Cooking, Summer Cooking.* New York: Knopf, 1980.

————, *English Breads and Yeast Cookery.* London: Penguin, 1977.

————, *French Provincial Cooking.* London: Penguin, 1960.

————, *Italian Food.* London: Penguin, 1976.

————, *Spices, Salt and Aromatics in the English Kitchen.* London: Penguin, 1970.

Escoffier, A., *The Escoffier Cook Book.* New York: Crown, 1941.

Filippini, Alessandro, *The Table: How to Buy Food, How to Cook It, and How to Serve It.* New York: Charles L. Webster, 1890.

Fisher, M.F.K., *Consider the Oyster.* New York: Duell, Sloan and Pearce, 1941.

————, *A Considerable Town.* New York: Knopf, 1978.

————, *A Cordiall Water.* San Francisco: North Point Press, 1981.

————, *The Gastronomical Me.* New York: Duell, Sloan and Pearce, 1943.

————, *How to Cook a Wolf.* New York: World, 1944.

————, *Serve It Forth.* New York: Harper and Brothers, 1937.

————, *With Bold Knife and Fork.* New York: Putnam's, 1968.

Goldstein, Joyce Esersky, *Feedback.* New York: Richard Marek, 1976.

The Gourmet Cookbook. New York: Gourmet, 1950.

Grigson, Jane, *Charcuterie and French Pork Cookery.* London: Penguin, 1967.

————, *The Mushroom Feast.* New York: Knopf, 1975.

de Groot, Roy Andries, *The Auberge of the Flowering Hearth.* Indianapolis and New York: Bobbs-Merrill, 1973.

Guérard, Michel, *La Cuisine Gourmande.* Paris: Robert Laffont, 1978.

Guerot, Alfred, *French Cooking for Everyone.* New York: Golden Press, 1963.

Harris, Lloyd J., *The Book of Garlic.* New York: Holt, Rinehart and Winston, Panjandrum Press, 1974, 1975.

Hartley, Dorothy, *Food in England.* London: Macdonald and Jane's, 1954.

Jaffrey, Madhur, *An Invitation to Indian Cooking.* New York: Random House, Vintage Books, 1973.

Johnson, Hugh, *The World Atlas of Wine.* New York: Simon and Schuster, 1971.

Johnston, Mireille, *Cuisine of the Sun.* New York: Random House, 1976.

Jones, Evan. *The World of Cheese.* New York: Knopf, 1979.

Kamman, Madeleine M., *When French Women Cook: A Gastronomic Memoir.* New York: Atheneum, 1976.

Kennedy, Diana, *The Cuisines of Mexico.* New York: Harper and Row, 1972.

————, *Recipes from the Regional Cooks of Mexico.* New York: Harper and Row, 1978.

————, *The Tortilla Book.* New York: Harper and Row, 1975.

Lucas, Dione, *The Cordon Bleu Cook Book.* Boston: Little, Brown, 1947.

Macdougall, Allan Ross, *The Gourmet's Almanac.* London: Desmond Harmsworth, 1931.

Marshall, A. B., *Ices Plain and Fancy.* New York: The Metropolitan Museum of Art, 1976.

Montagne, Prosper, *Larousse Gastronomique.* New York: Crown, 1961.

Moraud, Simone, *Gastronomie Bretonne d'Hier et d'Aujourd'hui.* Paris: Flammarion, 1965.

Oliver, Raymond, *La Cuisine.* Translated and edited by Nika Standen Hazelton and Jack Van Bibber. New York: Tudor, 1969.

————, *Gastronomy of France.* Translated from the French by Claude Durrell. New York: The Wine and Food Society in association with World Publishing Company, 1967.

Olney, Richard, *The French Menu Cookbook.* New York: Simon and Schuster, 1970.

————(ed.), *The Good Cook, Technique and Recipes.* Alexandria, Va.: Time-Life Books, 1979.

————, *Simple French Food.* New York: Atheneum, 1974.

Peck, Paula, *The Art of Fine Baking.* New York: Simon and Schuster, 1961.

Pellaprat, Henri-Paul, *Modern French Culinary Art.* New York: World, 1966.

Pepin, Jacques, *A French Chef Cooks at Home.* New York: Simon and Schuster, 1975.

Pepin, Jacques, *La Méthode.* New York: Times Books, 1979.

————, *La Technique.* New York: Times Books, 1976.

Picture Cook Book. New York: Time Inc., 1958.

Point, Fernand, *Ma Gastronomie.* Wilton, Conn.: Lyceum Books, 1969.

Quimme, Peter, *The Signet Book of Cheeses.* New York: New American Library, Signet, 1976.

Ray, Elizabeth, *The Best of Eliza Acton.* Longmans, Green, 1968.

Reyniere, Grimod de la, *Almanach des Gourmands.* Paris: Pierre Waleffe, 1968.

Root, Waverly, *The Food of France.* New York: Random House, Vintage Books, 1977.

————, *The Food of Italy.* New York: Random House, Vintage Books, 1977.

Rouff, Marcel, *The Passionate Epicure.* Translated by Claude Durrell. New York: Dutton, 1962.

Schwabe, Calvin W., *Unmentionable Cuisine.* Charlottesville: University Press of Virginia, 1979.

Soldati, Mario, *Vino al Vino.* Rome: Mondadori, 1969, 1971.

Toklas, Alice B., *The Alice B. Toklas Cook Book.* Garden City, N.Y.: Doubleday, 1960.

Countess of Toulouse-Lautrec, *Chez Maxim's.* New York: McGraw-Hill, 1962.

Troisgros, Jean and Pierre, *Cuisiniers à Roanne.* Paris: Robert Laffont, 1977.

Tsuji, Kaichi, *Kaiseki: Zen Tastes in Japanese Cooking.* Tokyo and San Francisco: Kodansha International, 1972.

Tsuji, Shizuo, *Japanese Cooking: A Simple Art.* Tokyo and San Francisco: Kodansha International, 1980.

Vergé, Roger, *Roger Vergé's Cuisine of the South of France.* Translated by Roberta Wolfe Snoler. New York: William Morrow, 1980.

Viazzi, Alfredo, *Alfredo Viazzi's Italian Cooking.* New York: Random House, 1979.

Vidrine, Mercedes, *Quelque Chose Piquante: Acadian Meat and Fish Recipes.* Baton Rouge, La.: Claitor's Publishing Division, 1970.

Wechsberg, Joseph, *Blue Trout and Black Truffles.* New York: Knopf, 1953.

Wilson, Anne C., *Food and Drink in Britain.* London: Penguin, 1973.

Wolfert, Paula, *Couscous and Other Good Food from Morocco.* New York: Harper and Row, 1973.

INDEX

ABOUT THE AUTHOR

ALICE WATERS left Chatham, New Jersey, for Berkeley, California, where she can now be found cooking her delightful dishes. She has been the proprietor of Chez Panisse for more than ten years.